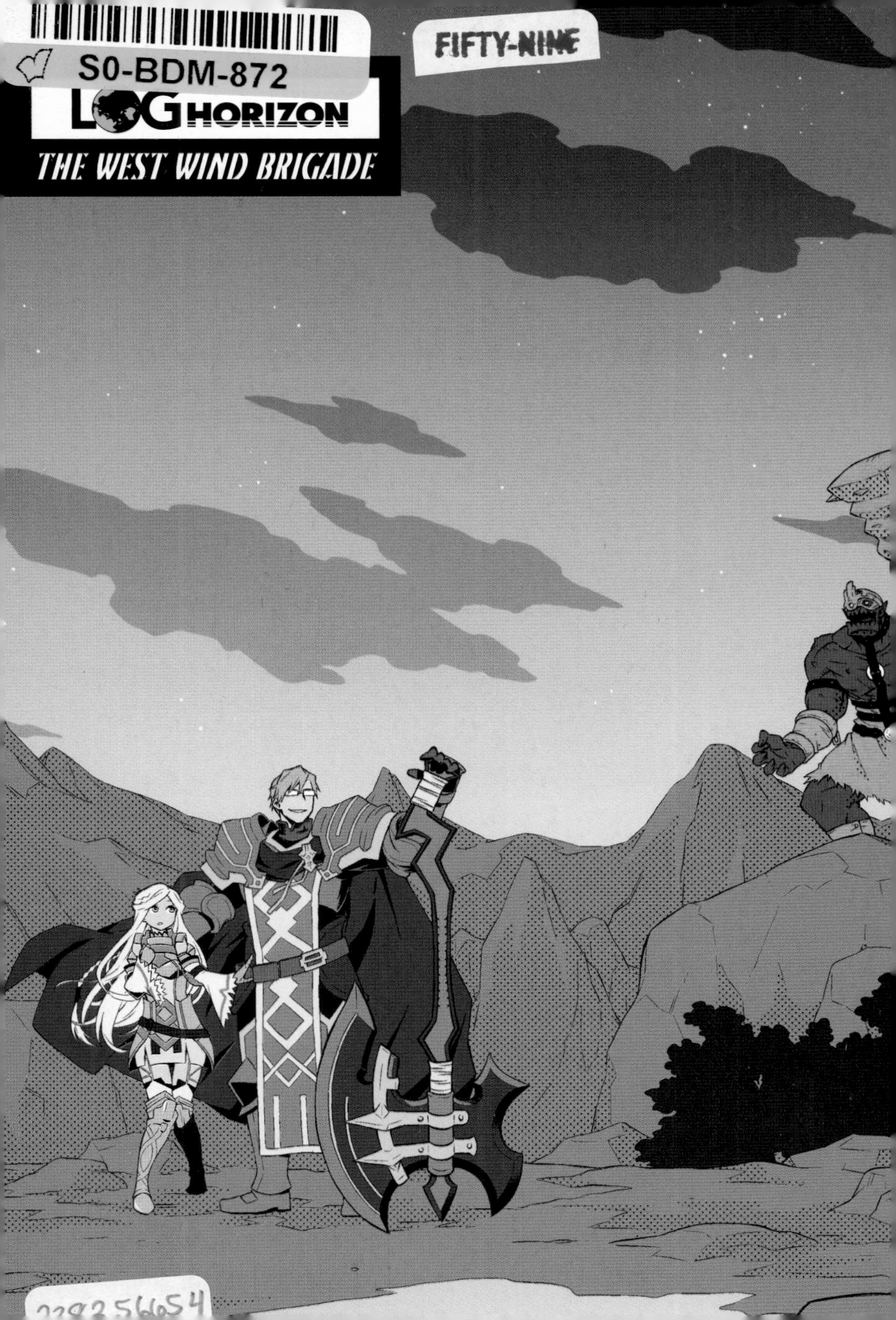
LOG HORIZON
THE WEST WIND BRIGADE

LOG HORIZON **THE WEST WIND BRIGADE** ◆8◆

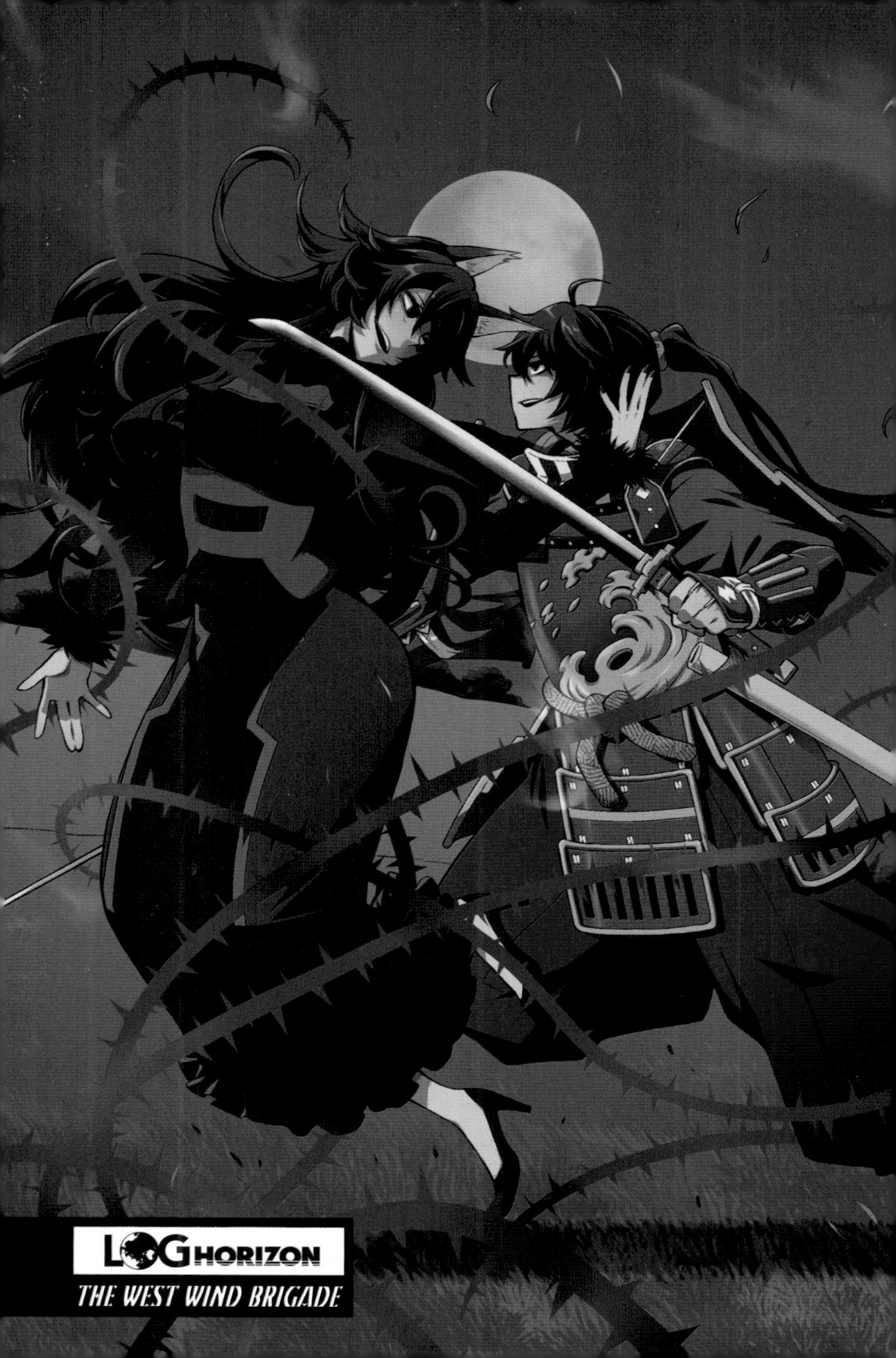
LOG HORIZON
THE WEST WIND BRIGADE

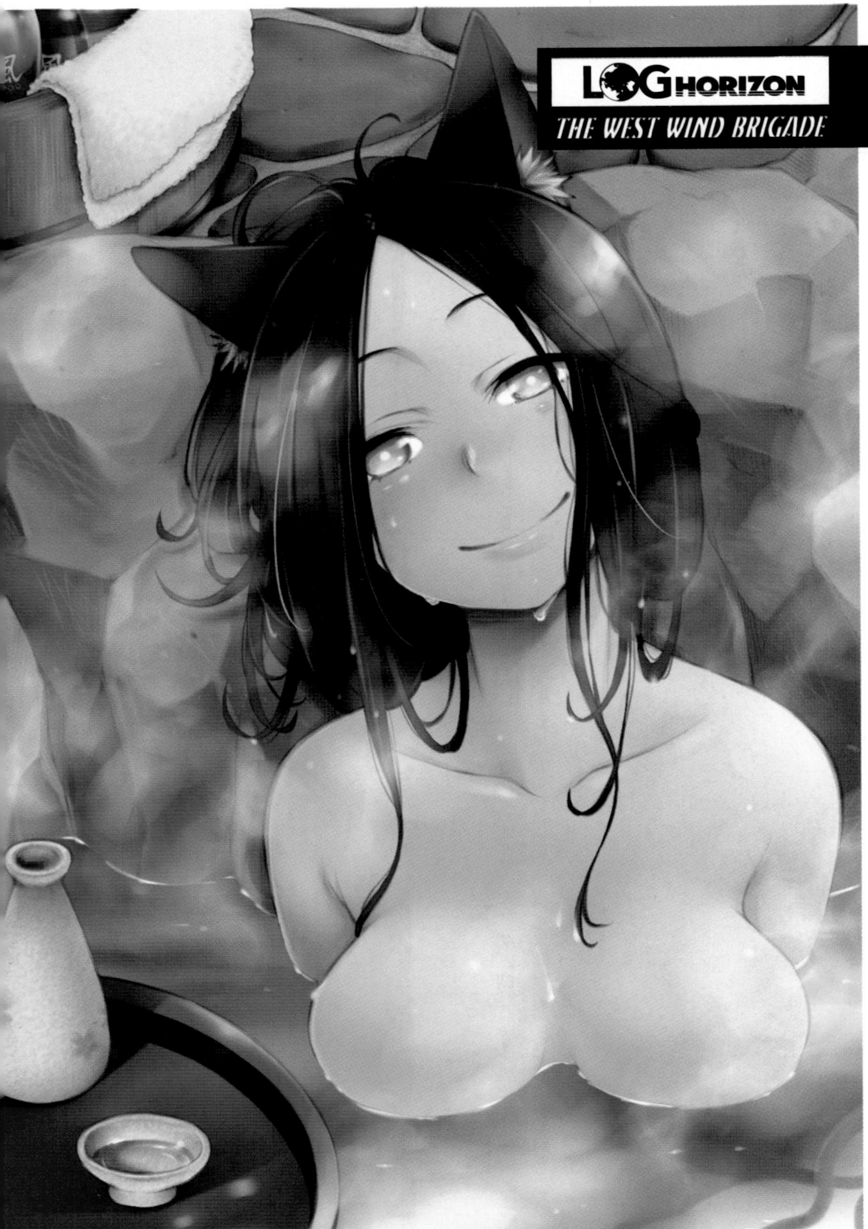
LOG HORIZON
THE WEST WIND BRIGADE

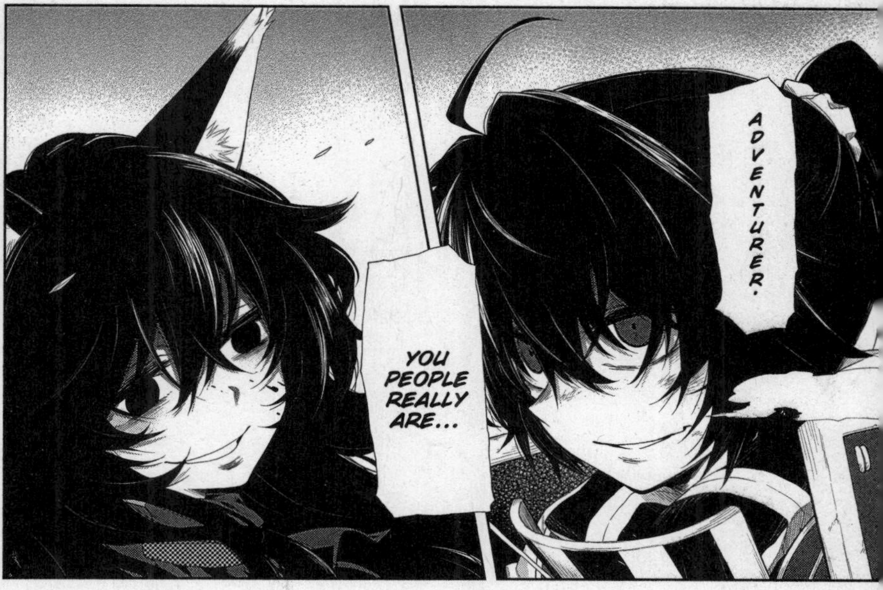
ADVENTURER.
YOU PEOPLE REALLY ARE...

CHAPTER: 42 To the Point of Lunacy

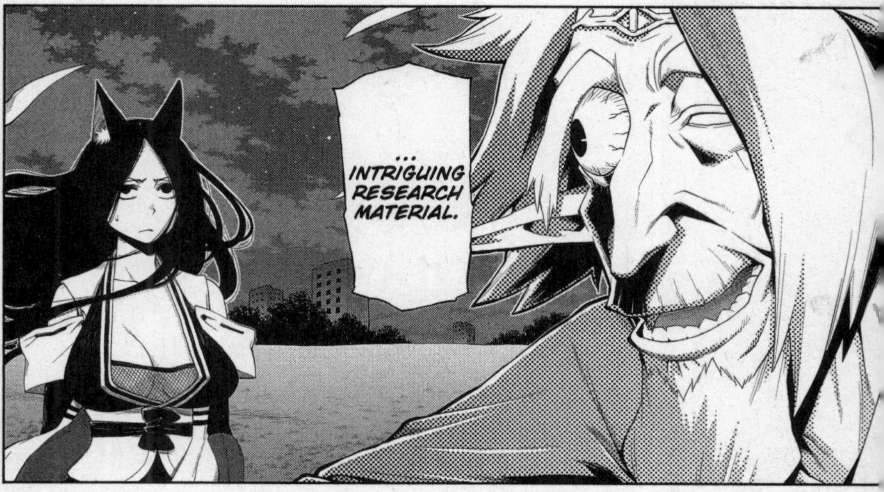
...INTRIGUING RESEARCH MATERIAL.

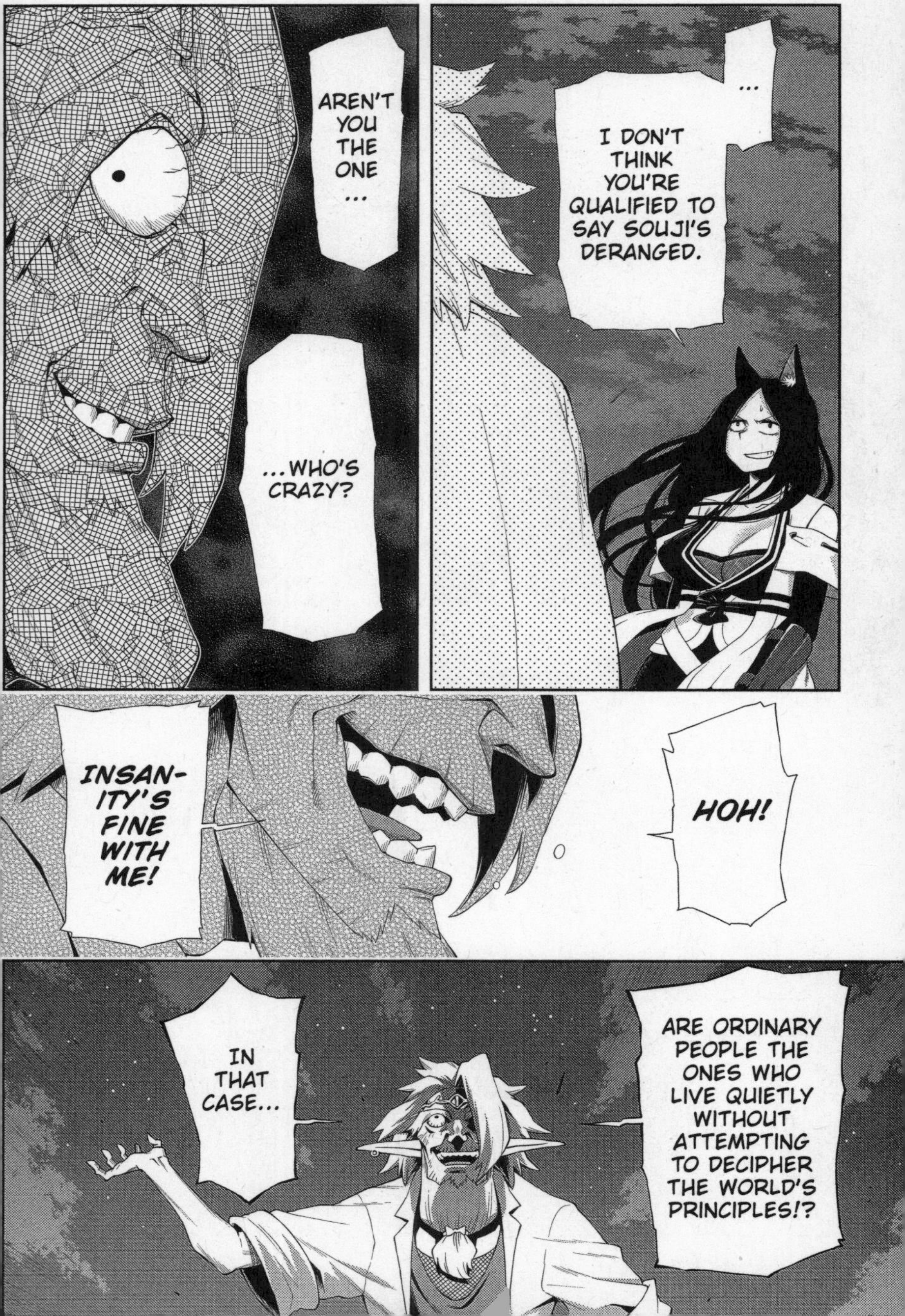
...
I DON'T THINK YOU'RE QUALIFIED TO SAY SOUJI'S DERANGED.
AREN'T YOU THE ONE ...
...WHO'S CRAZY?
HOH!
INSANITY'S FINE WITH ME!
IN THAT CASE...
ARE ORDINARY PEOPLE THE ONES WHO LIVE QUIETLY WITHOUT ATTEMPTING TO DECIPHER THE WORLD'S PRINCIPLES!?

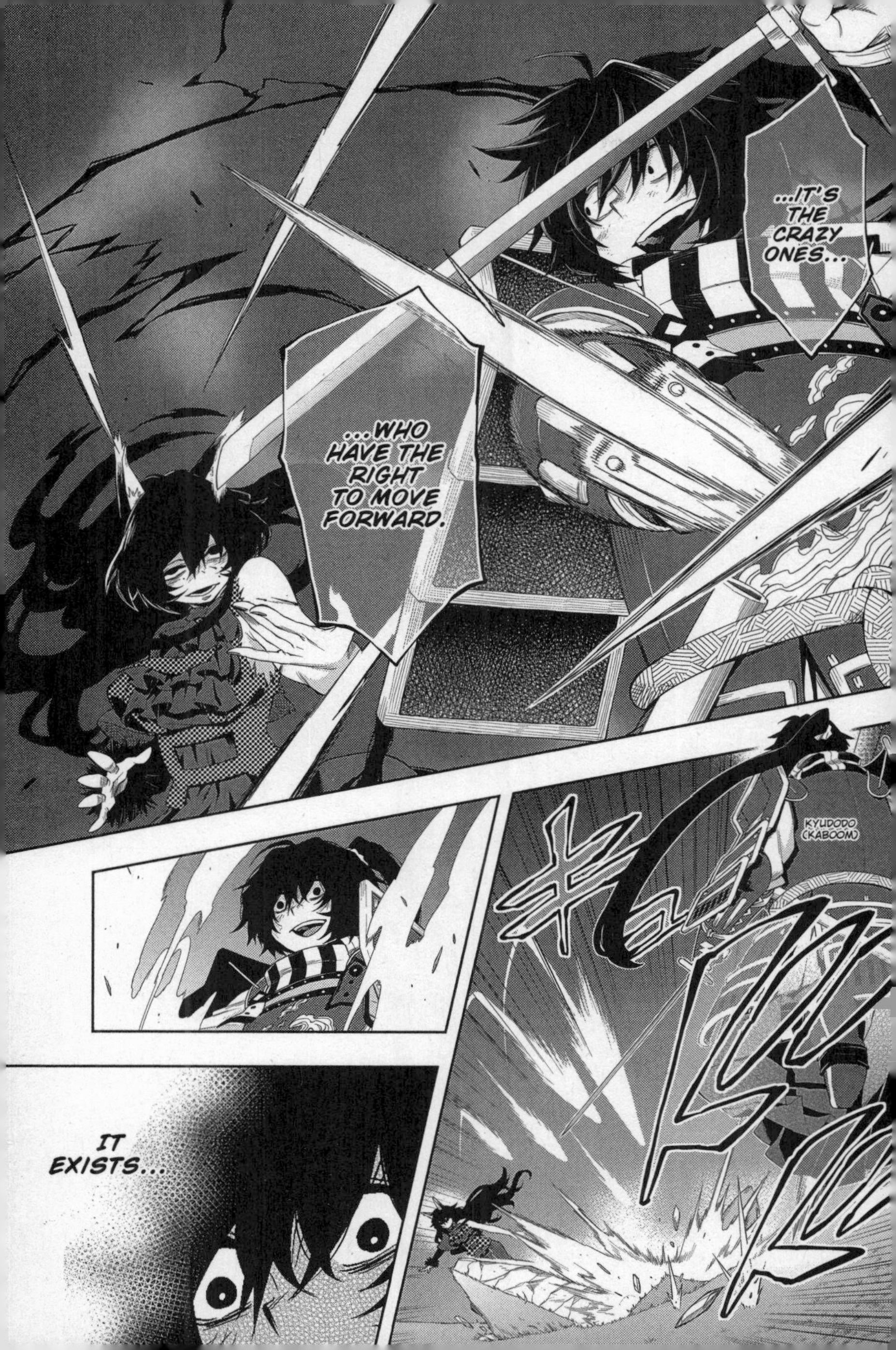
...IT'S THE CRAZY ONES...
...WHO HAVE THE RIGHT TO MOVE FORWARD.
KYUDODO (KABOOM)
IT EXISTS...

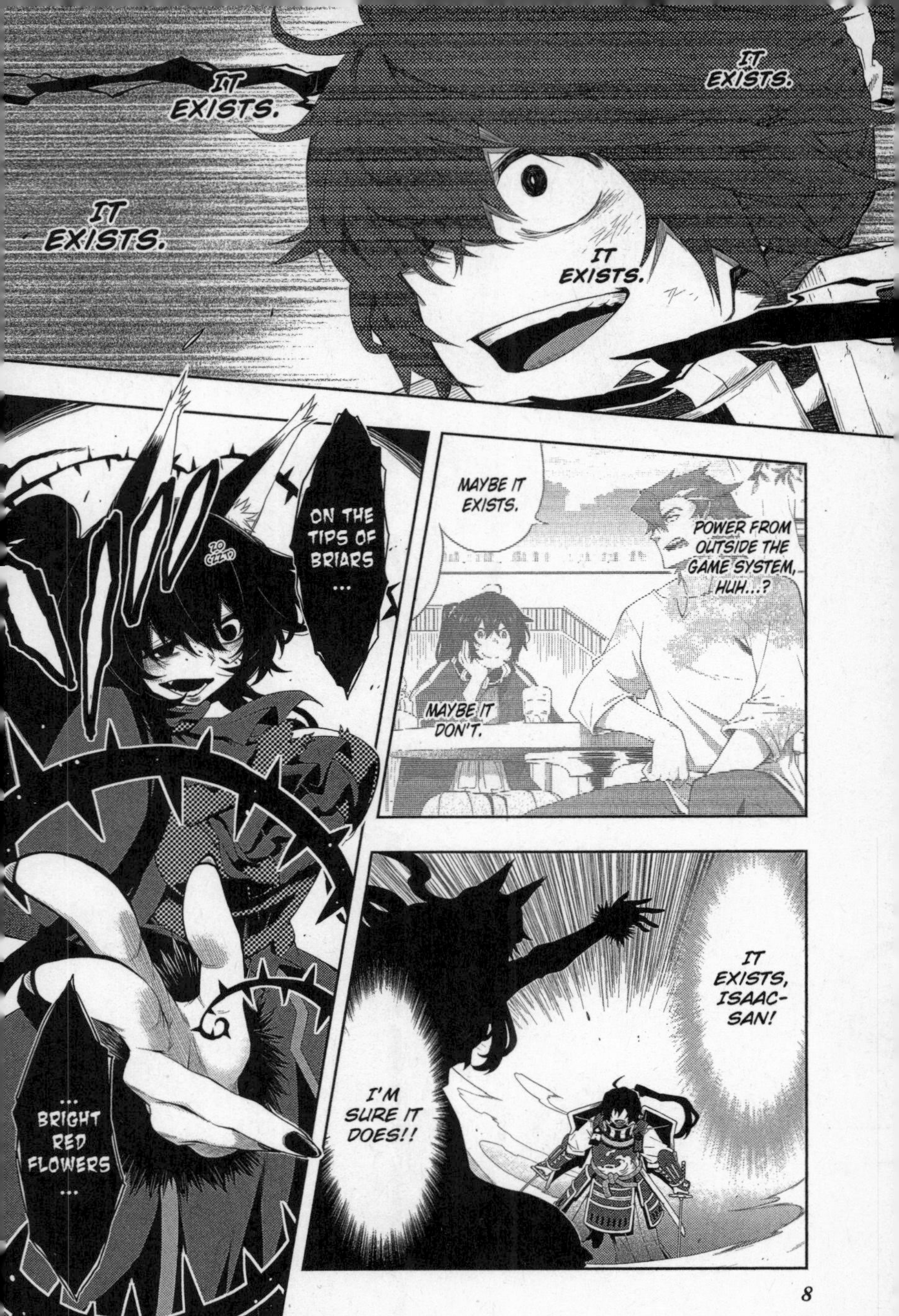
IT EXISTS.
IT EXISTS.
IT EXISTS.
IT EXISTS.
MAYBE IT EXISTS.
POWER FROM OUTSIDE THE GAME SYSTEM, HUH...?
MAYBE IT DON'T.
IT EXISTS, ISAAC-SAN!
I'M SURE IT DOES!!
ON THE TIPS OF BRIARS ...
... BRIGHT RED FLOWERS ...

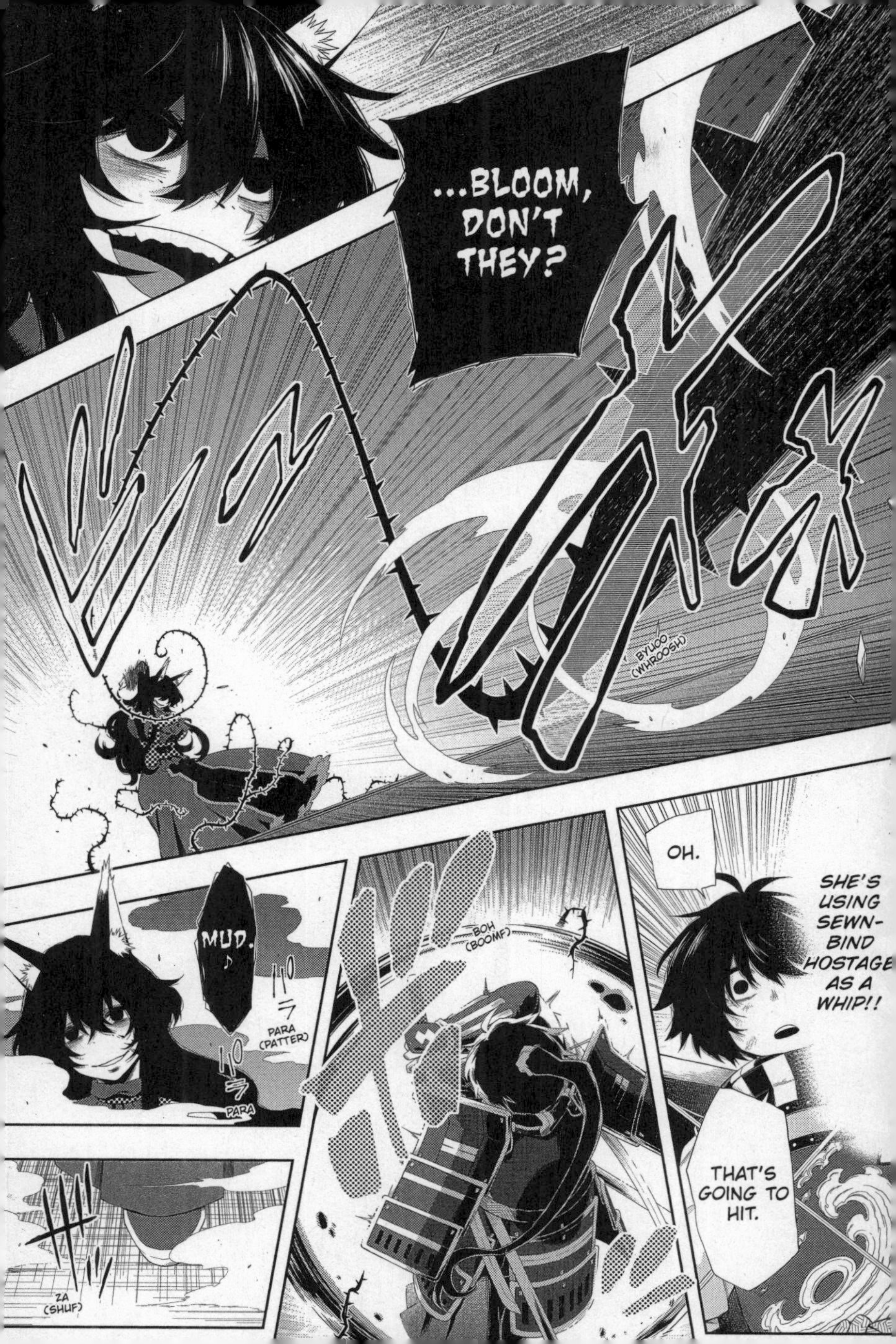
...BLOOM, DON'T THEY?
BYUOO (WHROOSH)
OH.
SHE'S USING SEWN-BIND HOSTAGE AS A WHIP!!
THAT'S GOING TO HIT.
BOH (BOOMF)
MUD. ♪
PARA (PATTER)
PARA
ZA (SHUF)

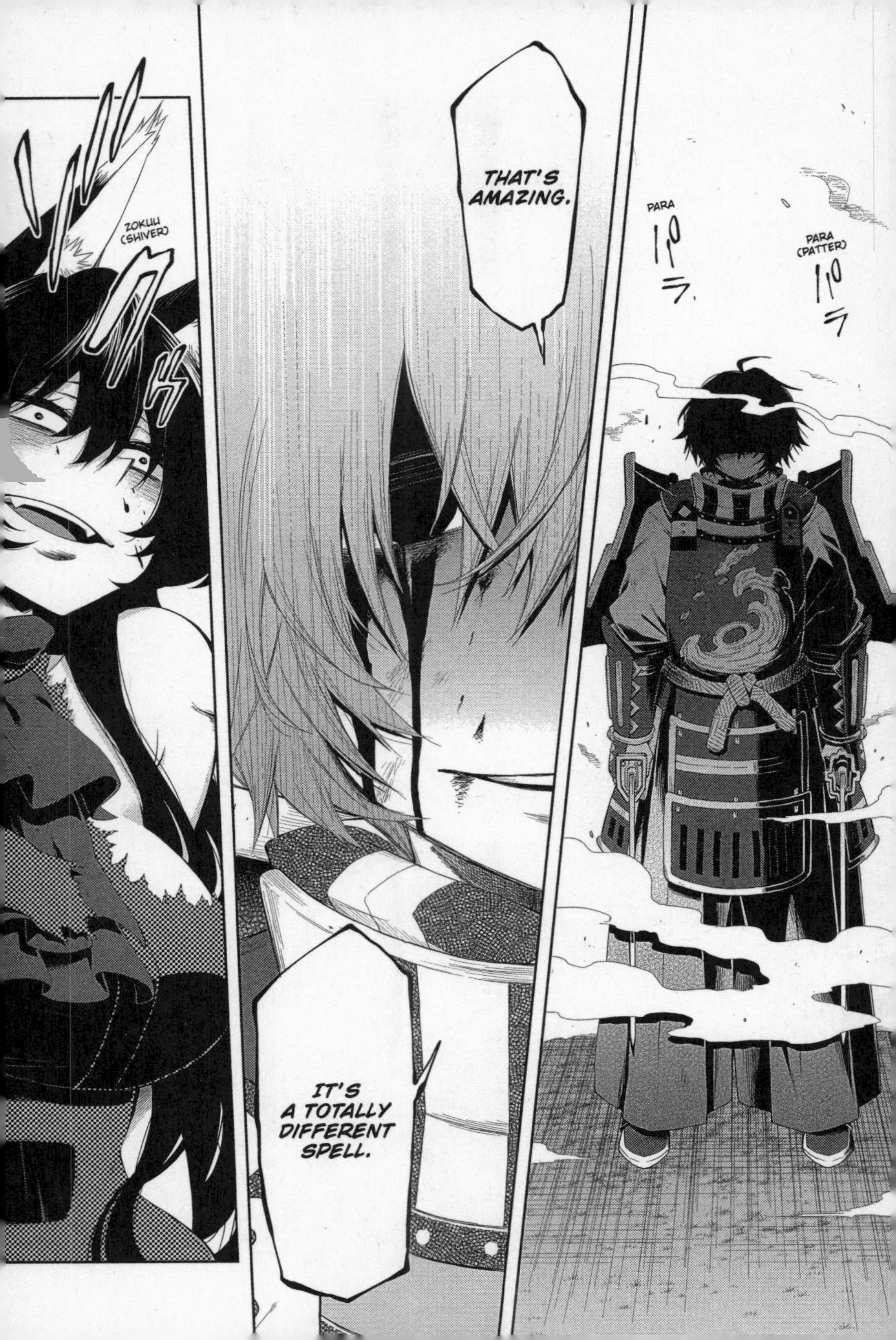
PARA
(PATTER)
PARA
THAT'S AMAZING.
IT'S A TOTALLY DIFFERENT SPELL.
ZOKUU
(SHIVER)

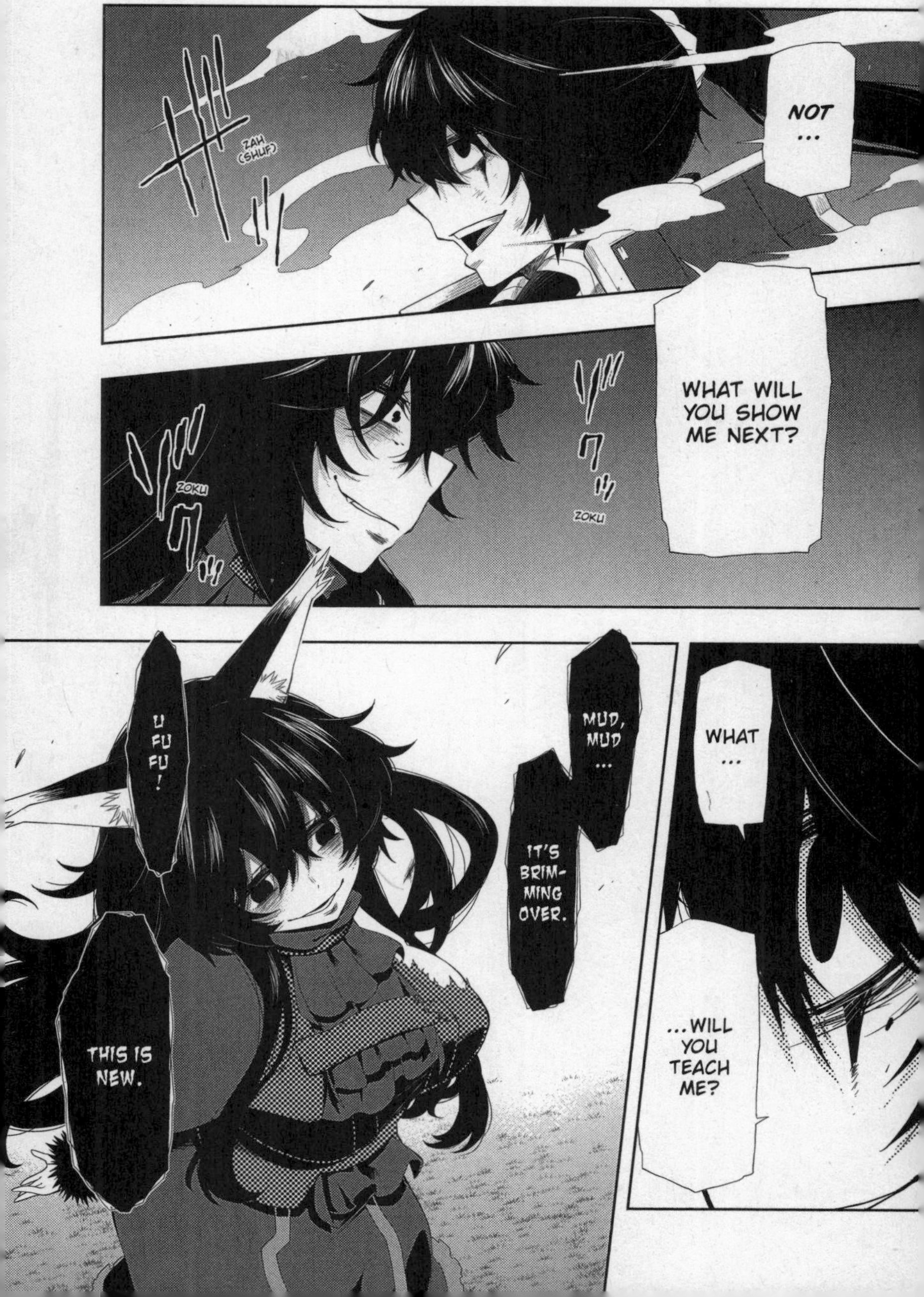
NOT ...
ZAH (SHUF)
WHAT WILL YOU SHOW ME NEXT?
ZOKU
ZOKU
WHAT ...
...WILL YOU TEACH ME?
MUD, MUD ...
IT'S BRIM-MING OVER.
UFUFU!
THIS IS NEW.

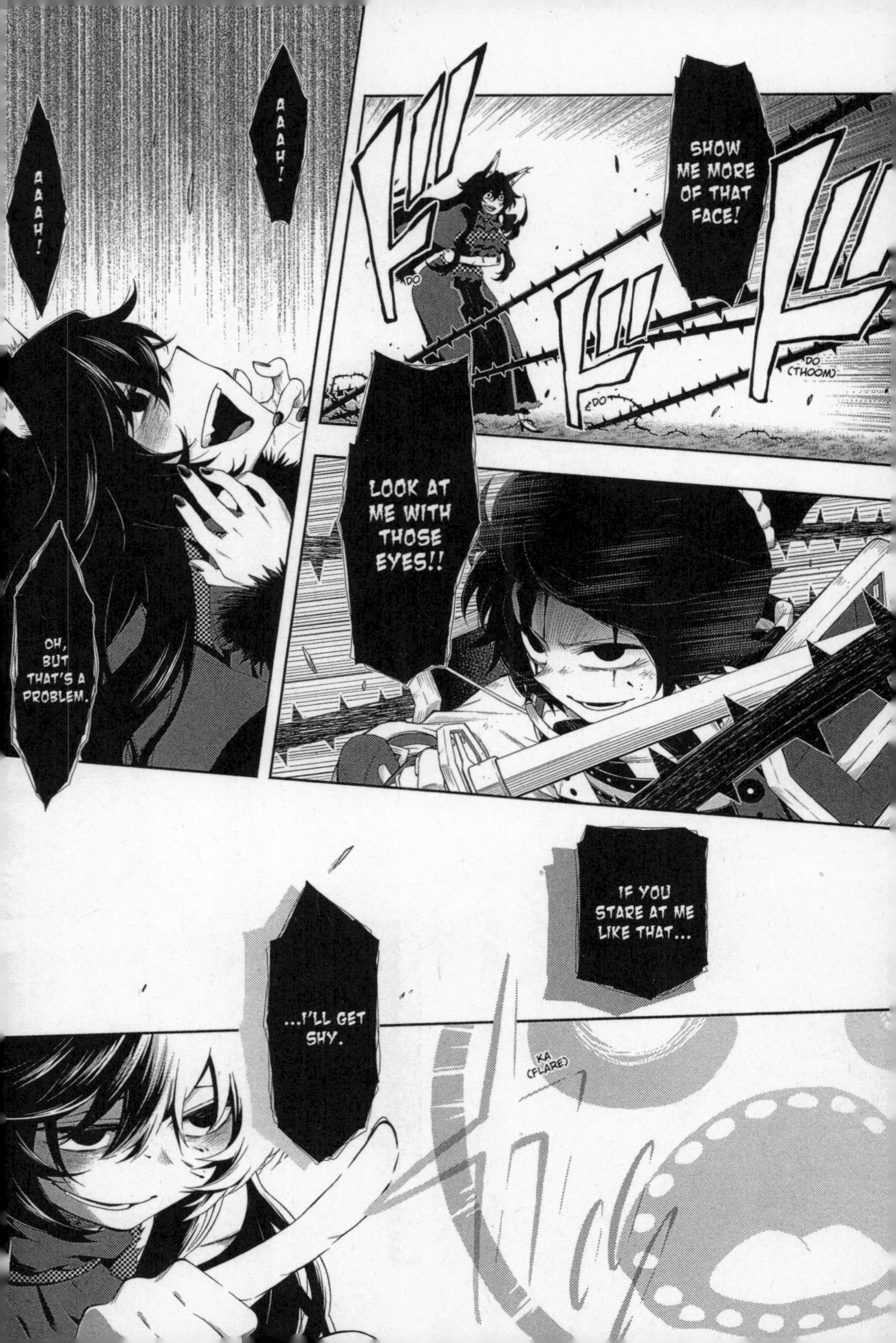
SHOW ME MORE OF THAT FACE!
DO
(THOOM)
DO
DO
LOOK AT ME WITH THOSE EYES!!
AAAH!
AAAH!
OH, BUT THAT'S A PROBLEM.
IF YOU STARE AT ME LIKE THAT...
...I'LL GET SHY.
KA
(FLARE)

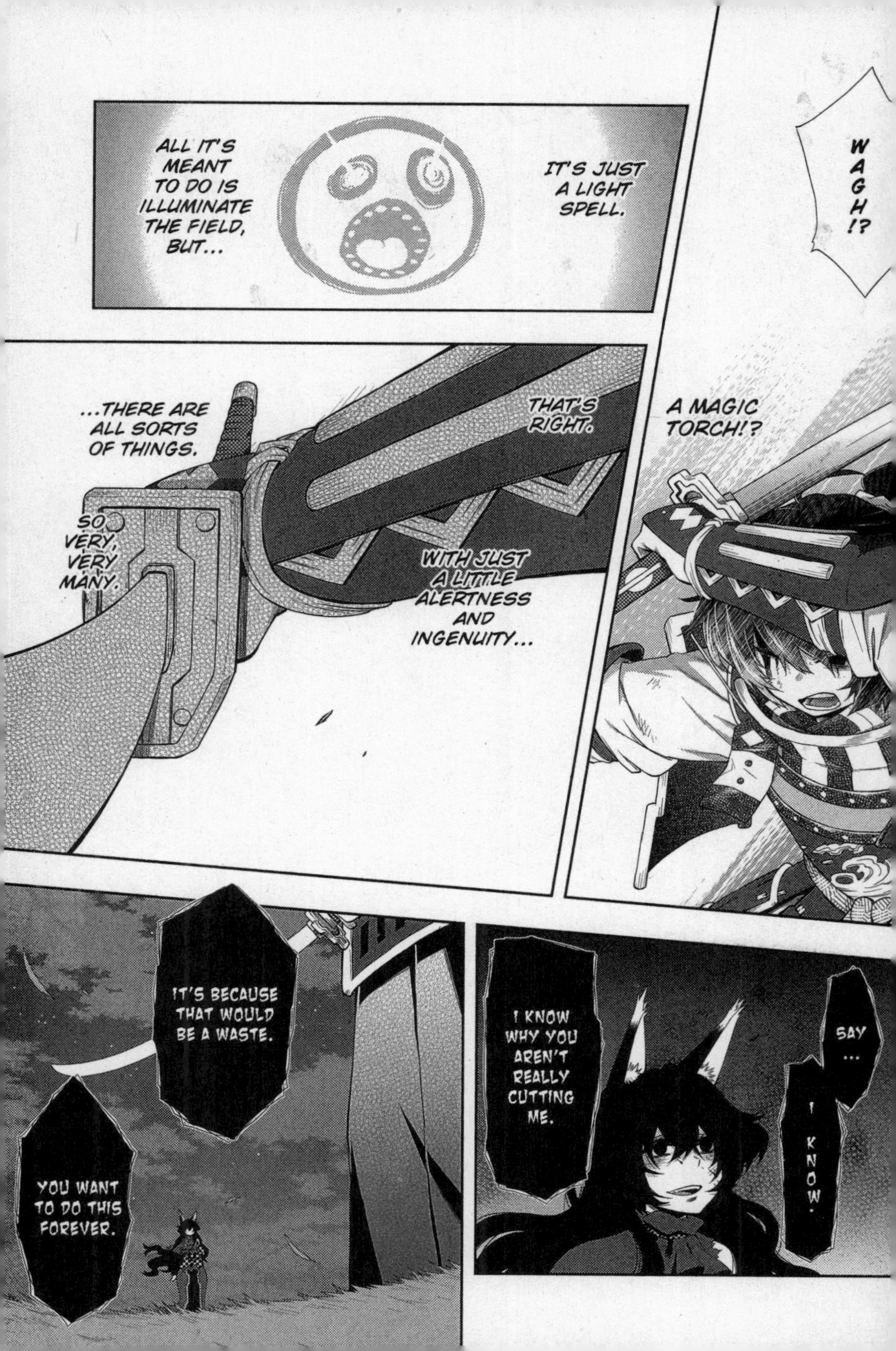
WAGH!?
A MAGIC TORCH!?
IT'S JUST A LIGHT SPELL.
ALL IT'S MEANT TO DO IS ILLUMINATE THE FIELD, BUT...
THAT'S RIGHT.
WITH JUST A LITTLE ALERTNESS AND INGENUITY...
...THERE ARE ALL SORTS OF THINGS.
SO VERY, VERY MANY.
SAY... I KNOW.
I KNOW WHY YOU AREN'T REALLY CUTTING ME.
IT'S BECAUSE THAT WOULD BE A WASTE.
YOU WANT TO DO THIS FOREVER.

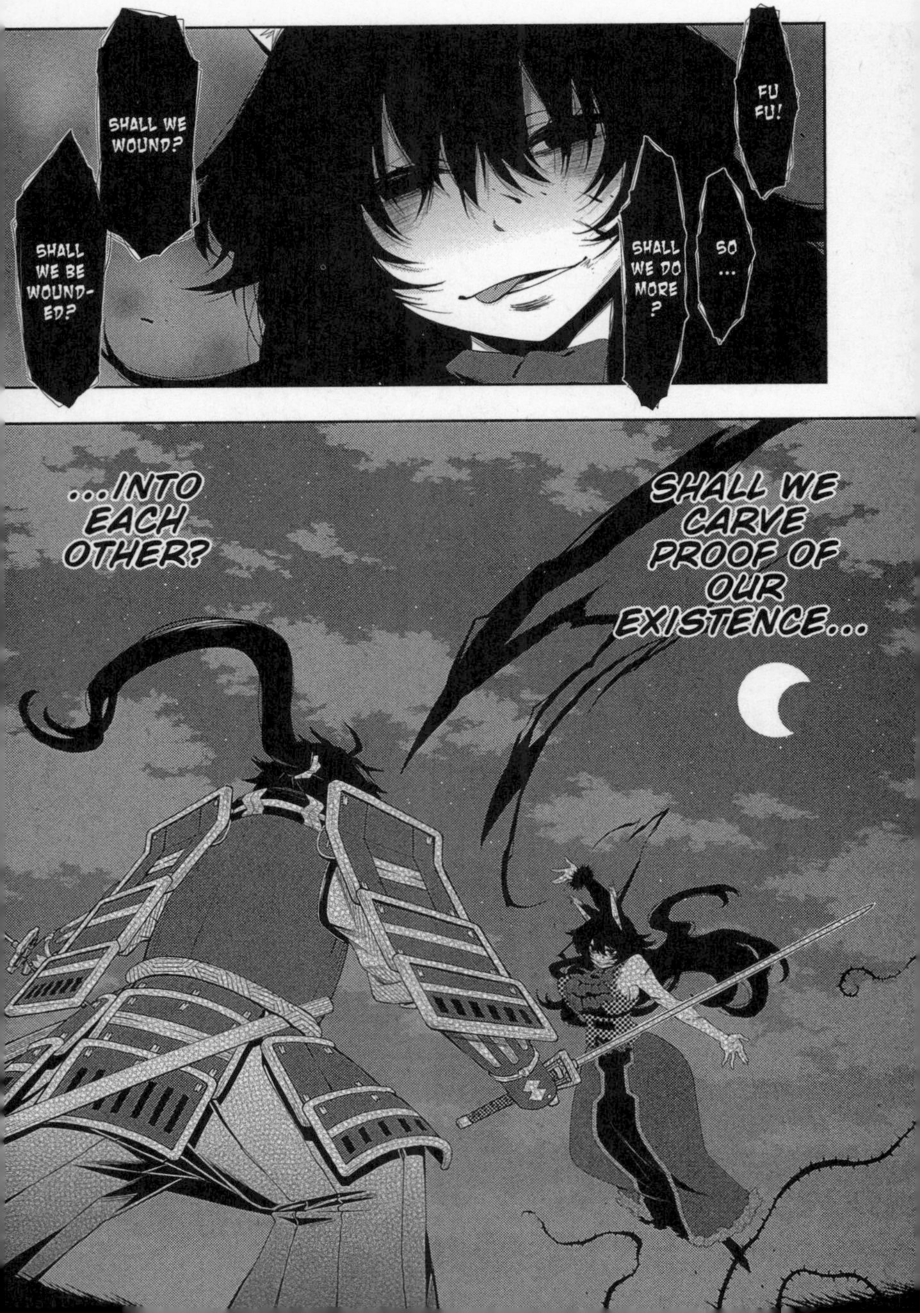
FU FU!
SO ...
SHALL WE DO MORE ?
SHALL WE WOUND?
SHALL WE BE WOUND-ED?
SHALL WE CARVE PROOF OF OUR EXISTENCE...
...INTO EACH OTHER?

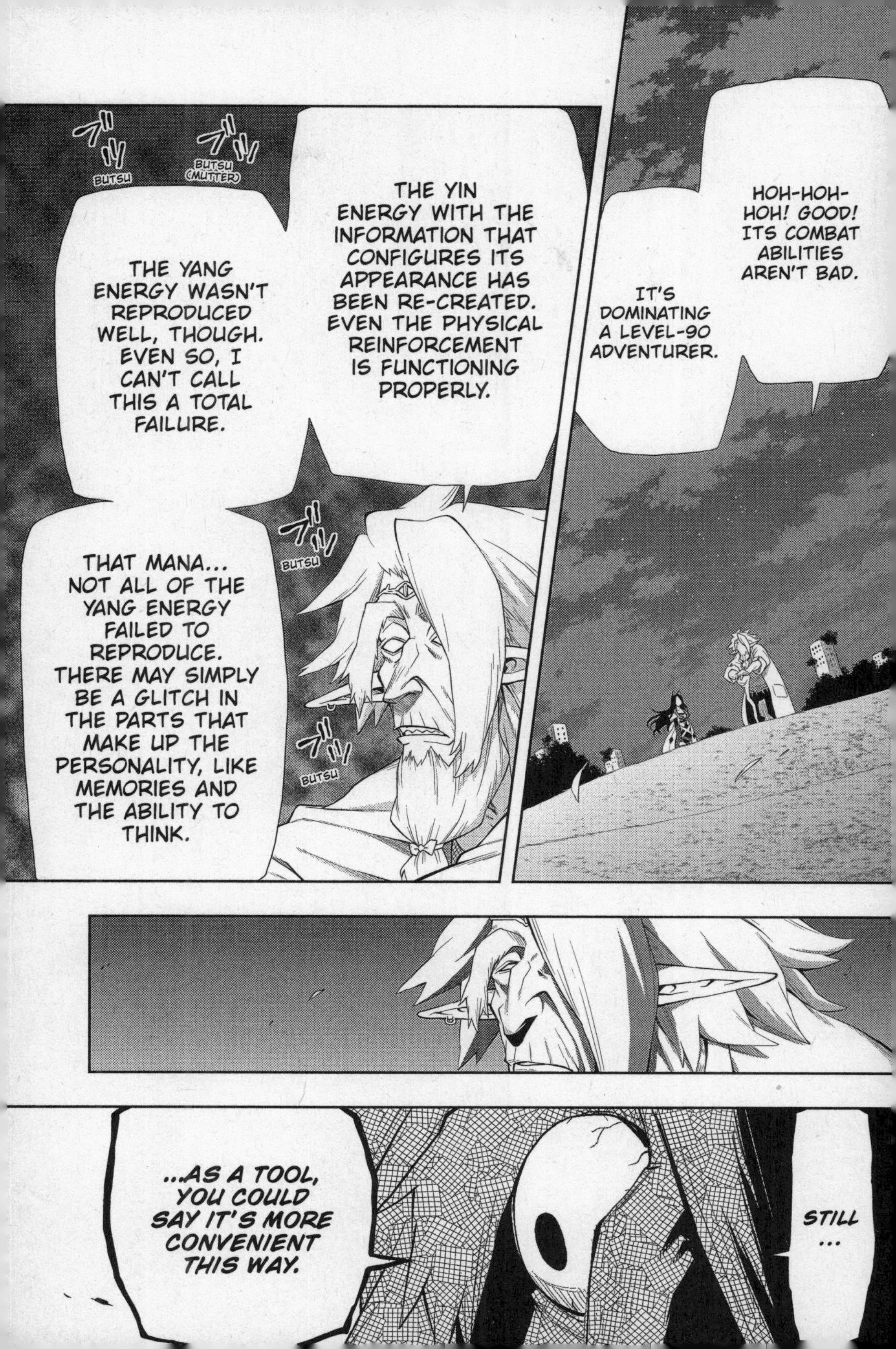
HOH-HOH-HOH! GOOD! ITS COMBAT ABILITIES AREN'T BAD.
IT'S DOMINATING A LEVEL-90 ADVENTURER.
BUTSU (MUTTER)
BUTSU
THE YIN ENERGY WITH THE INFORMATION THAT CONFIGURES ITS APPEARANCE HAS BEEN RE-CREATED. EVEN THE PHYSICAL REINFORCEMENT IS FUNCTIONING PROPERLY.
THE YANG ENERGY WASN'T REPRODUCED WELL, THOUGH. EVEN SO, I CAN'T CALL THIS A TOTAL FAILURE.
BUTSU
BUTSU
THAT MANA... NOT ALL OF THE YANG ENERGY FAILED TO REPRODUCE. THERE MAY SIMPLY BE A GLITCH IN THE PARTS THAT MAKE UP THE PERSONALITY, LIKE MEMORIES AND THE ABILITY TO THINK.
STILL...
...AS A TOOL, YOU COULD SAY IT'S MORE CONVENIENT THIS WAY.

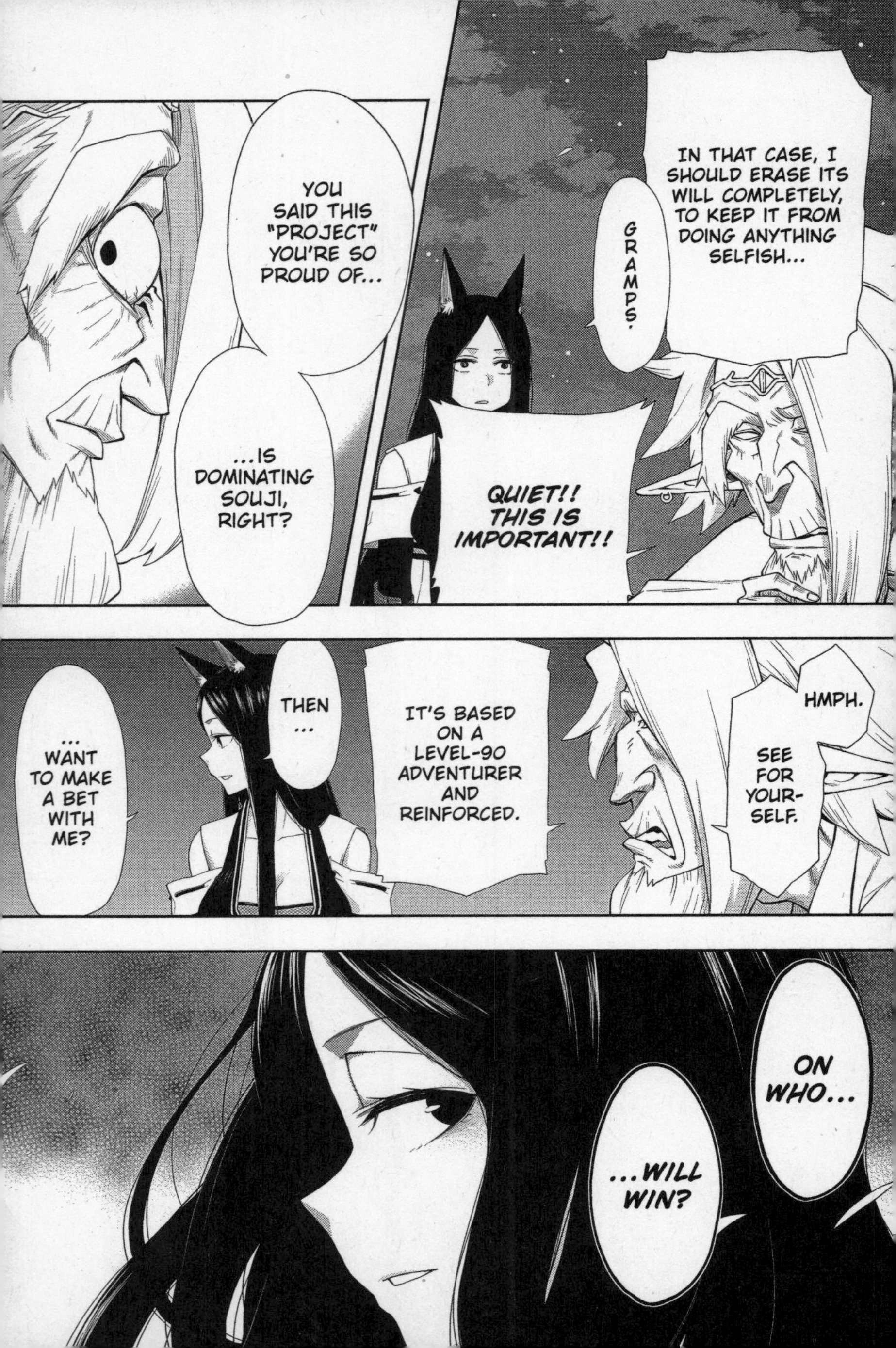

IN THAT CASE, I SHOULD ERASE ITS WILL COMPLETELY, TO KEEP IT FROM DOING ANYTHING SELFISH...
GRAMPS.
QUIET!! THIS IS IMPORTANT!!
YOU SAID THIS "PROJECT" YOU'RE SO PROUD OF...
...IS DOMINATING SOUJI, RIGHT?
HMPH.
SEE FOR YOURSELF.
IT'S BASED ON A LEVEL-90 ADVENTURER AND REINFORCED.
THEN...
...WANT TO MAKE A BET WITH ME?
ON WHO...
...WILL WIN?

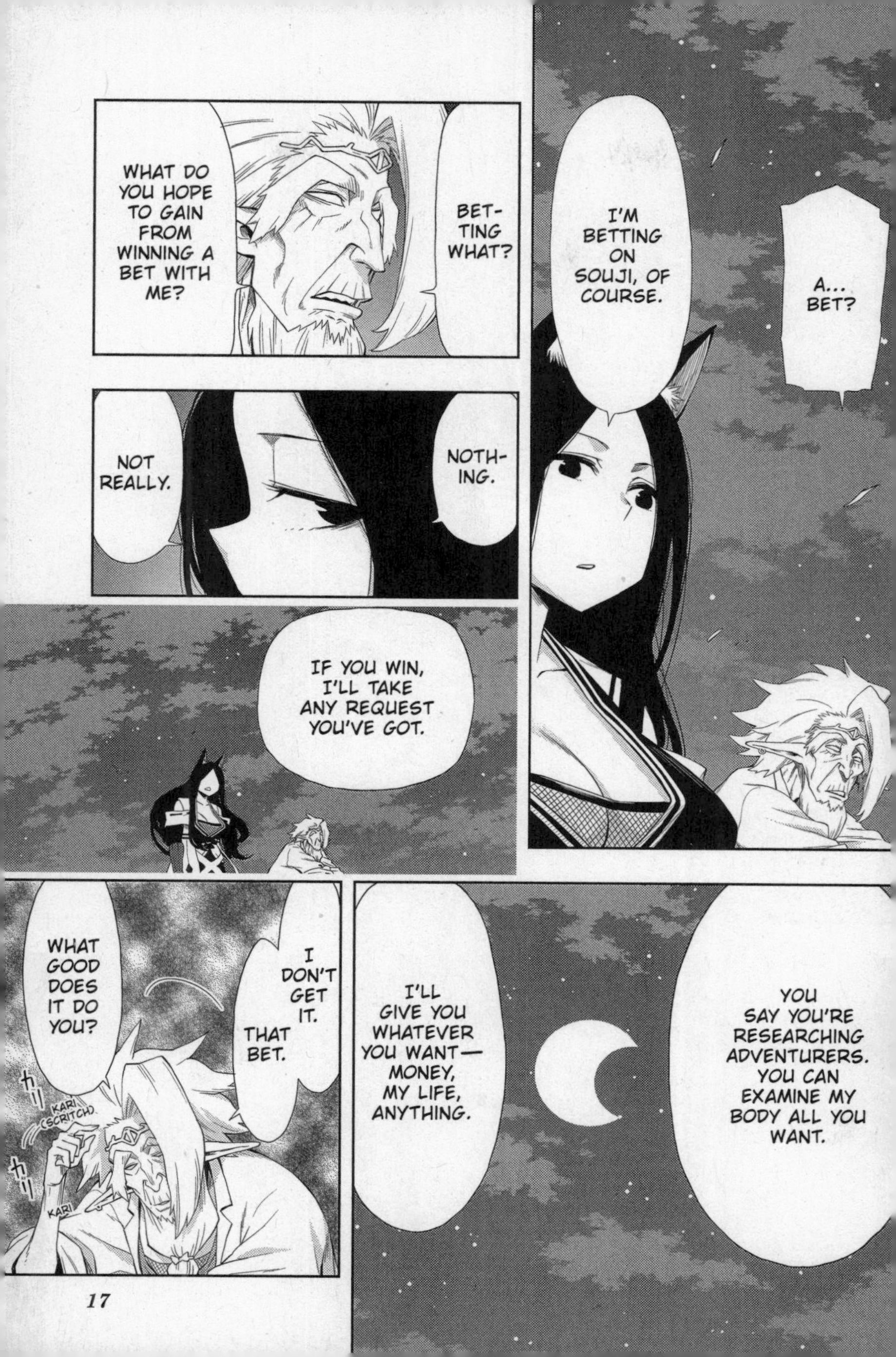
A... BET?
I'M BETTING ON SOUJI, OF COURSE.
BET-TING WHAT?
WHAT DO YOU HOPE TO GAIN FROM WINNING A BET WITH ME?
NOTH-ING.
NOT REALLY.
IF YOU WIN, I'LL TAKE ANY REQUEST YOU'VE GOT.
YOU SAY YOU'RE RESEARCHING ADVENTURERS. YOU CAN EXAMINE MY BODY ALL YOU WANT.
I'LL GIVE YOU WHATEVER YOU WANT—MONEY, MY LIFE, ANYTHING.
I DON'T GET IT.
THAT BET.
WHAT GOOD DOES IT DO YOU?
カリ KARI (SCRITCH)
カリ KARI

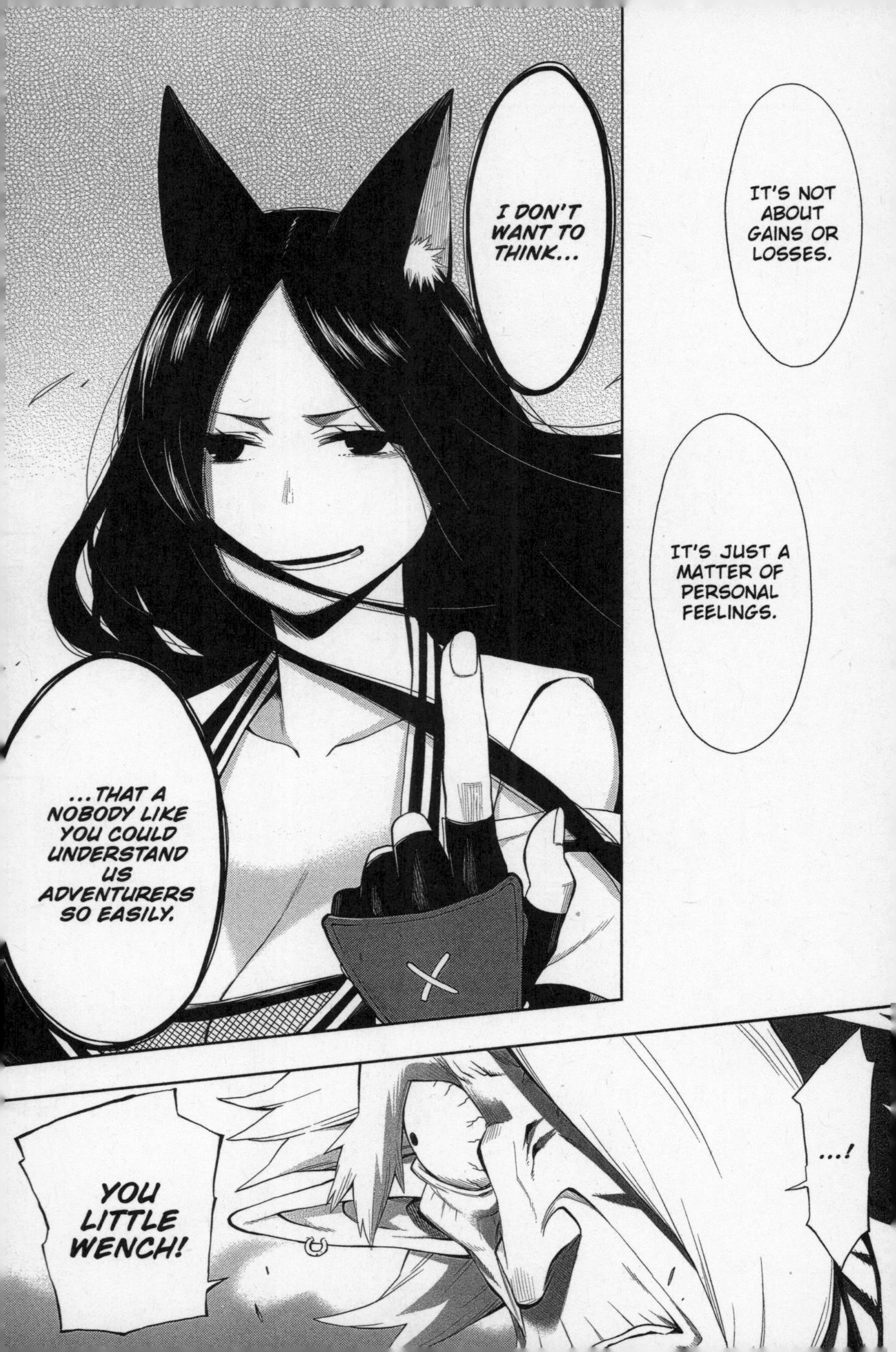
IT'S NOT ABOUT GAINS OR LOSSES.
IT'S JUST A MATTER OF PERSONAL FEELINGS.
I DON'T WANT TO THINK...
...THAT A NOBODY LIKE YOU COULD UNDERSTAND US ADVENTURERS SO EASILY.
...!
YOU LITTLE WENCH!

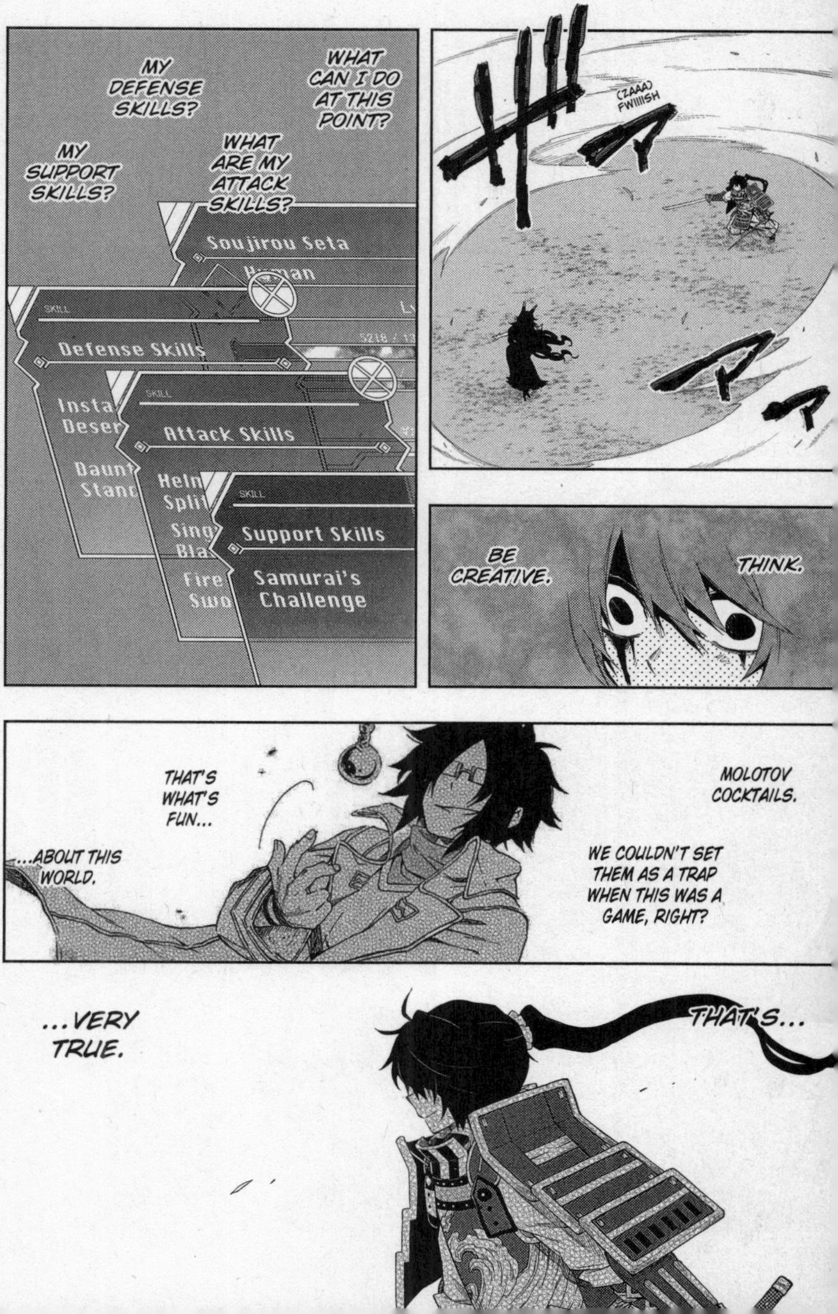
(ZAAA) FWIIIISH
THINK.
BE CREATIVE.
WHAT CAN I DO AT THIS POINT?
MY DEFENSE SKILLS?
WHAT ARE MY ATTACK SKILLS?
MY SUPPORT SKILLS?
Soujirou Seta
SKILL
Defense Skills
SKILL
Attack Skills
SKILL
Support Skills
Samurai's Challenge
MOLOTOV COCKTAILS.
WE COULDN'T SET THEM AS A TRAP WHEN THIS WAS A GAME, RIGHT?
THAT'S WHAT'S FUN...
...ABOUT THIS WORLD.
THAT'S...
...VERY TRUE.

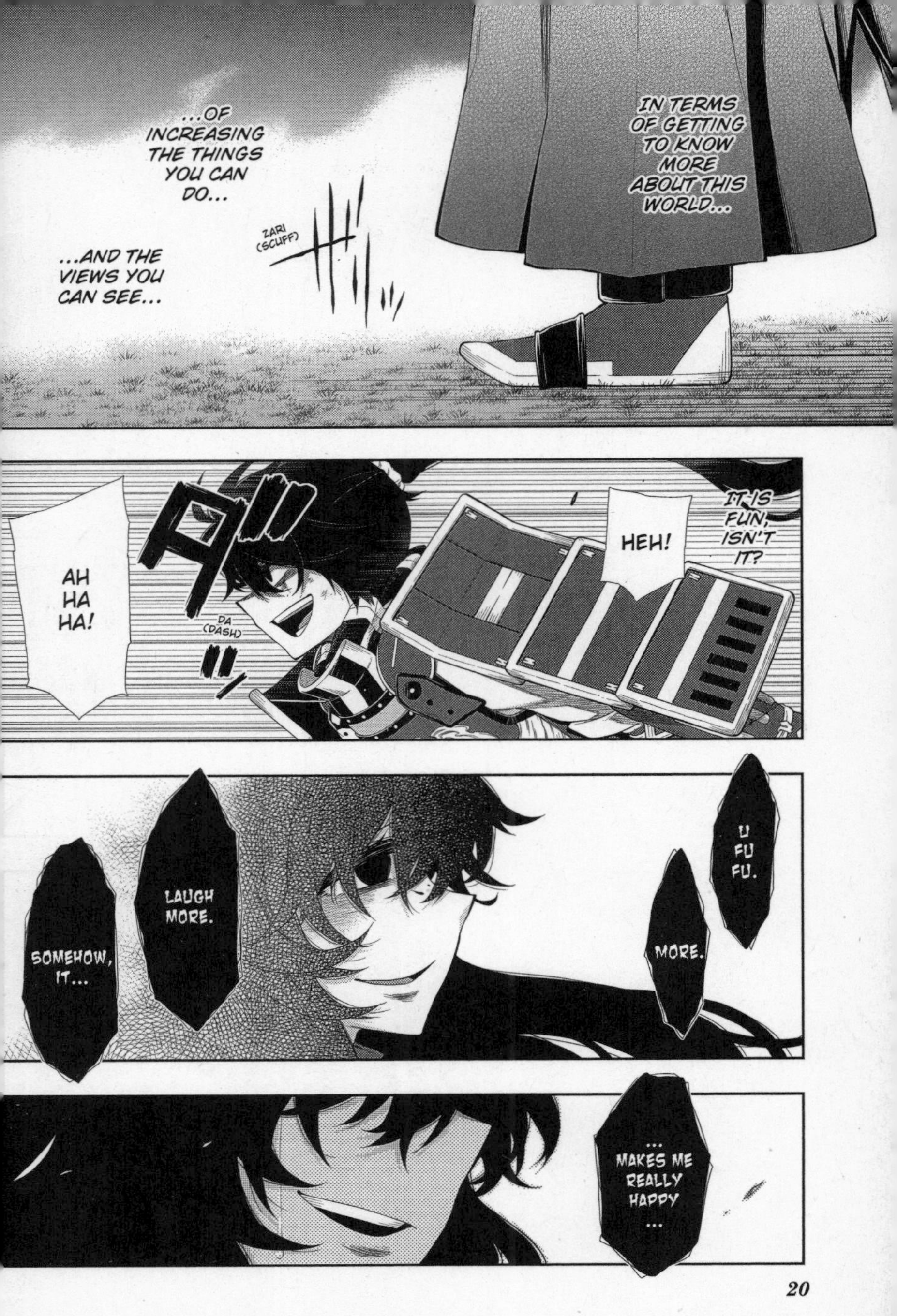
IN TERMS OF GETTING TO KNOW MORE ABOUT THIS WORLD...
...OF INCREASING THE THINGS YOU CAN DO...
ZARI (SCUFF)
...AND THE VIEWS YOU CAN SEE...
IT IS FUN, ISN'T IT?
HEH!
DA (DASH)
AH HA HA!
U FU FU.
MORE.
LAUGH MORE.
SOMEHOW, IT...
...MAKES ME REALLY HAPPY...

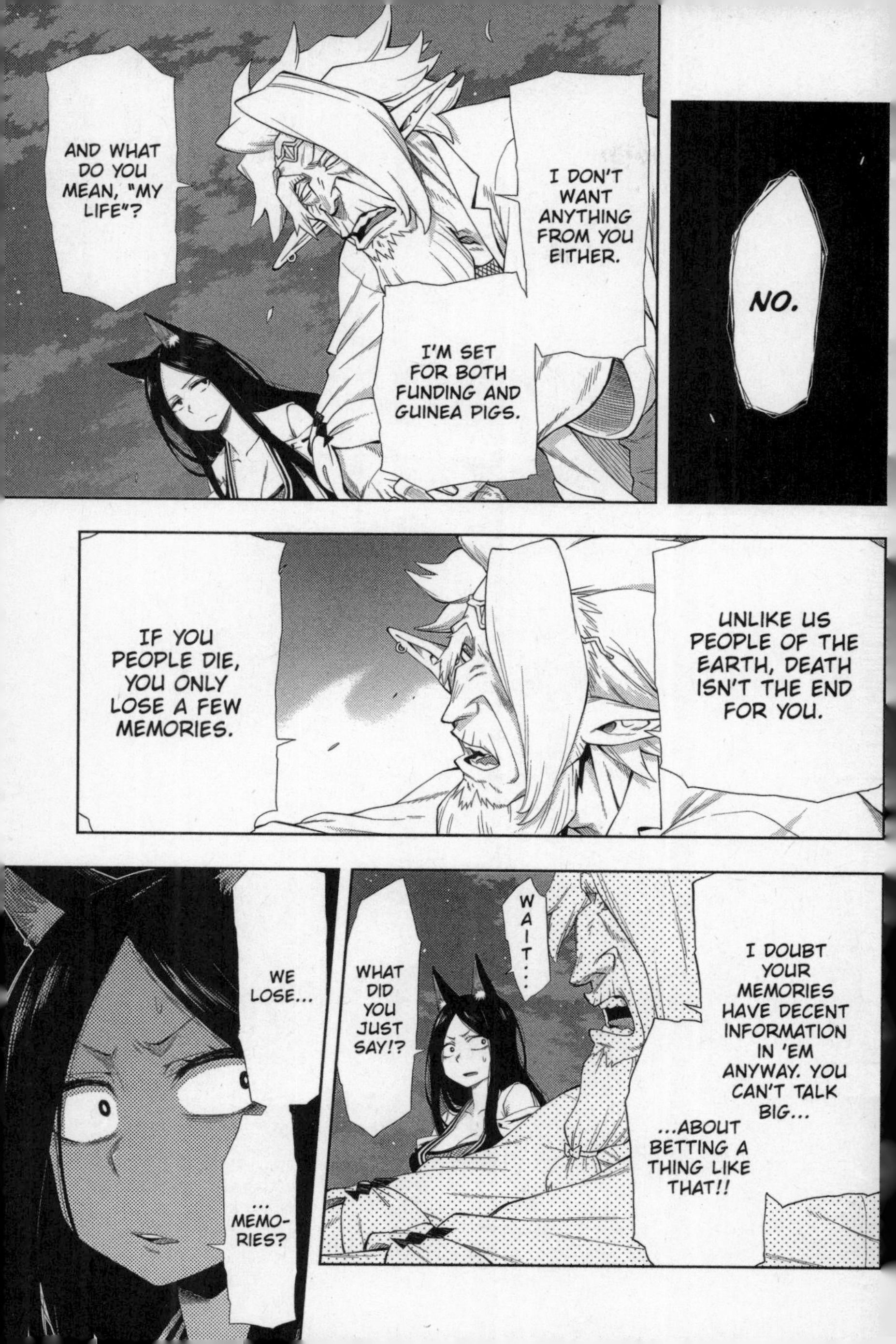
NO.
I DON'T WANT ANYTHING FROM YOU EITHER.
I'M SET FOR BOTH FUNDING AND GUINEA PIGS.
AND WHAT DO YOU MEAN, "MY LIFE"?
UNLIKE US PEOPLE OF THE EARTH, DEATH ISN'T THE END FOR YOU.
IF YOU PEOPLE DIE, YOU ONLY LOSE A FEW MEMORIES.
I DOUBT YOUR MEMORIES HAVE DECENT INFORMATION IN 'EM ANYWAY. YOU CAN'T TALK BIG...
...ABOUT BETTING A THING LIKE THAT!!
WAIT...
WHAT DID YOU JUST SAY!?
WE LOSE...
...MEMORIES?

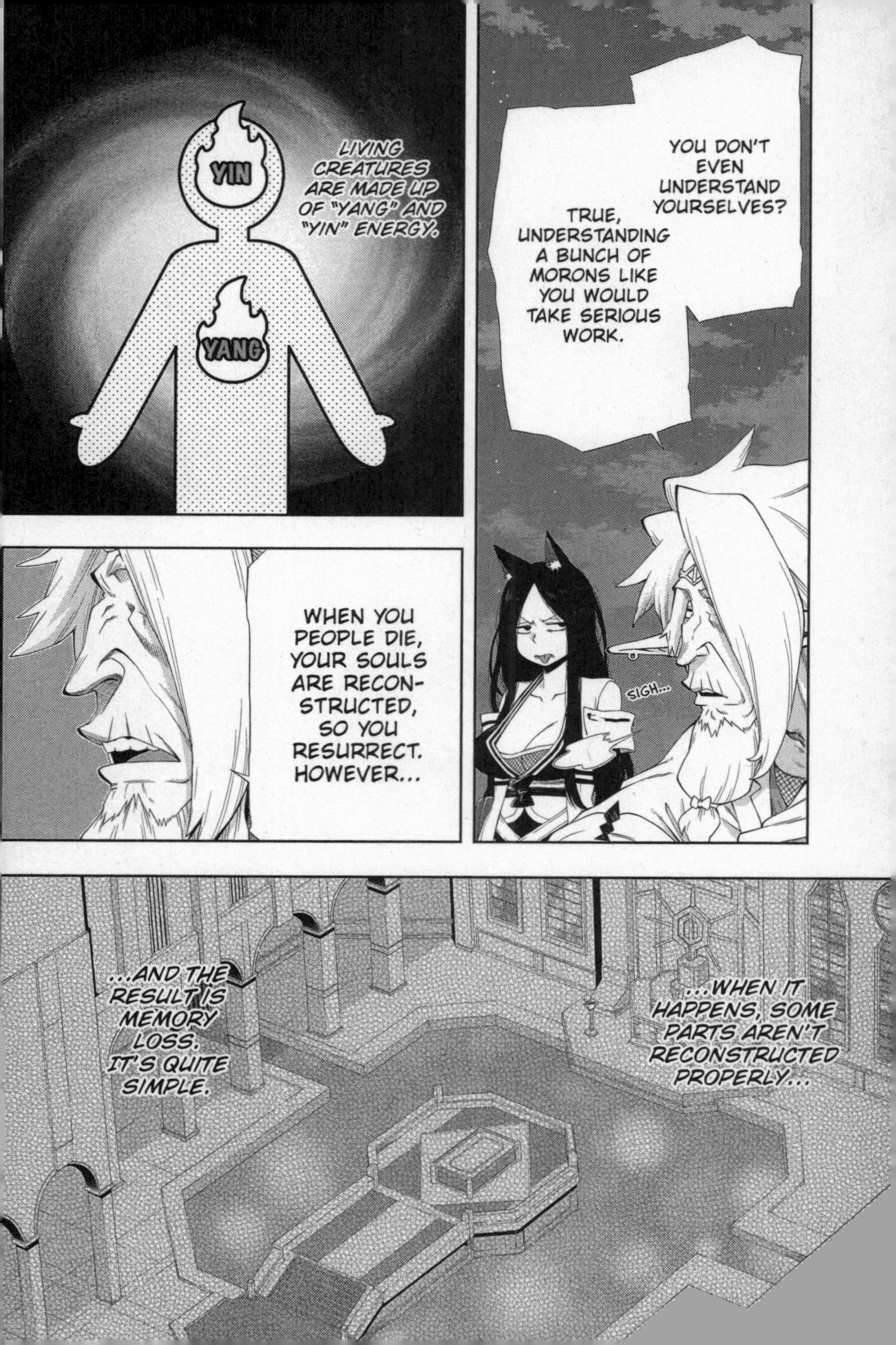
YOU DON'T EVEN UNDERSTAND YOURSELVES?
TRUE, UNDERSTANDING A BUNCH OF MORONS LIKE YOU WOULD TAKE SERIOUS WORK.
SIGH...
LIVING CREATURES ARE MADE UP OF "YANG" AND "YIN" ENERGY.
YIN
YANG
WHEN YOU PEOPLE DIE, YOUR SOULS ARE RECON-STRUCTED, SO YOU RESURRECT. HOWEVER...
...WHEN IT HAPPENS, SOME PARTS AREN'T RECONSTRUCTED PROPERLY...
...AND THE RESULT IS MEMORY LOSS. IT'S QUITE SIMPLE.

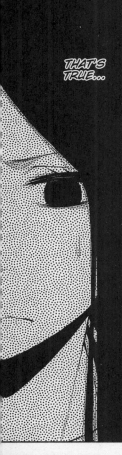

THAT...
...WAS ALSO MADE BY DUPLICATING INFORMATION, BASED ON THE SPIRIT THEORY. THAT'S ALL.
THAT'S TRUE...
IN THE GAME, WHEN YOU DIED, YOU LOST SOME EXP AS A PENALTY.
Smash
Race: Wolf-Fang
Swashbuckler LV.90
Dread Back
LEVEL DOWN
DEAD
Smash
Race: Wolf-Fang
Swashbuckler LV.88
Dread
Status Info
You lost 1,811,933 experience points as compensation.
THE EXPERIENCE WE'D BUILT UP... OUR KNOWLEDGE AND TECHNIQUES... YOU COULD TAKE THAT TO MEAN WE LOST MEMORIES.

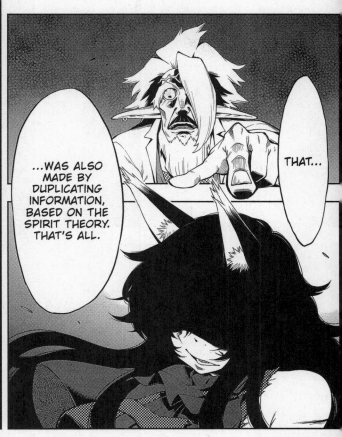

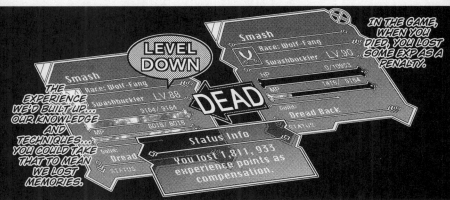

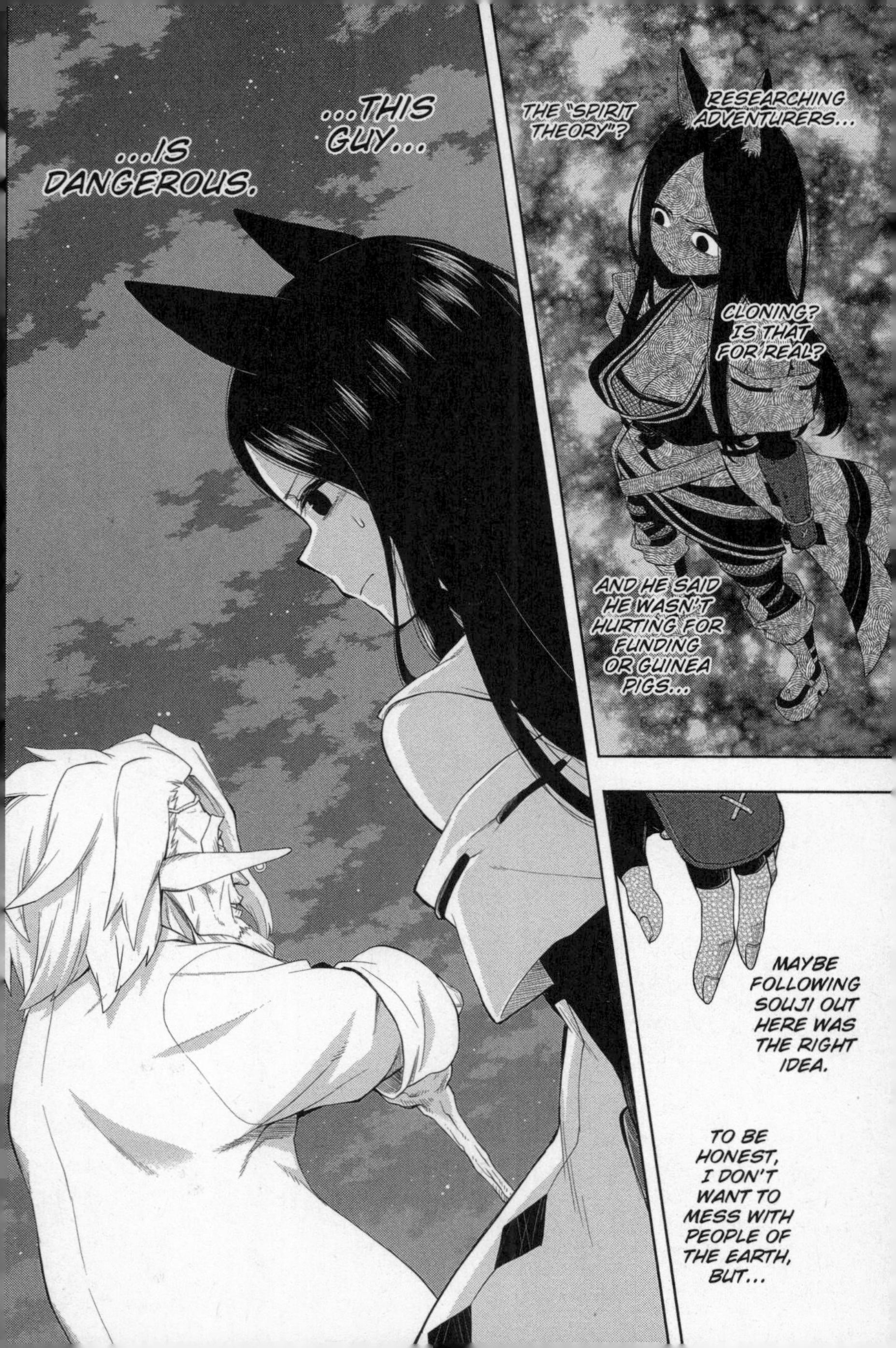
RESEARCHING ADVENTURERS...
THE "SPIRIT THEORY"?
CLONING? IS THAT FOR REAL?
AND HE SAID HE WASN'T HURTING FOR FUNDING OR GUINEA PIGS...
MAYBE FOLLOWING SOUJI OUT HERE WAS THE RIGHT IDEA.
TO BE HONEST, I DON'T WANT TO MESS WITH PEOPLE OF THE EARTH, BUT...
...THIS GUY...
...IS DANGEROUS.

LOG HORIZON
THE WEST WIND BRIGADE

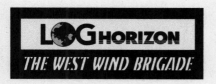

LOG HORIZON

THE WEST WIND BRIGADE

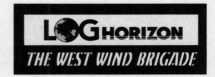

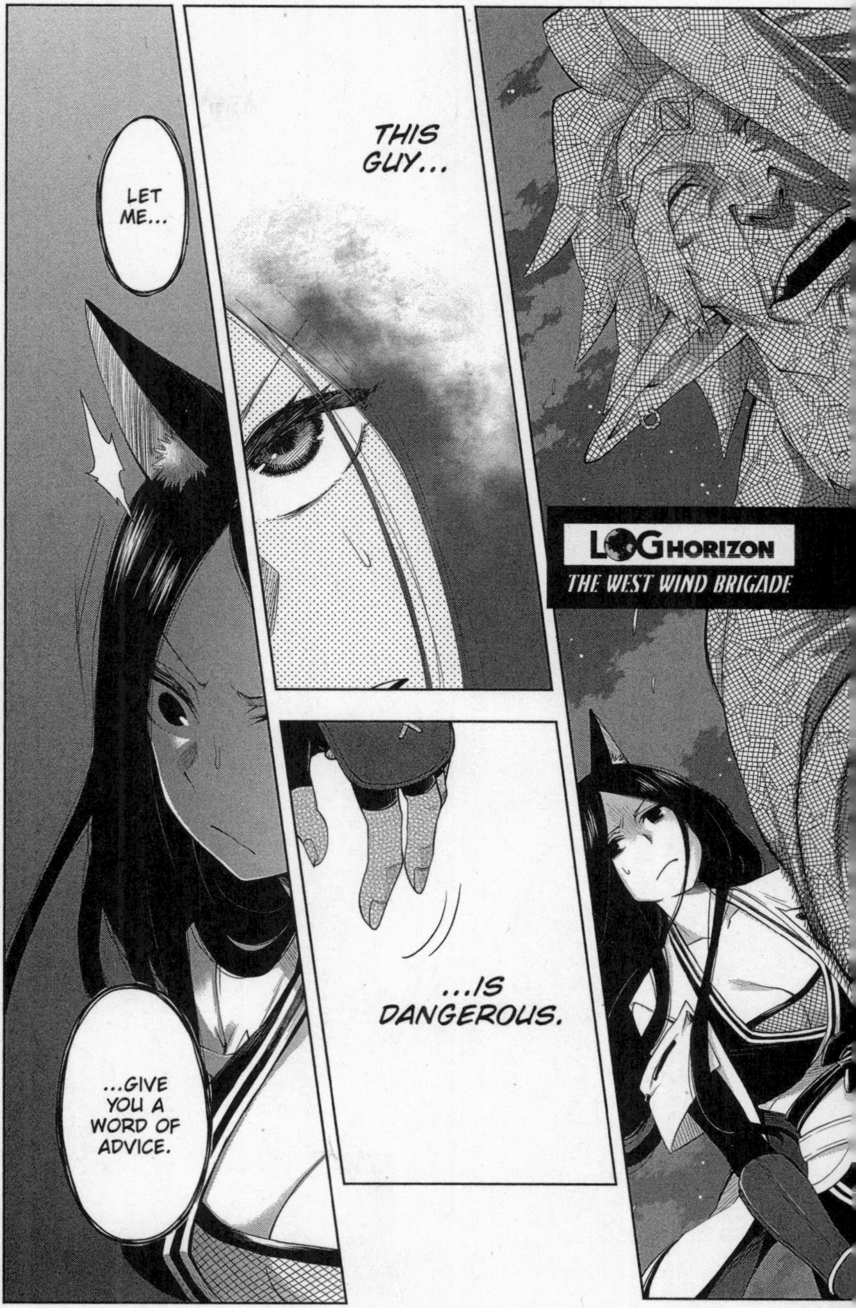
LOG HORIZON
THE WEST WIND BRIGADE
THIS GUY...
...IS DANGEROUS.
LET ME...
...GIVE YOU A WORD OF ADVICE.

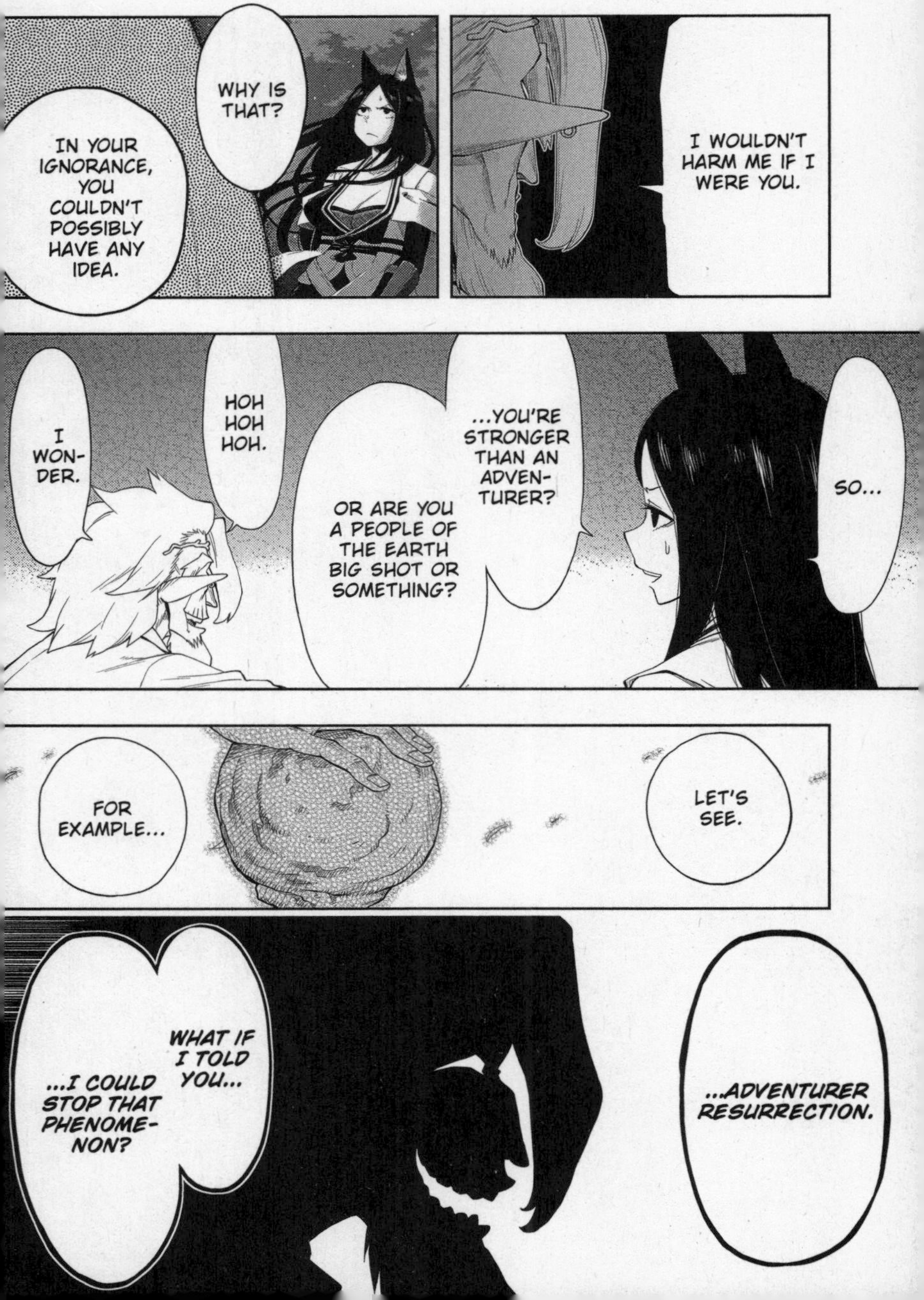
I WOULDN'T HARM ME IF I WERE YOU.
WHY IS THAT?
IN YOUR IGNORANCE, YOU COULDN'T POSSIBLY HAVE ANY IDEA.
SO...
...YOU'RE STRONGER THAN AN ADVENTURER?
OR ARE YOU A PEOPLE OF THE EARTH BIG SHOT OR SOMETHING?
HOH HOH HOH.
I WONDER.
LET'S SEE.
FOR EXAMPLE...
...ADVENTURER RESURRECTION.
WHAT IF I TOLD YOU...
...I COULD STOP THAT PHENOMENON?

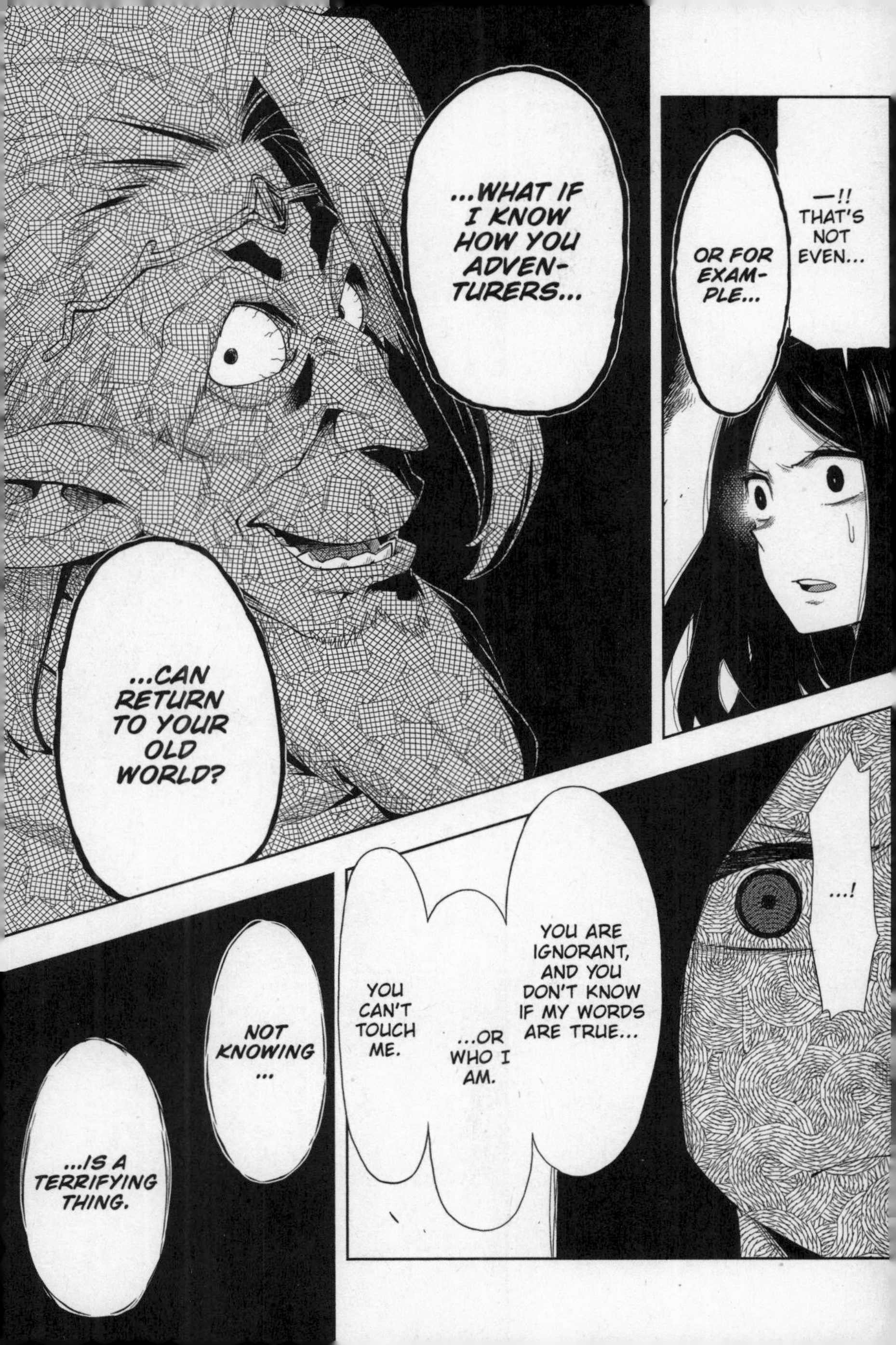
—!! THAT'S NOT EVEN...
OR FOR EXAMPLE...
...WHAT IF I KNOW HOW YOU ADVENTURERS...
...CAN RETURN TO YOUR OLD WORLD?
...!
YOU ARE IGNORANT, AND YOU DON'T KNOW IF MY WORDS ARE TRUE...
...OR WHO I AM.
YOU CAN'T TOUCH ME.
NOT KNOWING...
...IS A TERRIFYING THING.

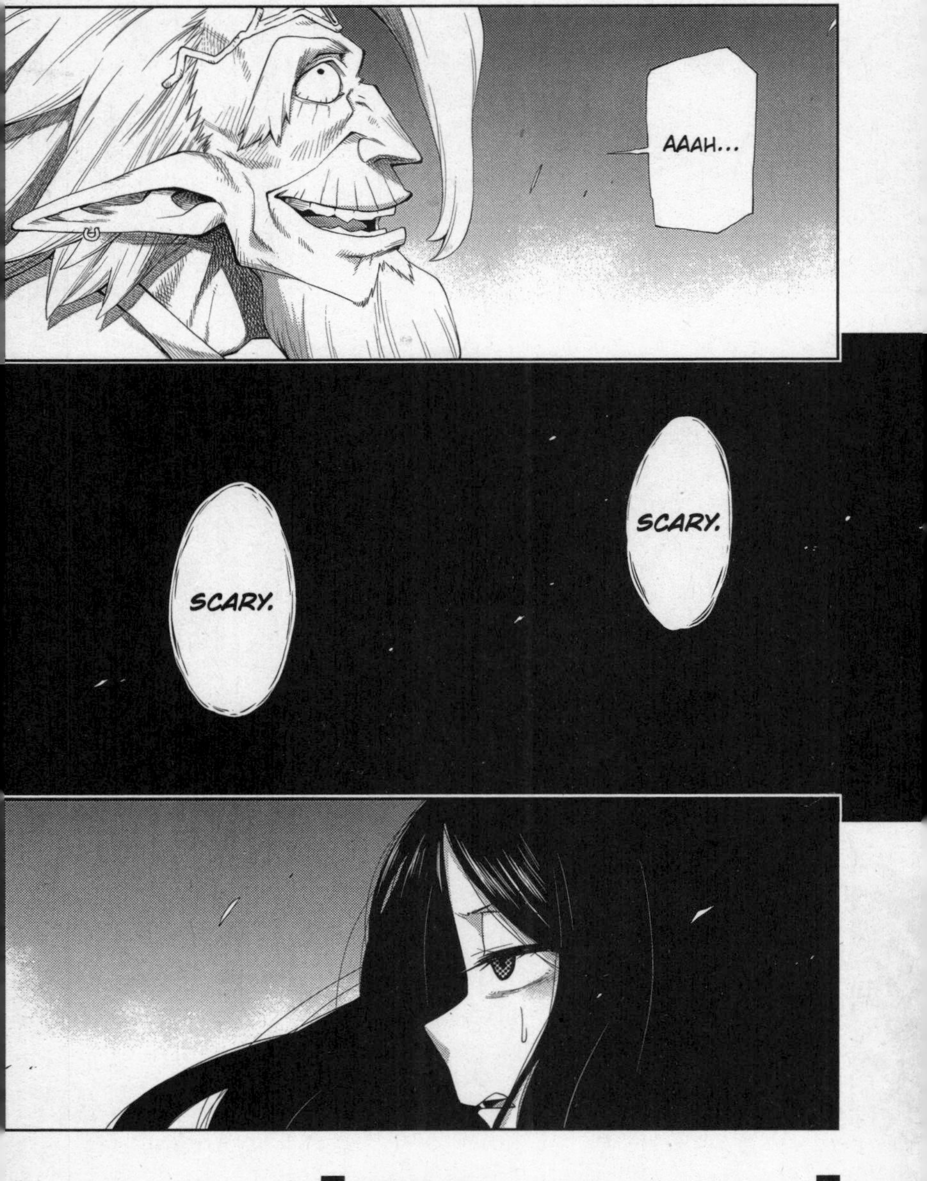
AAAH...
SCARY.
SCARY.

CHAPTER: 43 Because You Smiled

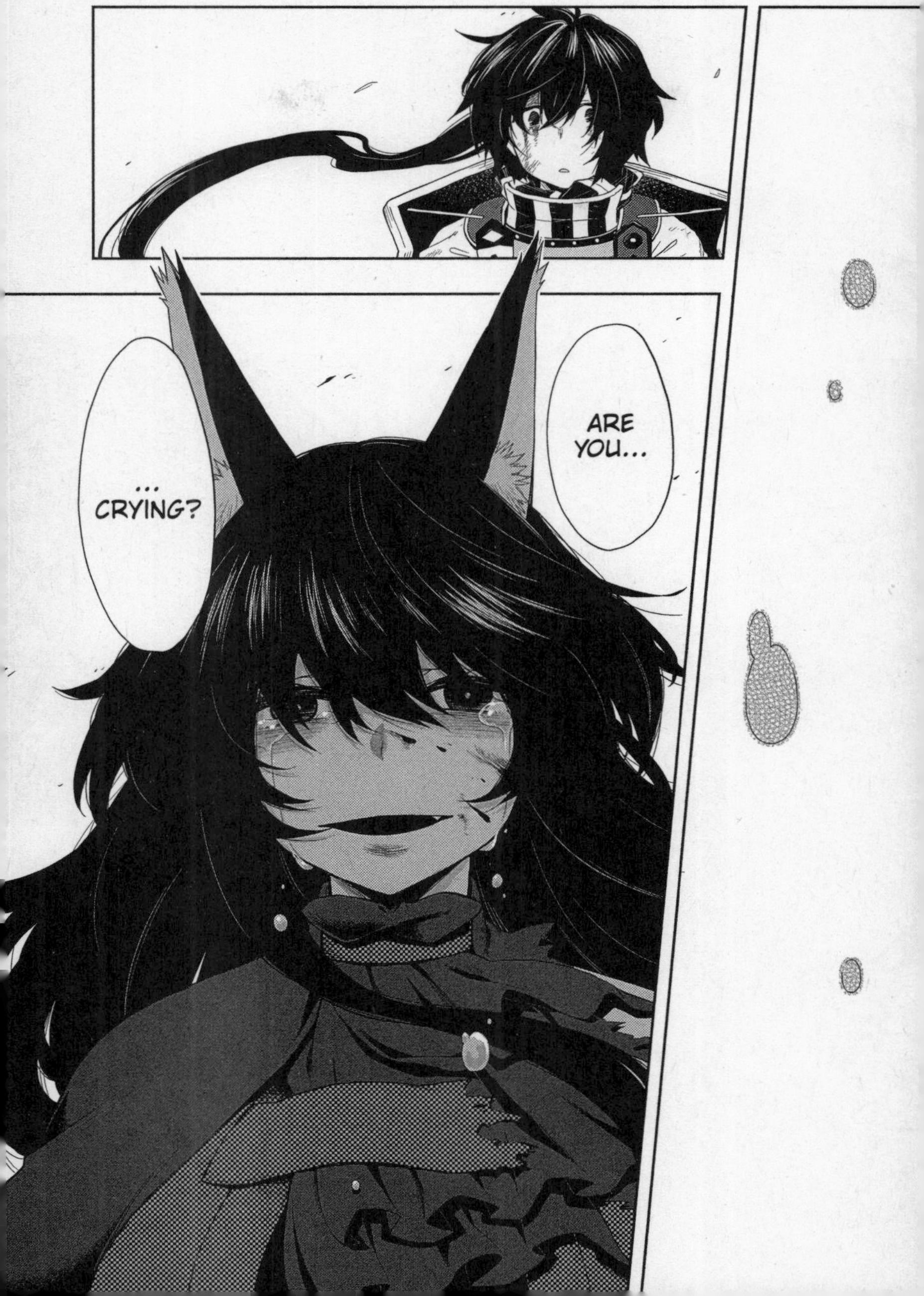
ARE YOU...
...CRYING?

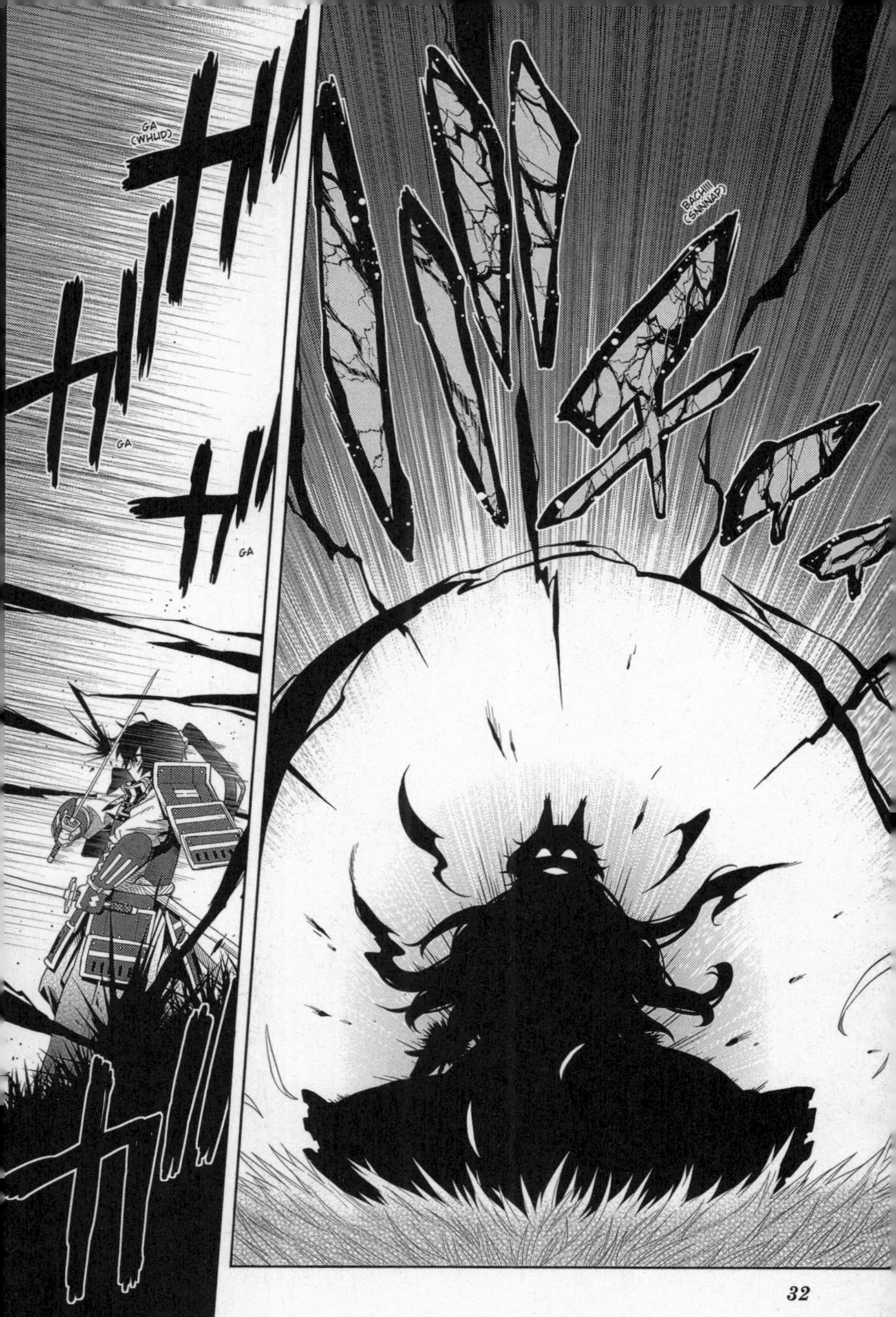
BACHIII (SNNNAP)
GA (WHUD)
GA
GA

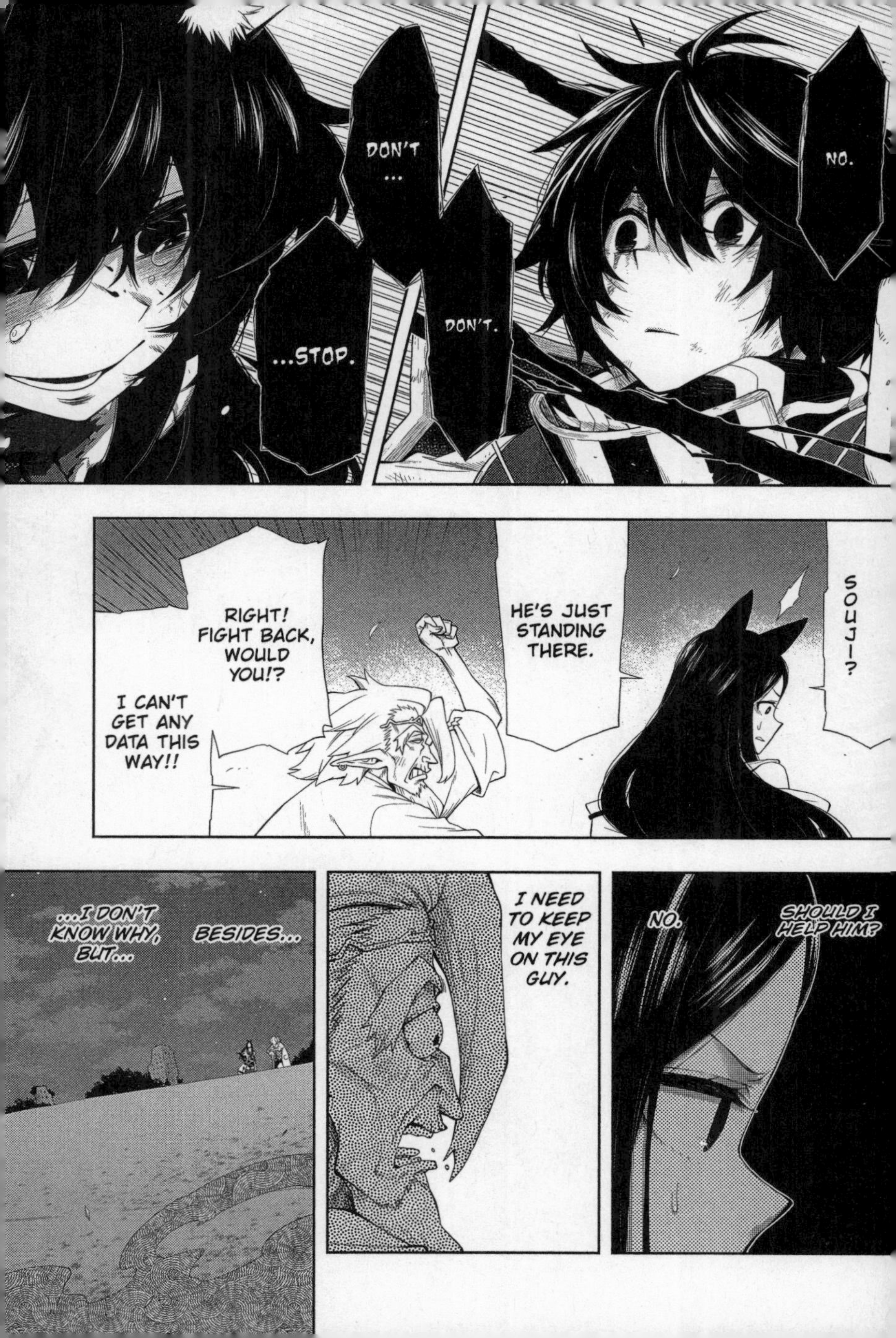
NO.
DON'T ...
DON'T.
...STOP.
SOUJI—?
HE'S JUST STANDING THERE.
RIGHT! FIGHT BACK, WOULD YOU!?
I CAN'T GET ANY DATA THIS WAY!!
SHOULD I HELP HIM?
NO.
I NEED TO KEEP MY EYE ON THIS GUY.
BESIDES...
...I DON'T KNOW WHY, BUT...

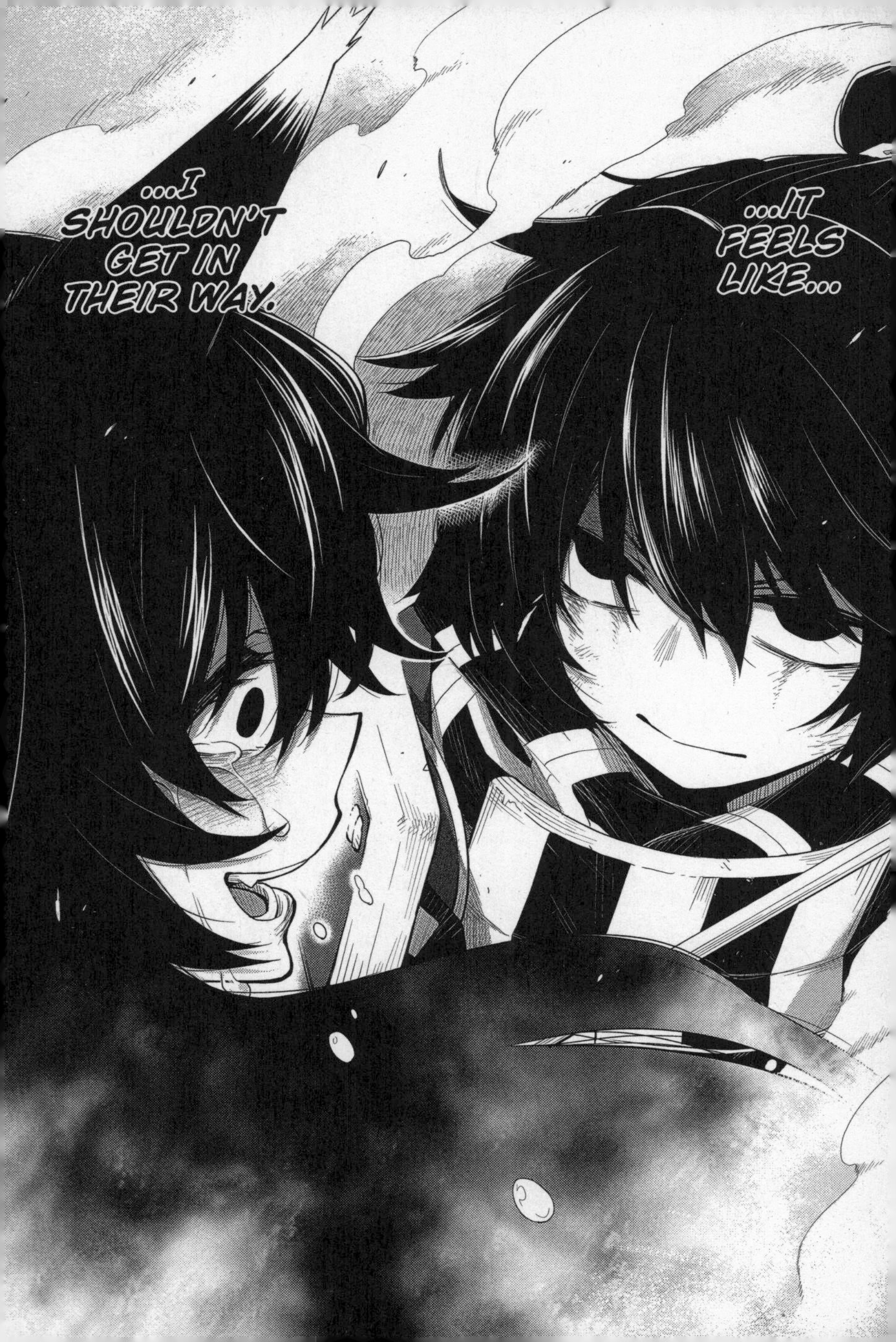
...IT FEELS LIKE...
...I SHOULDN'T GET IN THEIR WAY.

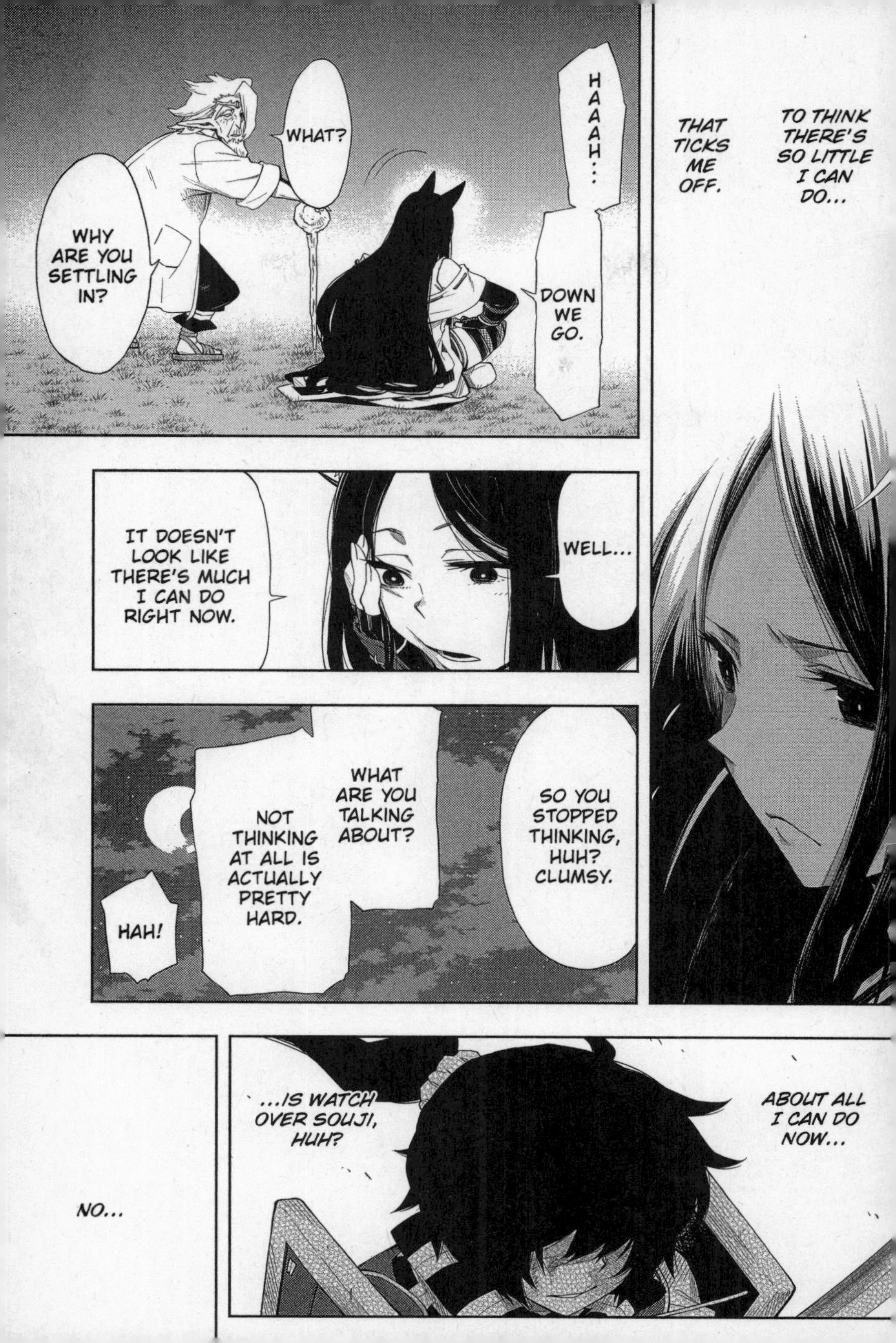
TO THINK THERE'S SO LITTLE I CAN DO...
THAT TICKS ME OFF.
HAAAH...
DOWN WE GO.
WHAT?
WHY ARE YOU SETTLING IN?
WELL...
IT DOESN'T LOOK LIKE THERE'S MUCH I CAN DO RIGHT NOW.
SO YOU STOPPED THINKING, HUH? CLUMSY.
WHAT ARE YOU TALKING ABOUT?
NOT THINKING AT ALL IS ACTUALLY PRETTY HARD.
HAH!
ABOUT ALL I CAN DO NOW...
...IS WATCH OVER SOUJI, HUH?
NO...

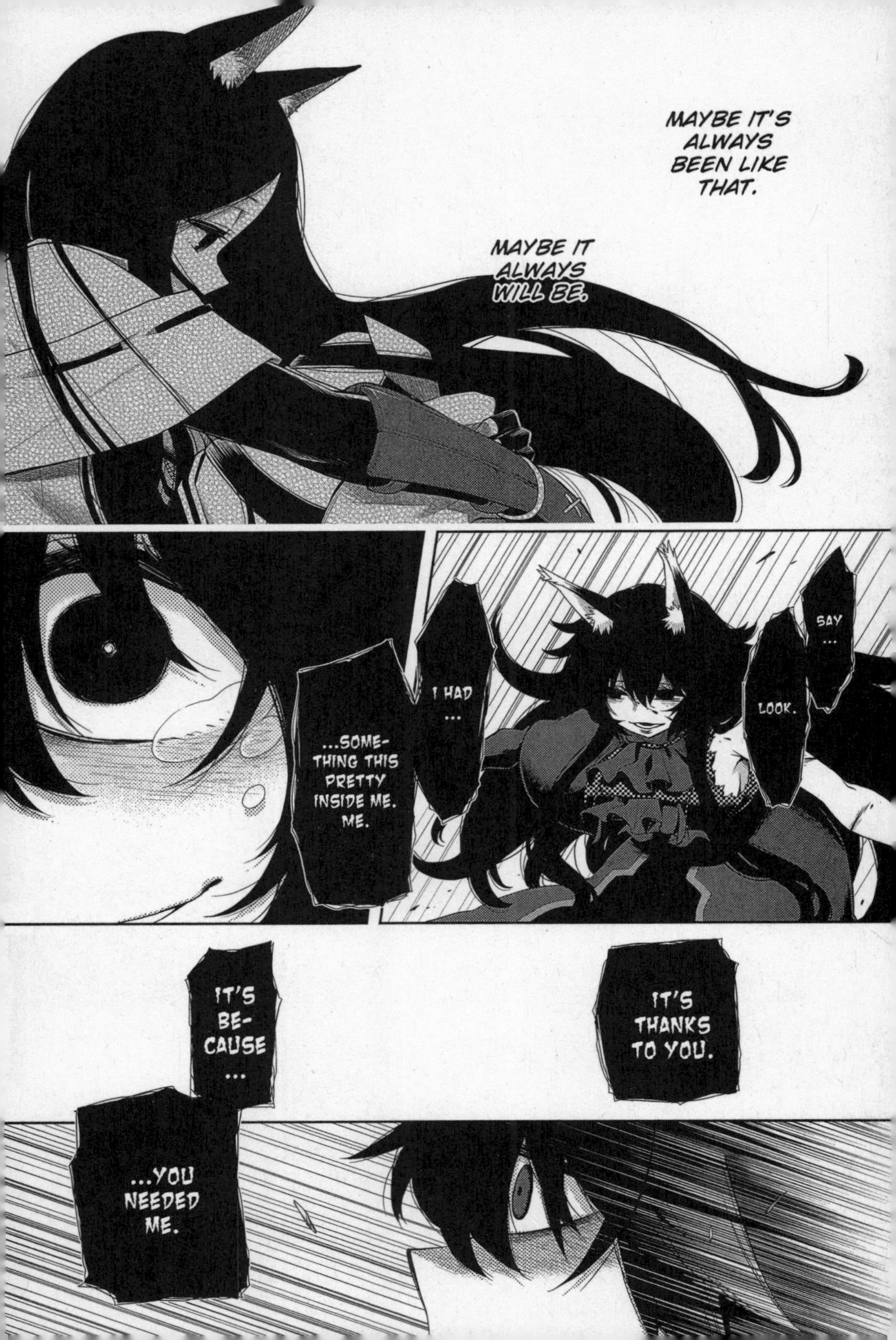
MAYBE IT'S ALWAYS BEEN LIKE THAT.
MAYBE IT ALWAYS WILL BE.
SAY...
LOOK.
I HAD...
...SOME-THING THIS PRETTY INSIDE ME. ME.
IT'S THANKS TO YOU.
IT'S BE-CAUSE...
...YOU NEEDED ME.

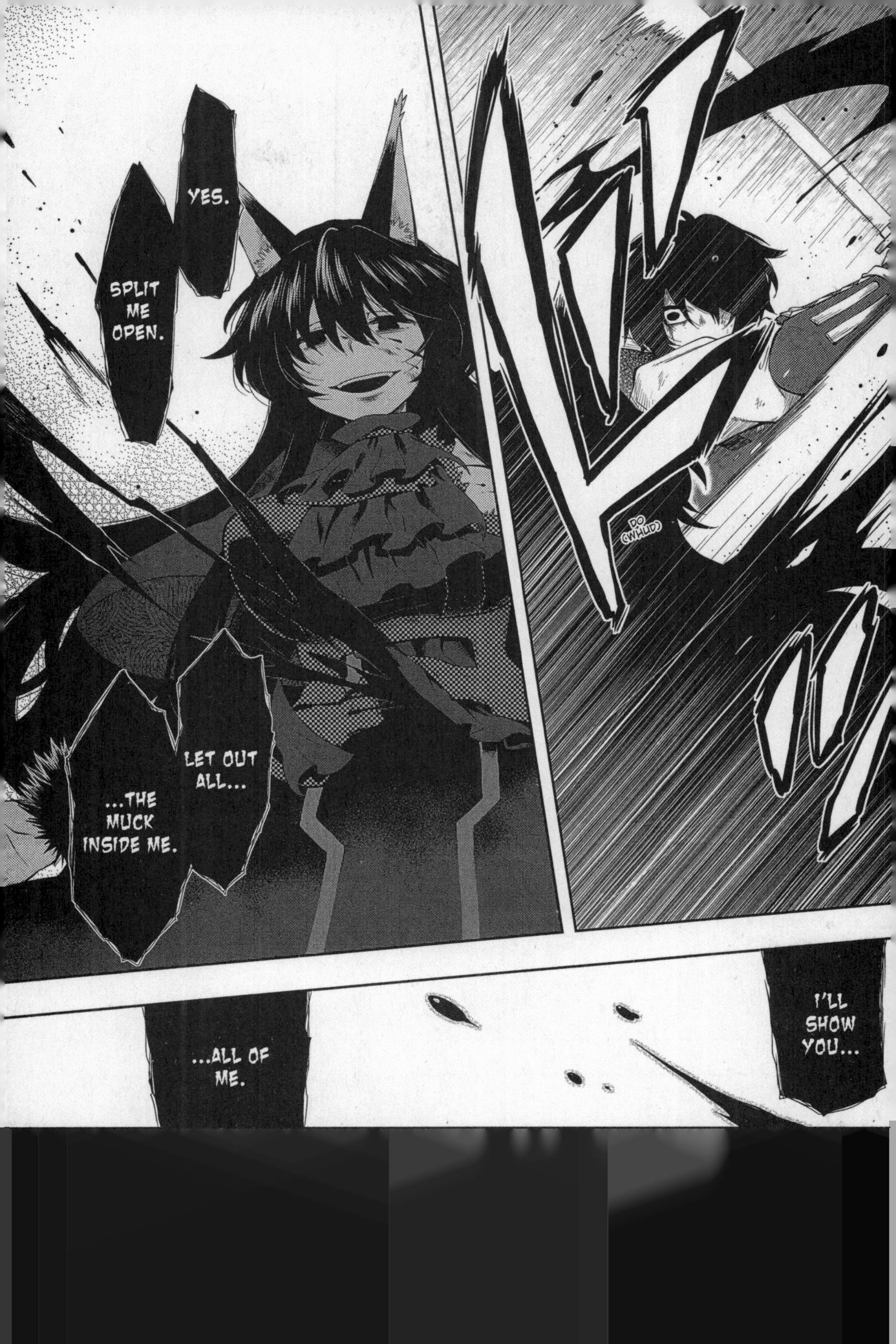
DO (WHUD)
YES.
SPLIT ME OPEN.
LET OUT ALL...
...THE MUCK INSIDE ME.
I'LL SHOW YOU...
...ALL OF ME.

I'M...
...TRASH.
I'M AN IMPURITY.
THE EYES THAT WATCH ME...
...SEE SOMETHING DIRTY.
ALWAYS, ALWAYS ...
IT'S BEEN THAT WAY FOR A VERY LONG TIME.
ONLY ...

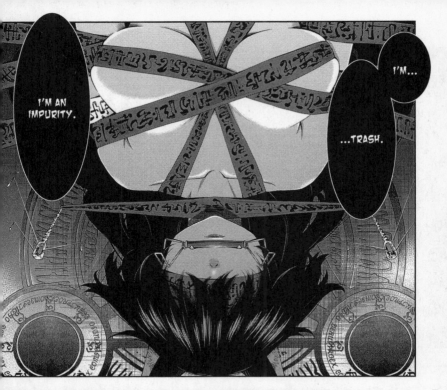

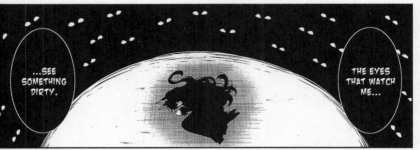

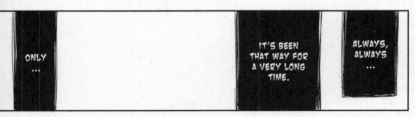

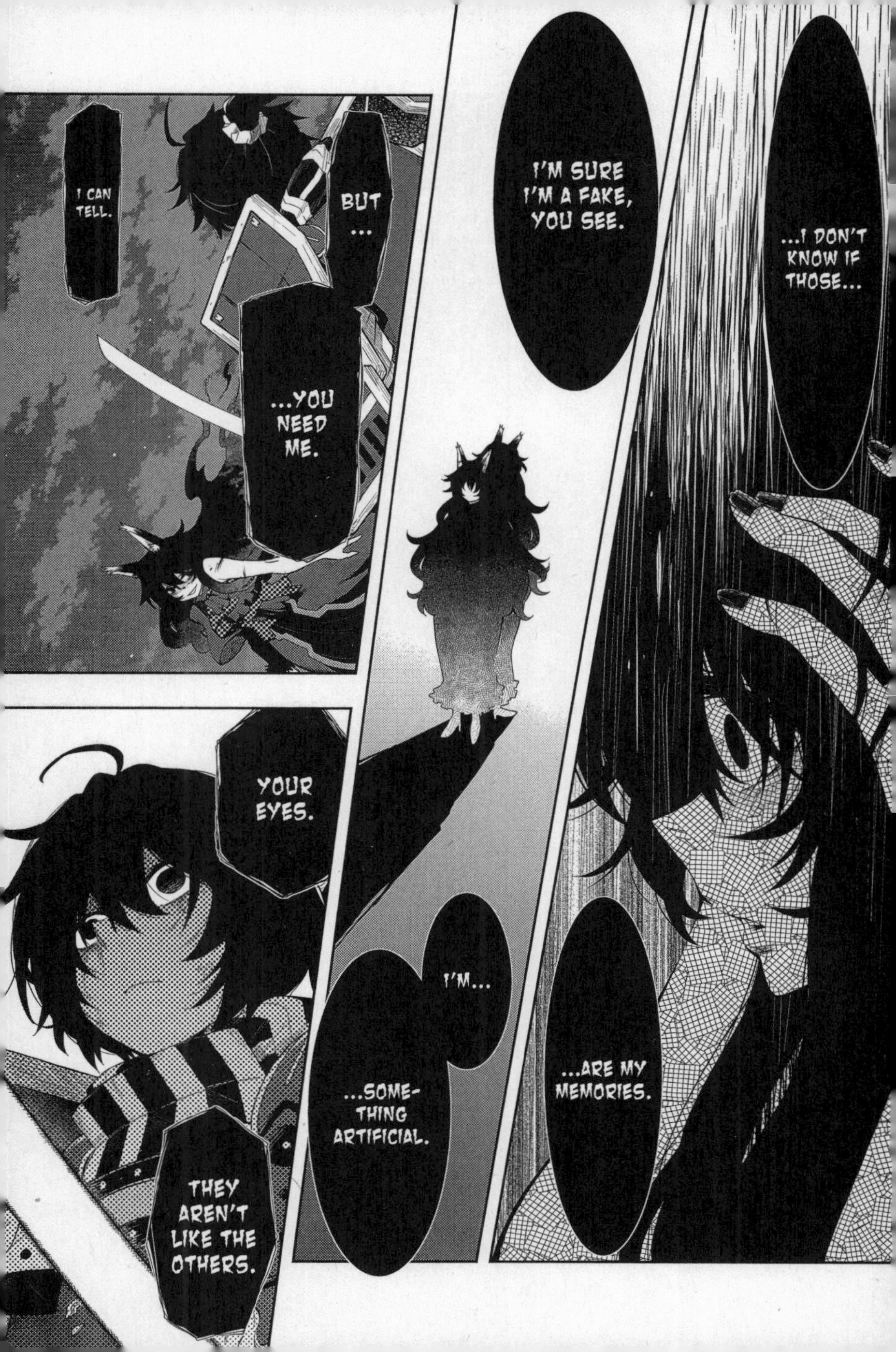
...I DON'T KNOW IF THOSE...
...ARE MY MEMORIES.
I'M SURE I'M A FAKE, YOU SEE.
I'M...
...SOME-THING ARTIFICIAL.
BUT...
...YOU NEED ME.
I CAN TELL.
YOUR EYES.
THEY AREN'T LIKE THE OTHERS.

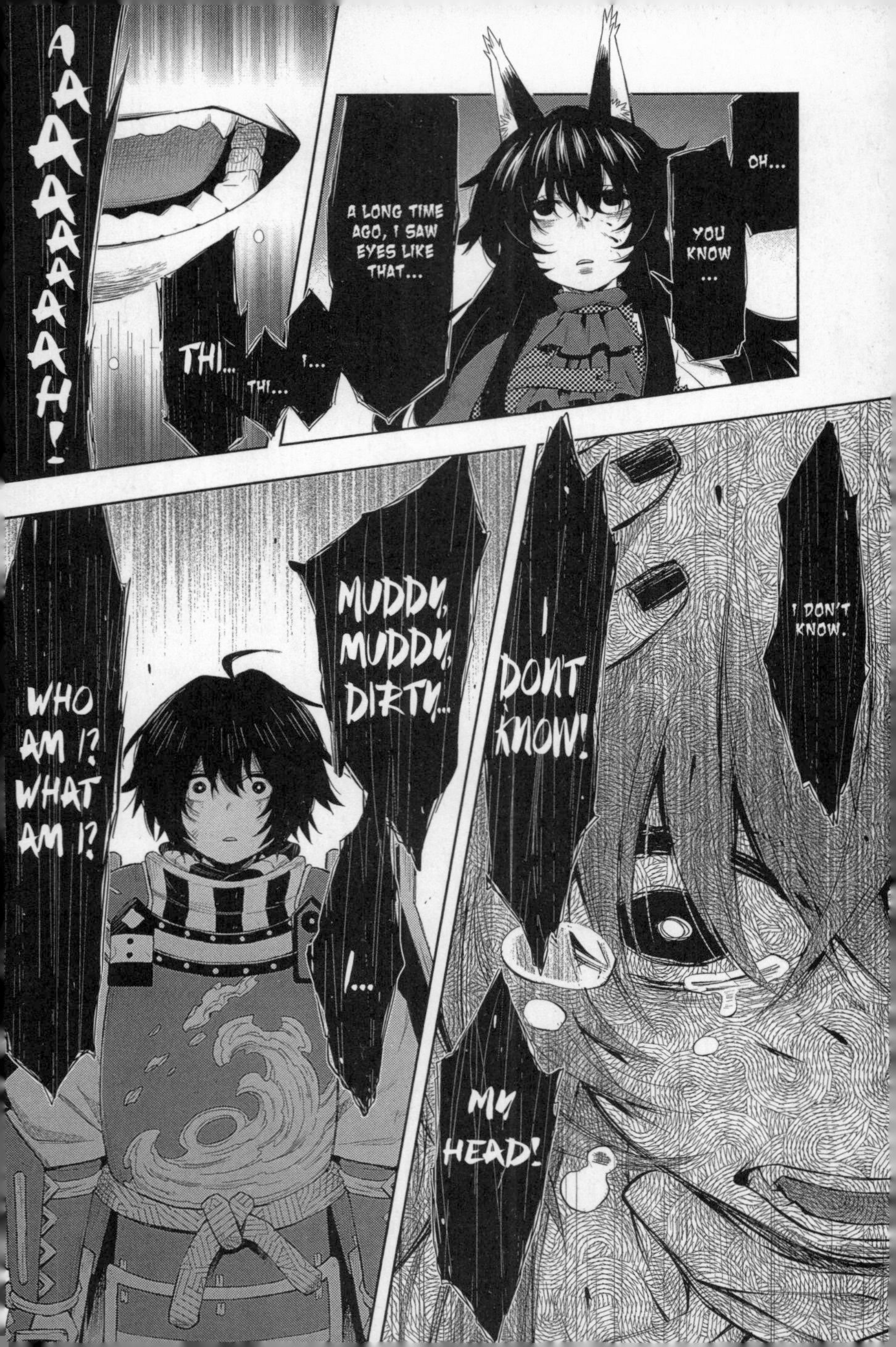
OH...
YOU KNOW ...
A LONG TIME AGO, I SAW EYES LIKE THAT...
THI...
I...
THI...
AAAAAAAAAH!
I DON'T KNOW.
I DONT KNOW!
MY HEAD!
MUDDY, MUDDY, DIRTY...
I...
WHO AM I? WHAT AM I?

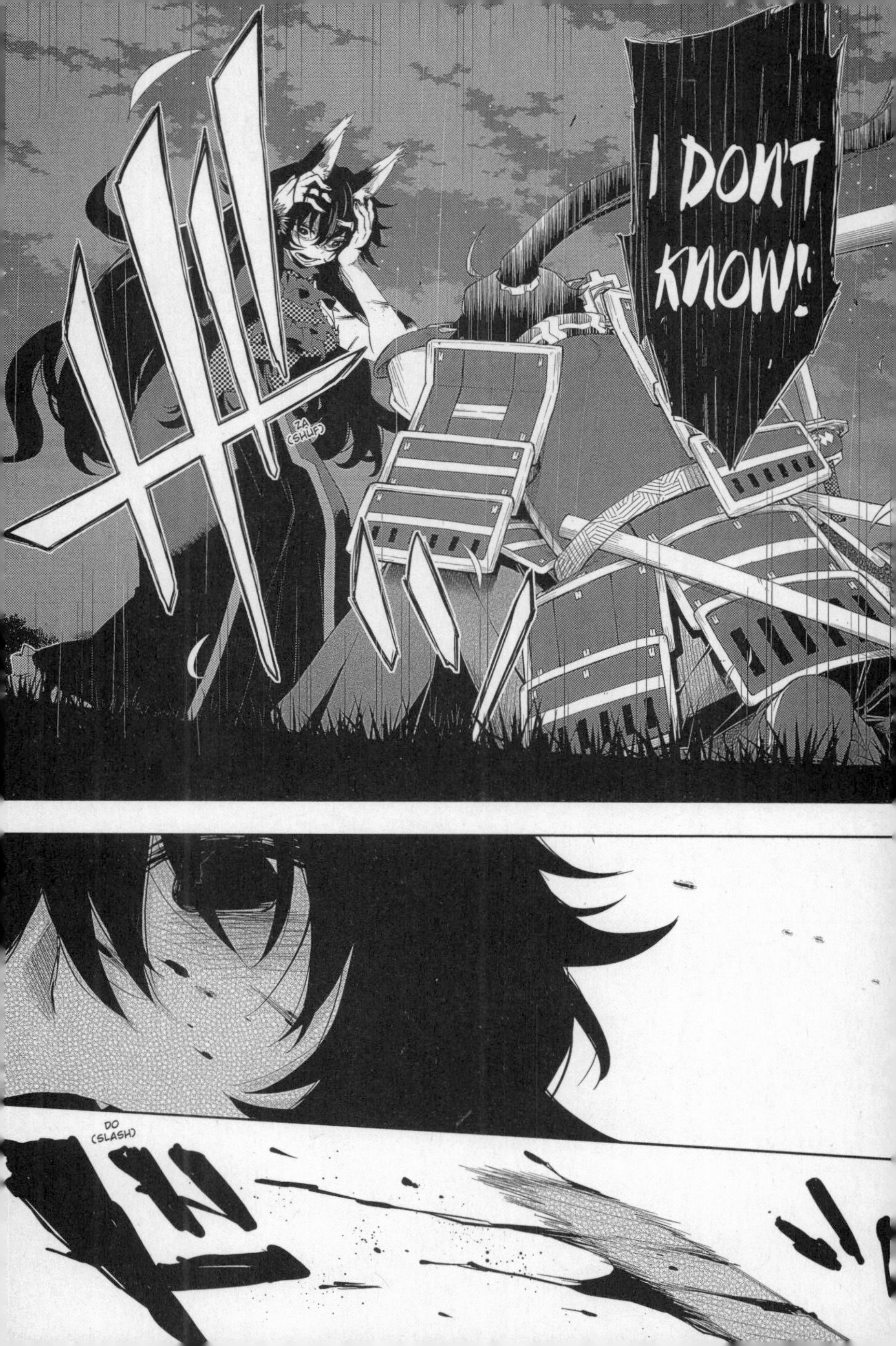
I DON'T KNOW!
ZA (SHUF)
DO (SLASH)

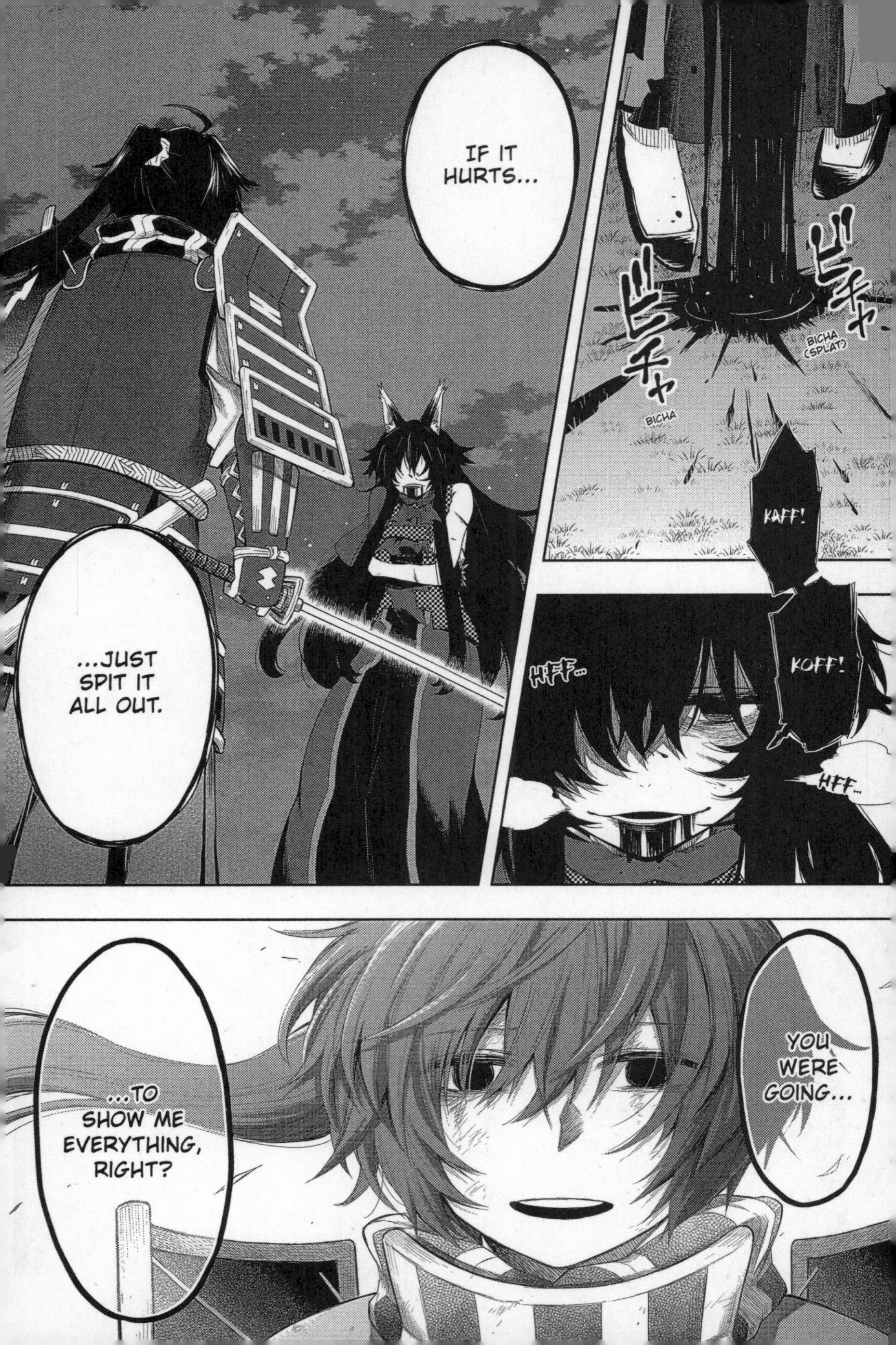
ビチャ
BICHA (SPLAT)
ビチャ
BICHA
KAFF!
KOFF!
HFF...
HFF...
IF IT HURTS...
...JUST SPIT IT ALL OUT.
YOU WERE GOING...
...TO SHOW ME EVERYTHING, RIGHT?

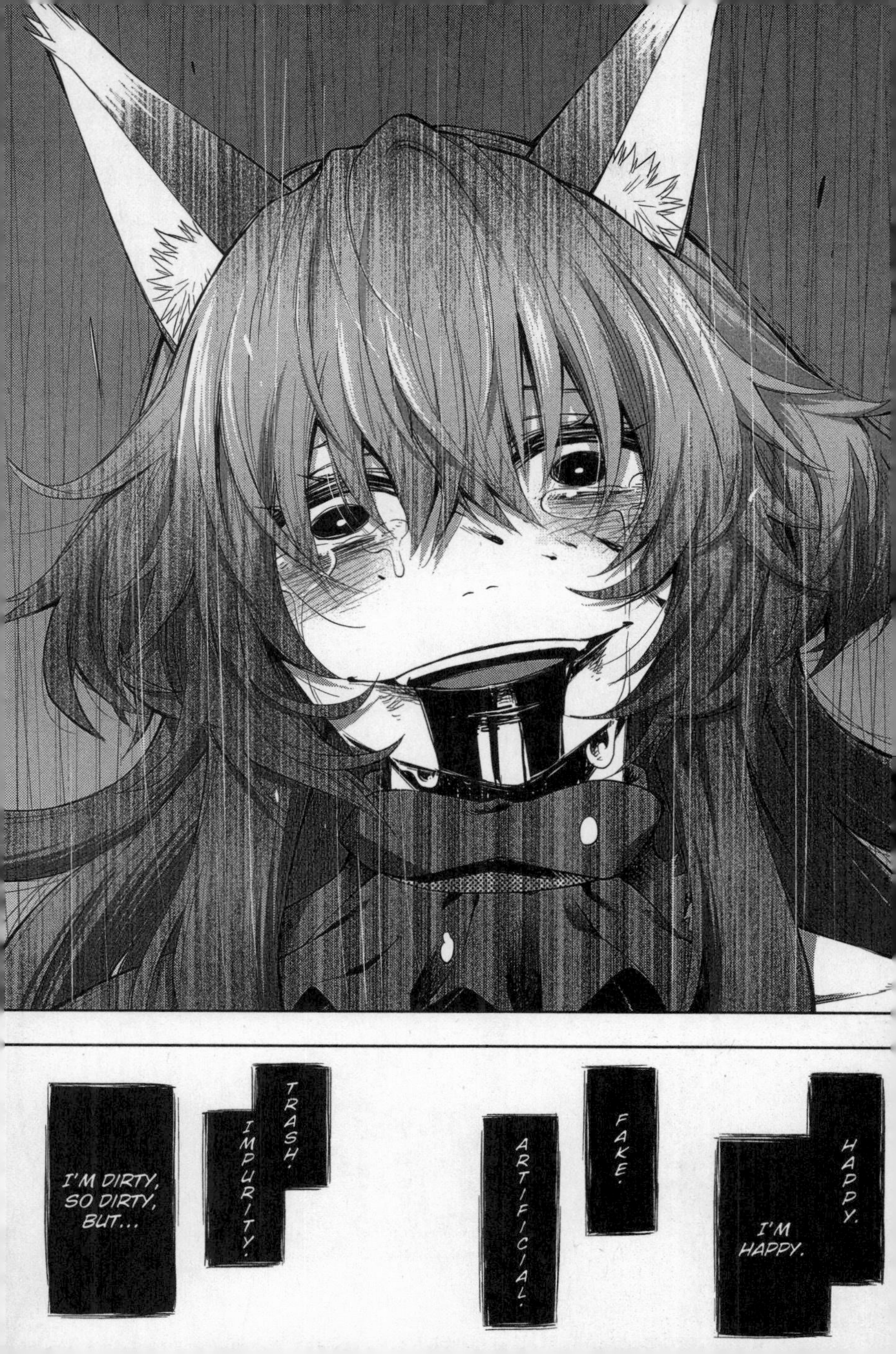
I'M DIRTY, SO DIRTY, BUT...
TRASH.
IMPURITY.
ARTIFICIAL.
FAKE.
HAPPY.
I'M HAPPY.

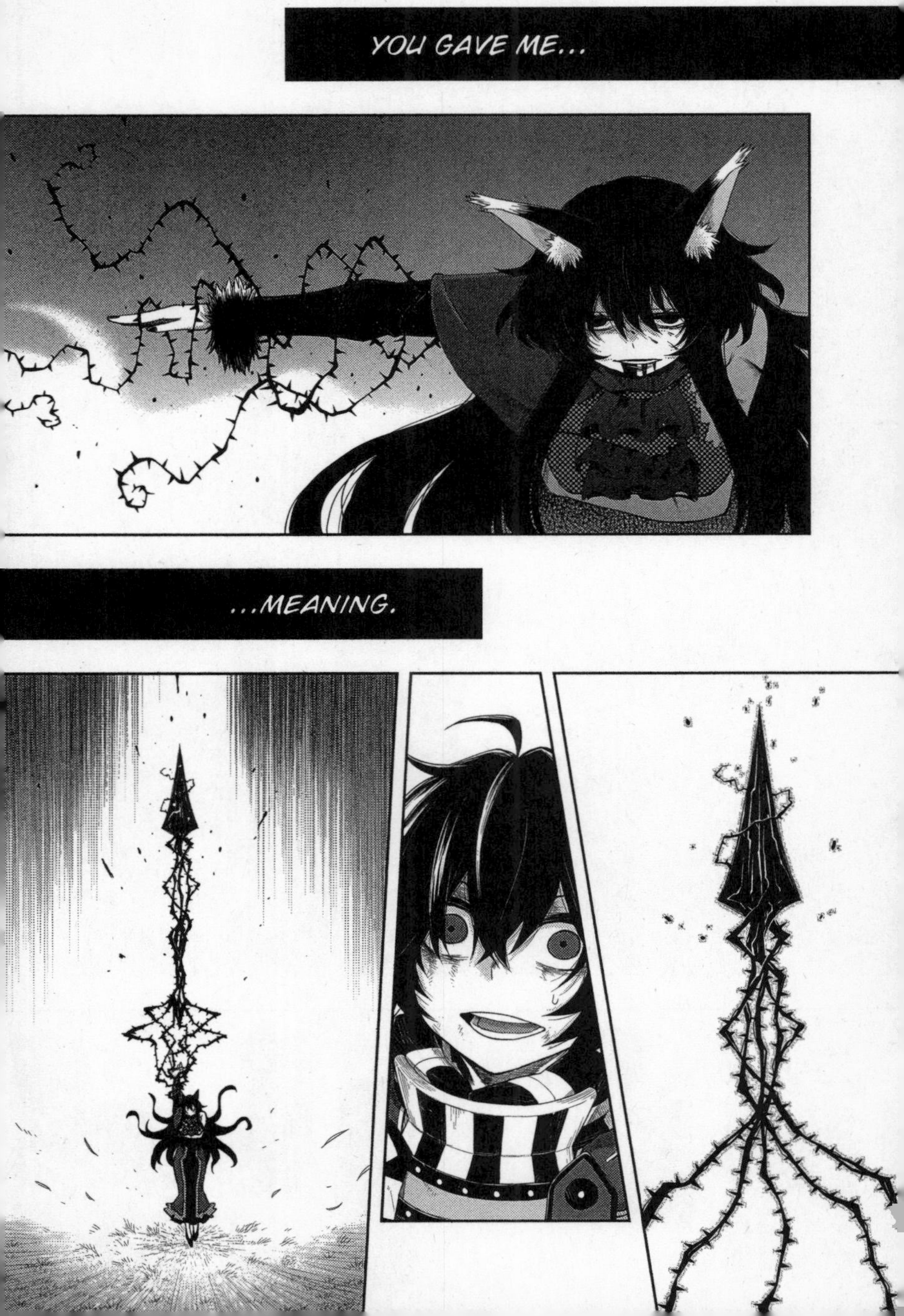
YOU GAVE ME...
...MEANING.

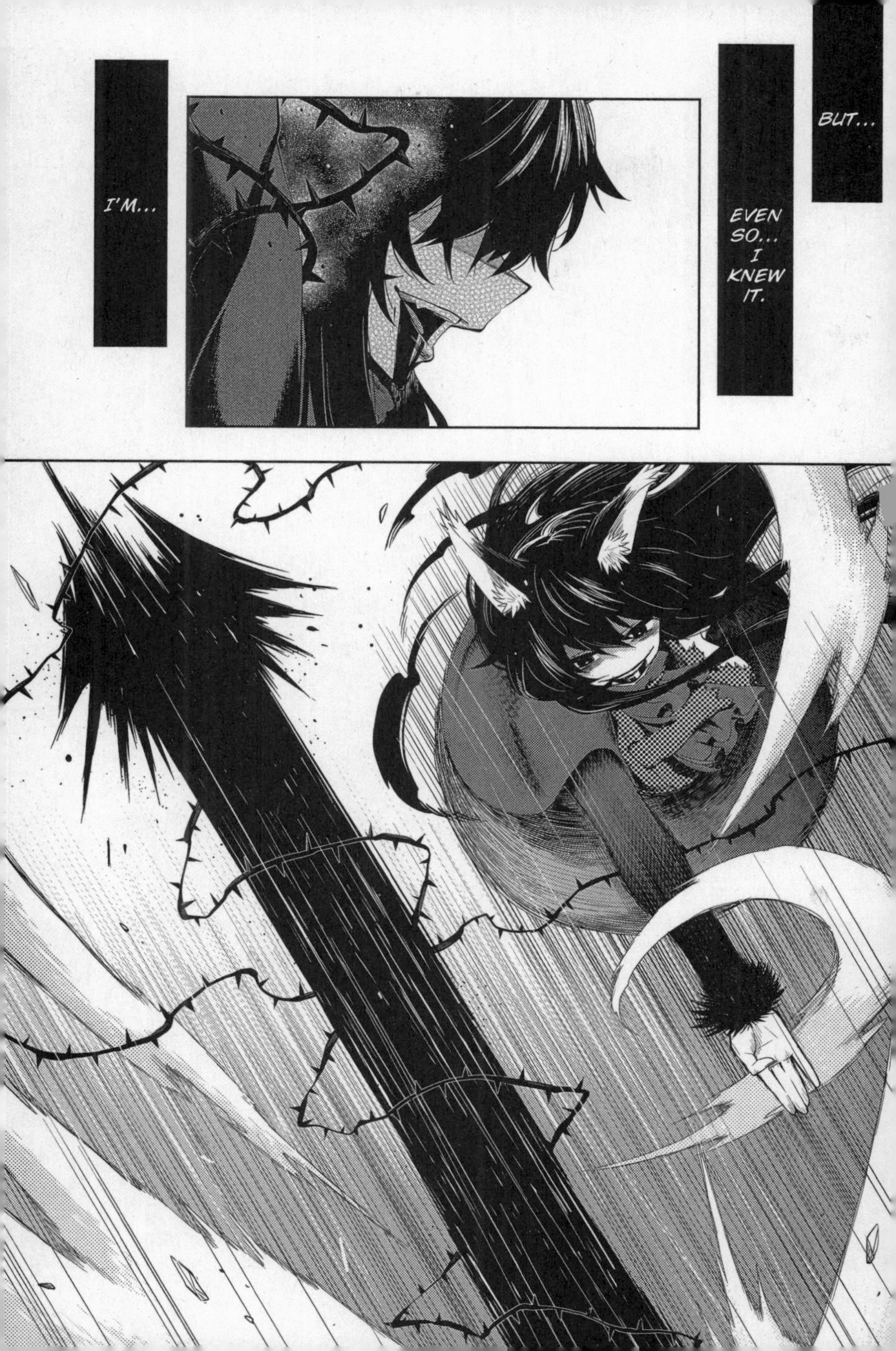
BUT...
EVEN SO... I KNEW IT.
I'M...

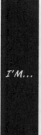

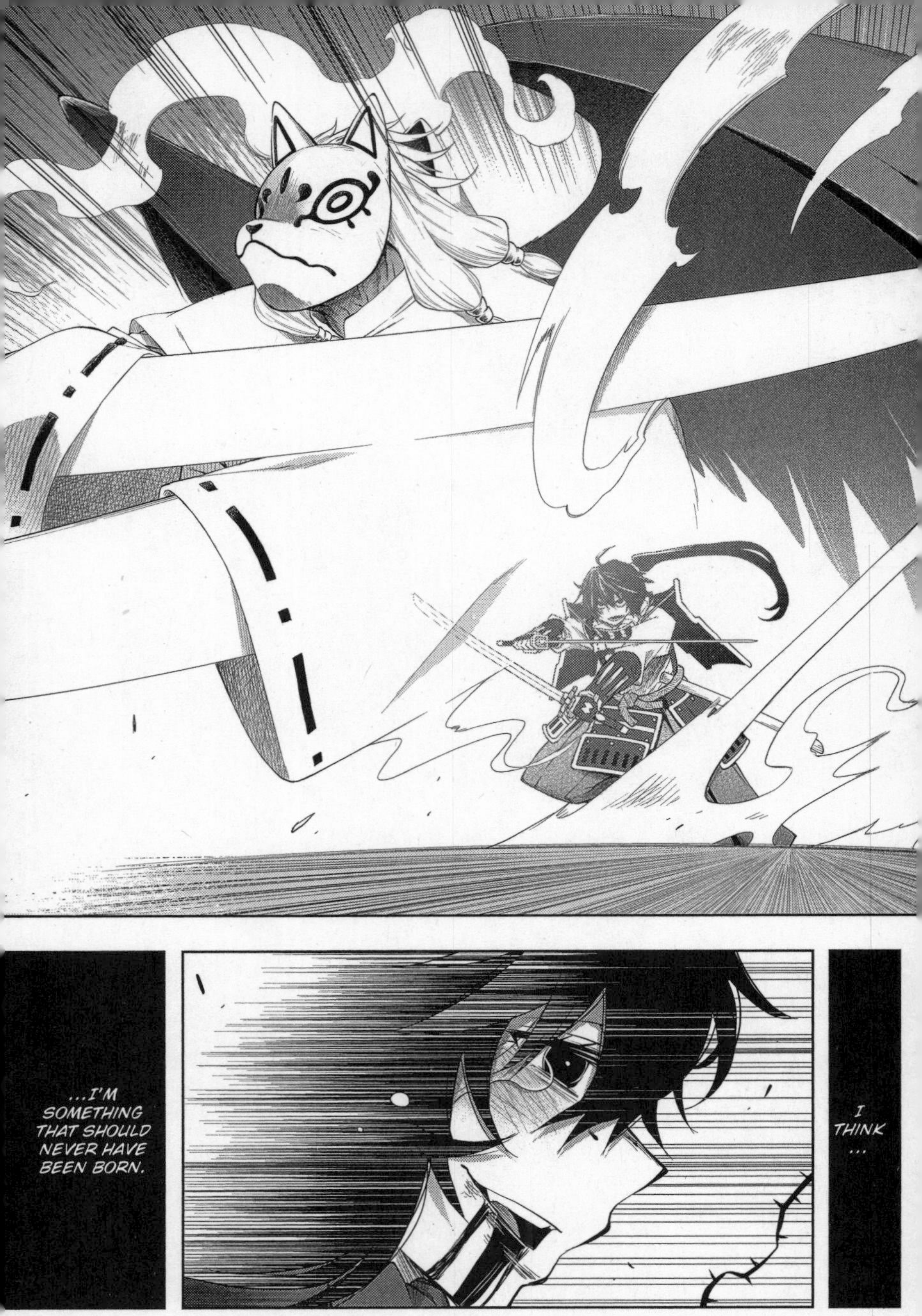
I THINK ...
...I'M SOMETHING THAT SHOULD NEVER HAVE BEEN BORN.

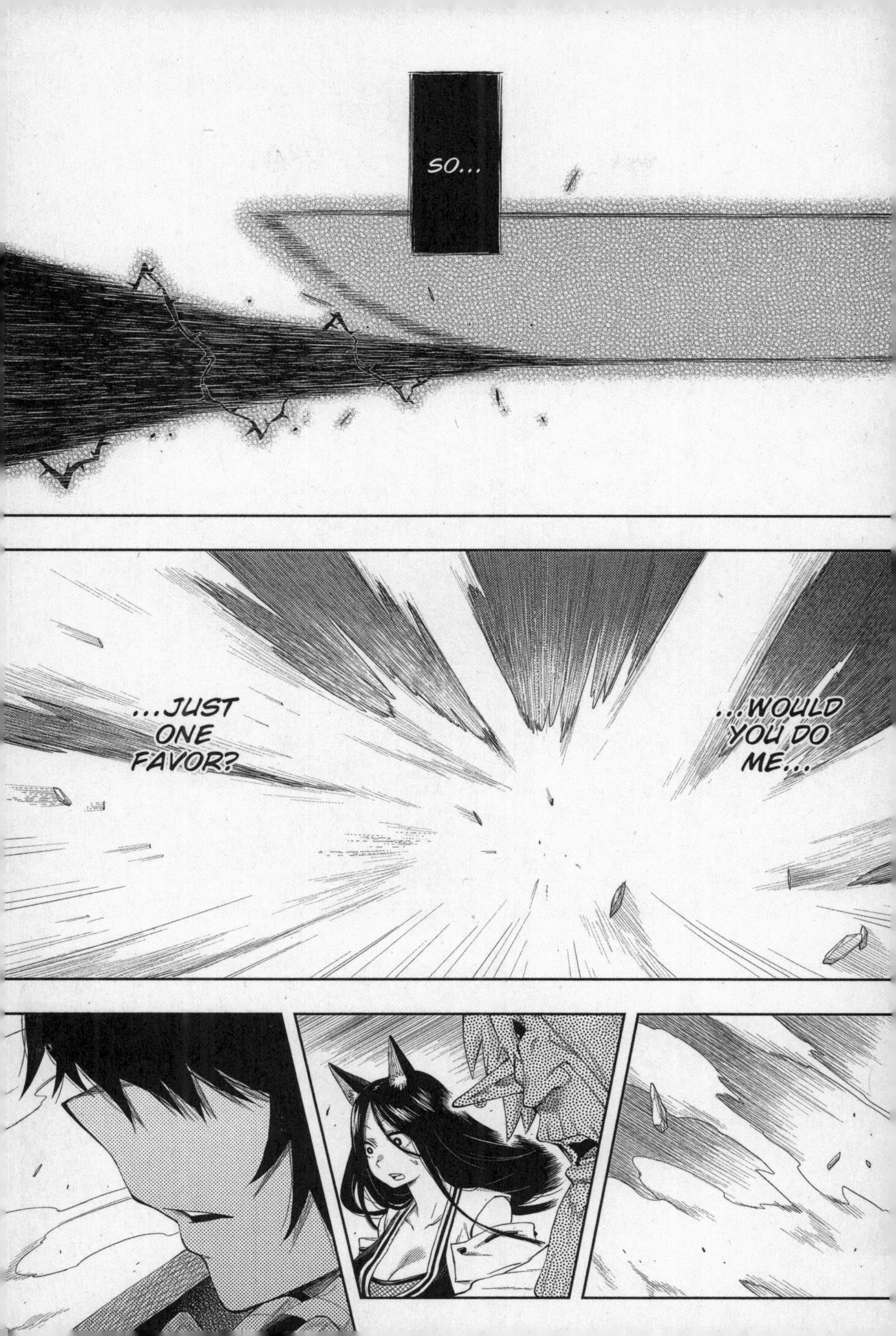
SO...
...WOULD YOU DO ME...
...JUST ONE FAVOR?

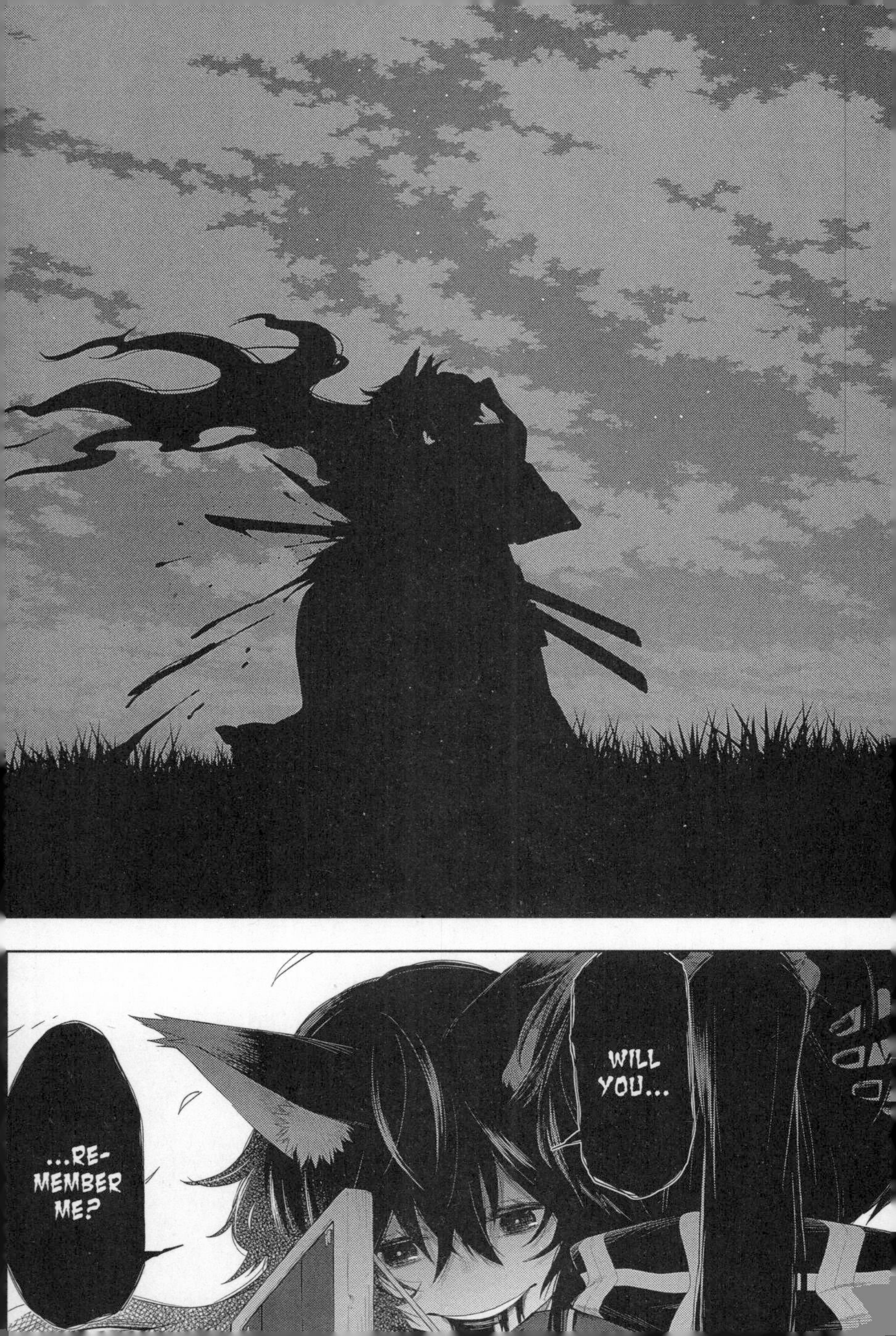
WILL YOU...
...RE-MEMBER ME?

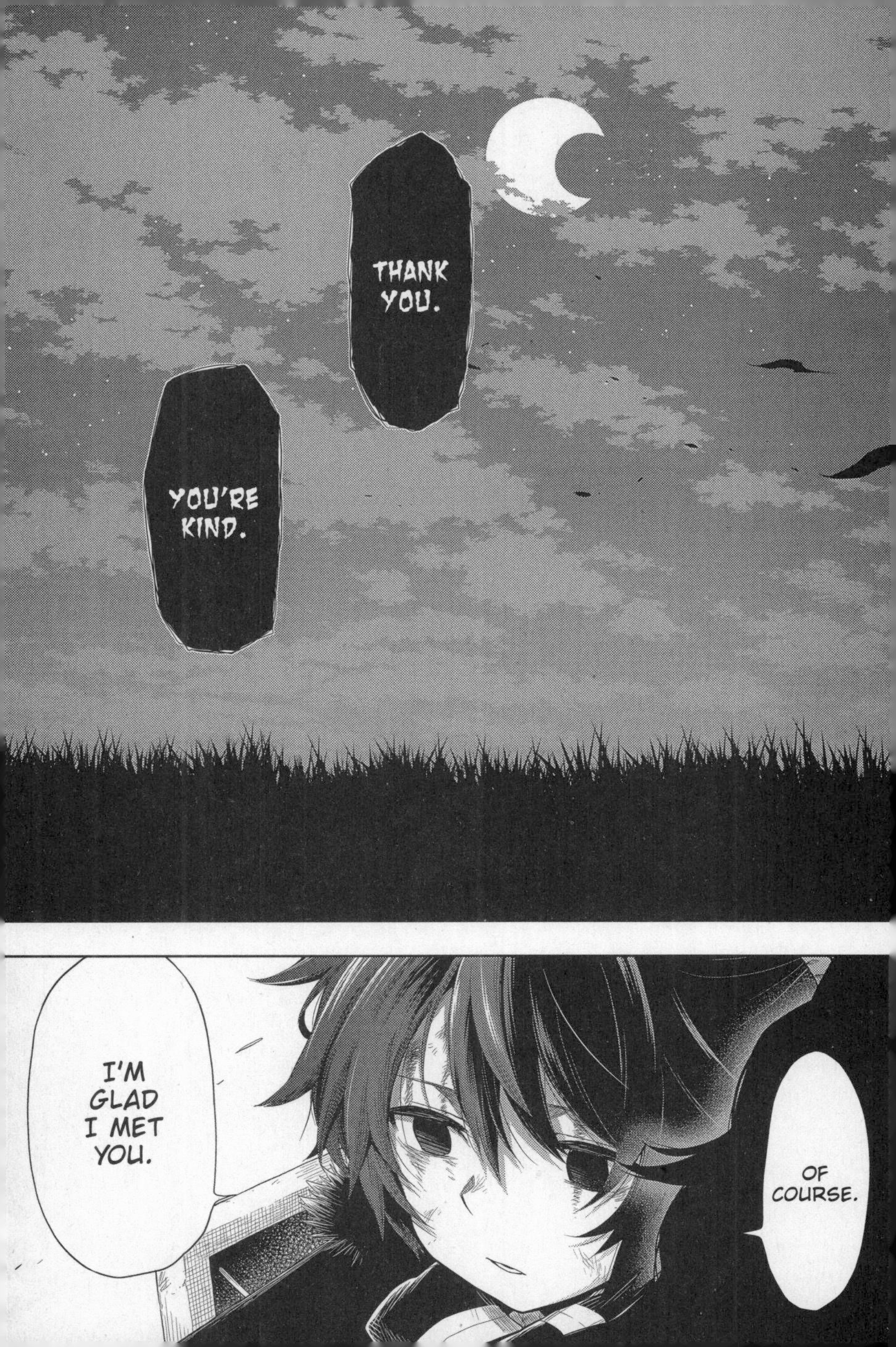
THANK YOU.
YOU'RE KIND.
OF COURSE.
I'M GLAD I MET YOU.

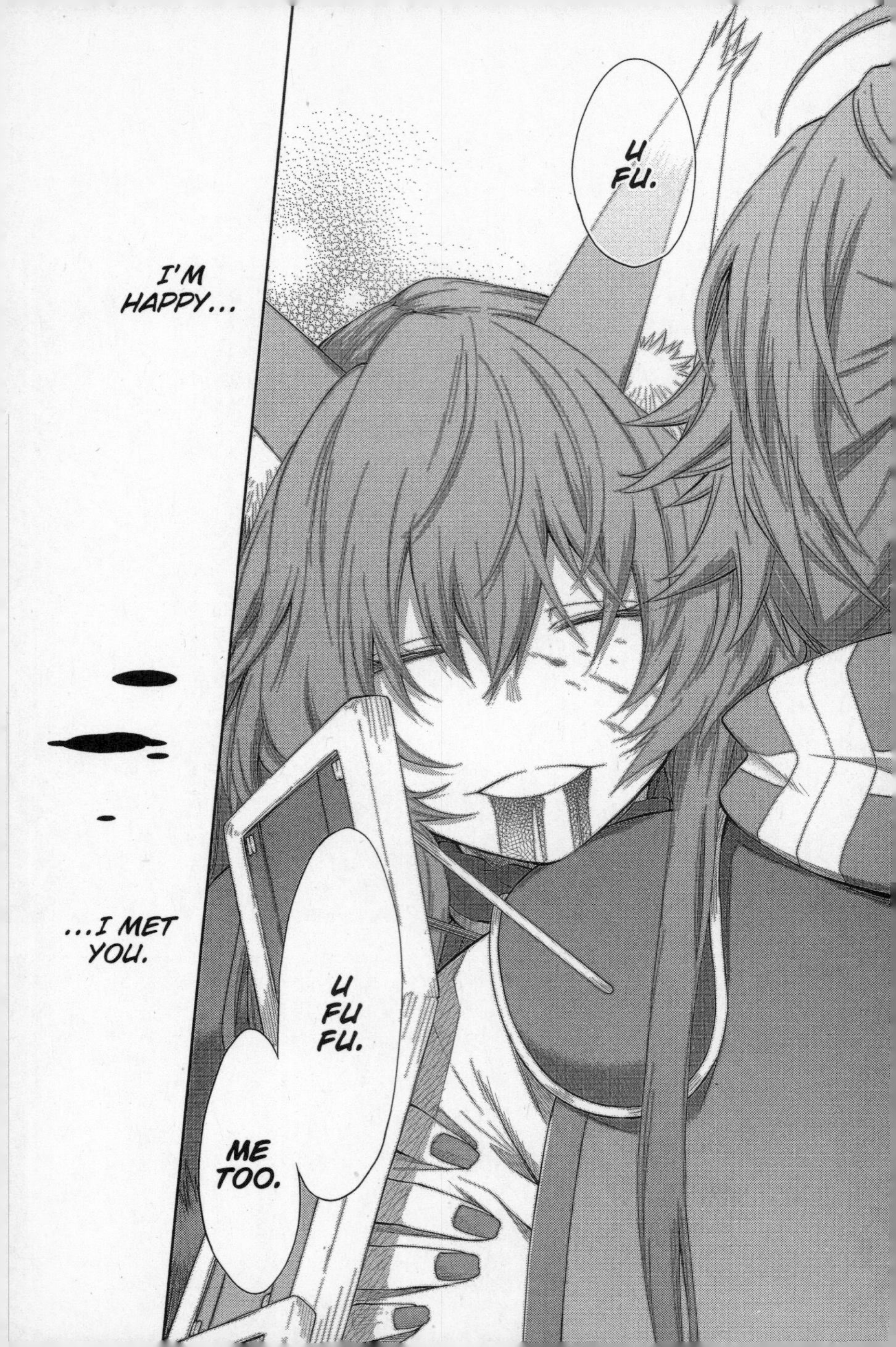
U FU.
U FU FU.
ME TOO.
I'M HAPPY...
...I MET YOU.

LOG HORIZON

THE WEST WIND BRIGADE

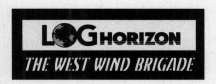

LOG HORIZON

THE WEST WIND BRIGADE

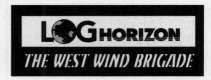

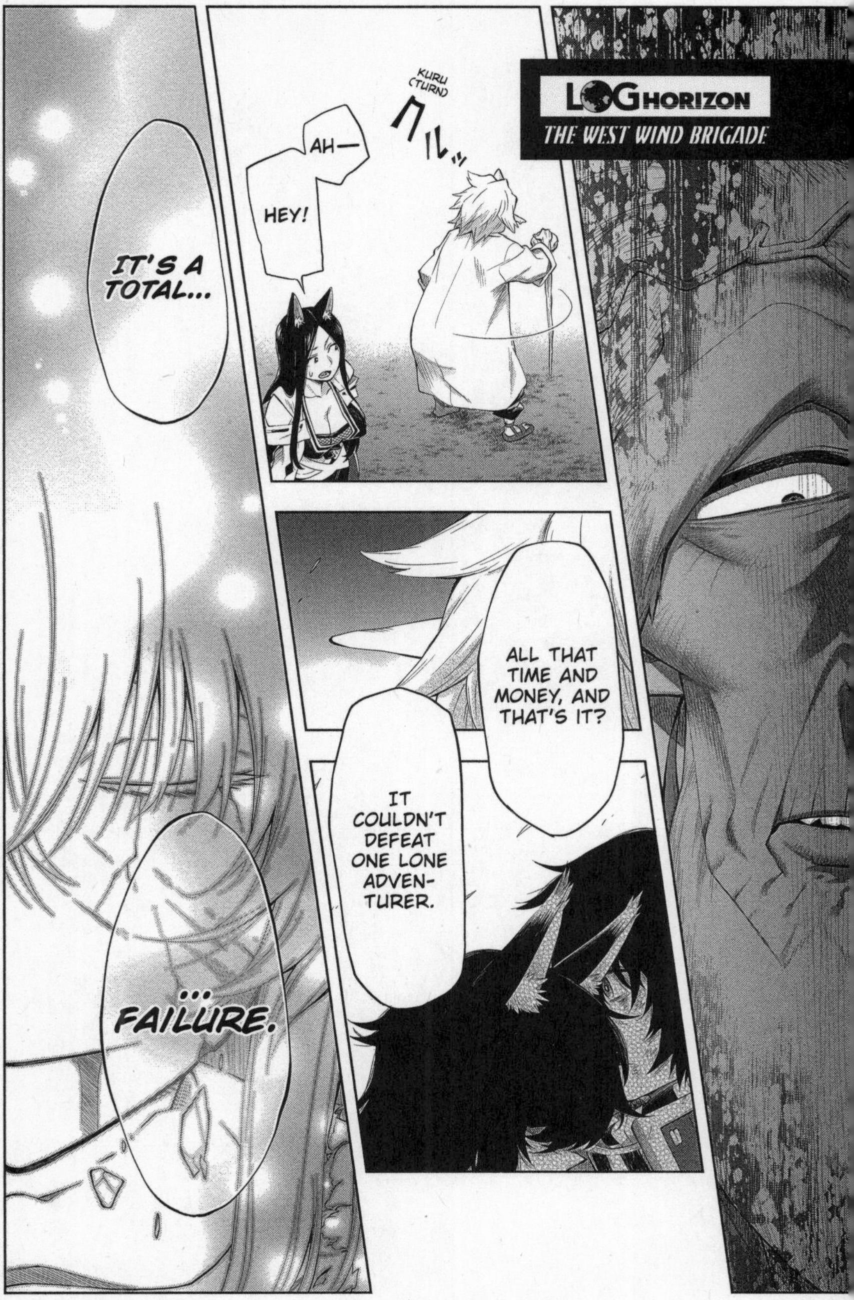
LOG HORIZON
THE WEST WIND BRIGADE
KURU (TURN)
AH—
HEY!
ALL THAT TIME AND MONEY, AND THAT'S IT?
IT COULDN'T DEFEAT ONE LONE ADVENTURER.
IT'S A TOTAL...
...FAILURE.

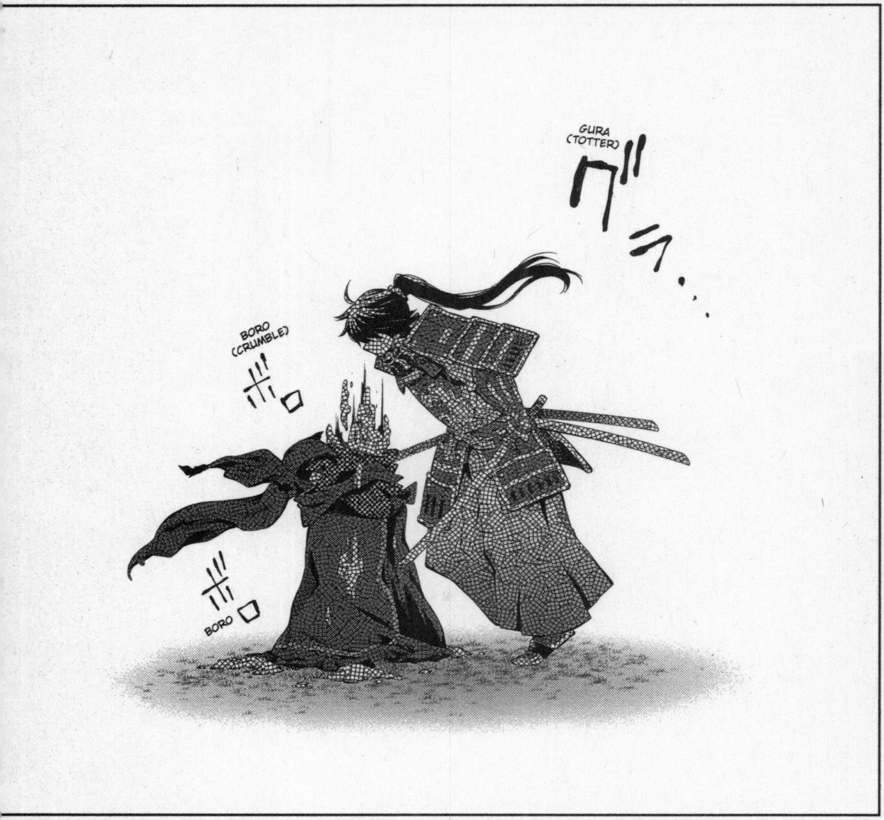
GURA (TOTTER)
BORO (CRUMBLE)
BORO

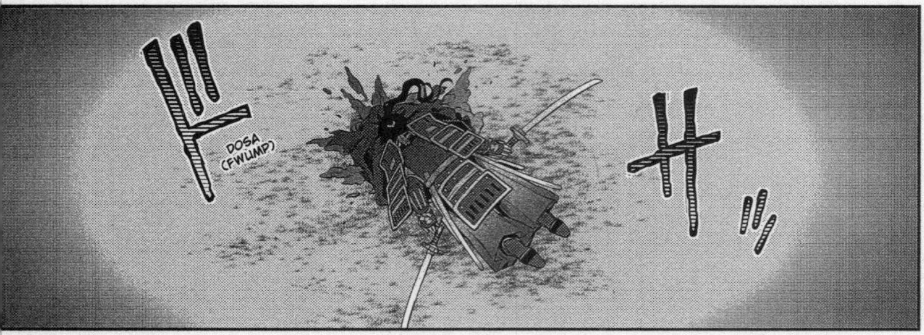
DOSA (FWUMP)

[CHAPTER : 44 Life and Death]

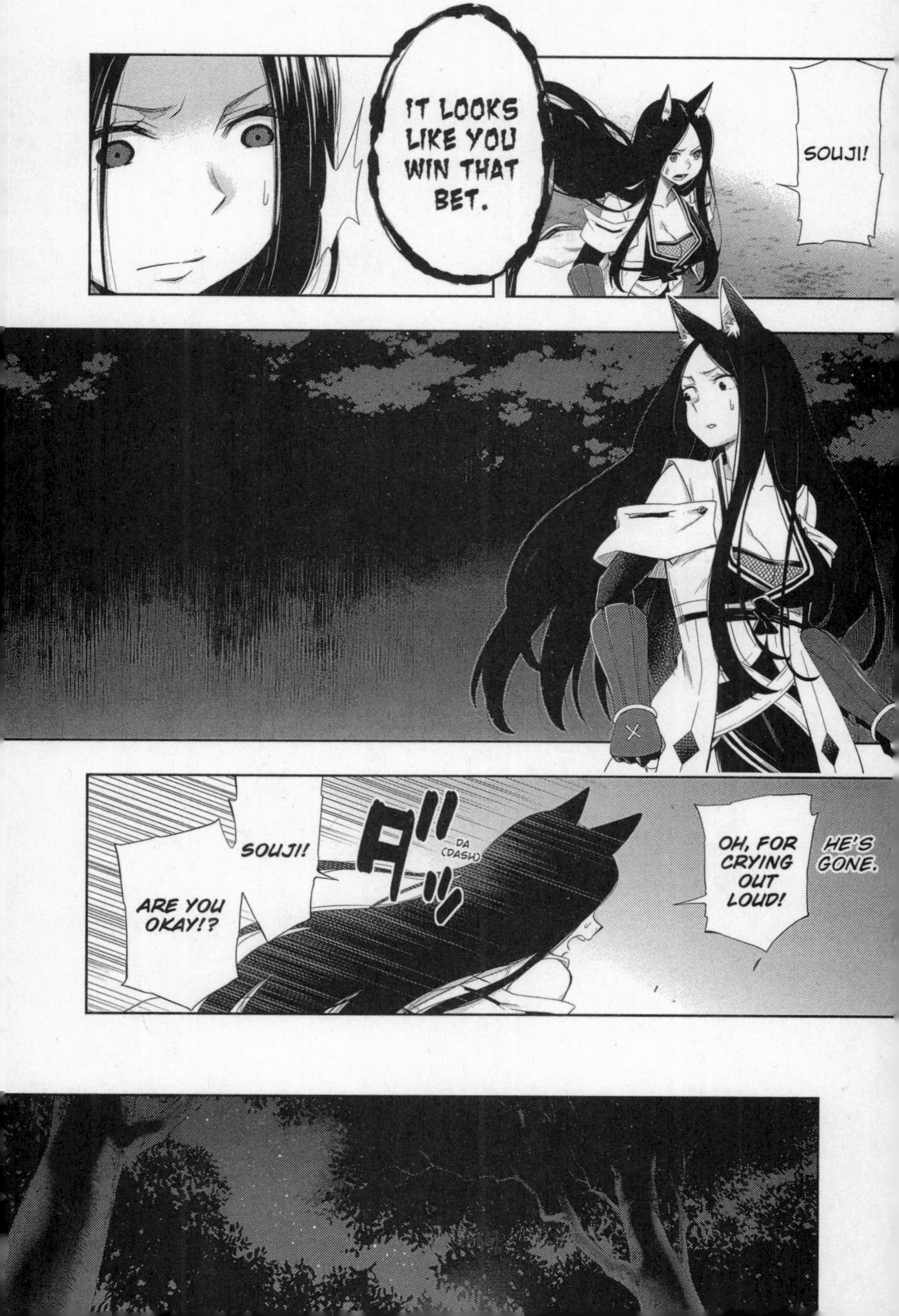
SOUJI!
IT LOOKS LIKE YOU WIN THAT BET.
HE'S GONE.
OH, FOR CRYING OUT LOUD!
DA (DASH)
SOUJI!
ARE YOU OKAY!?

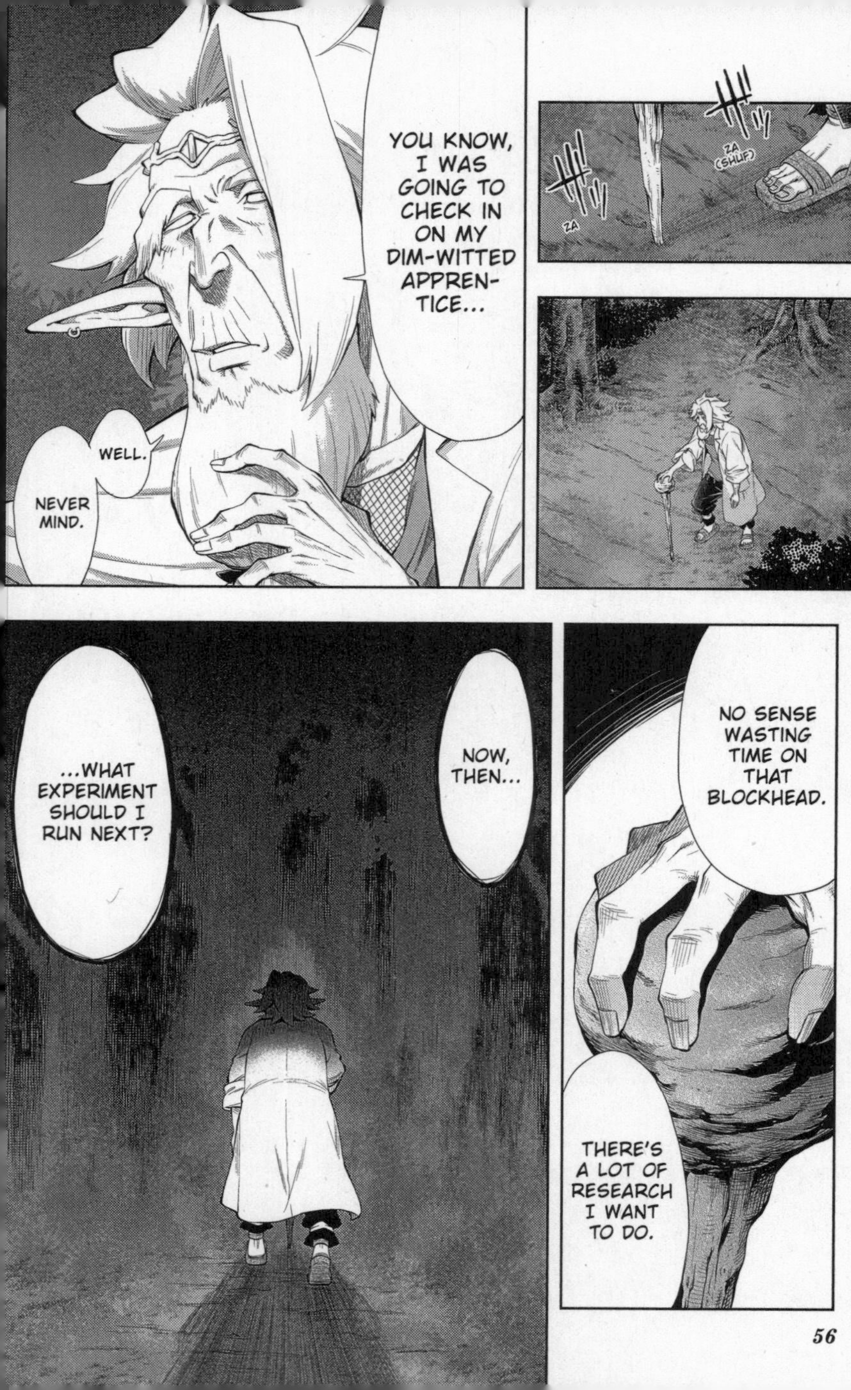
ZA
ZA (SHUF)
YOU KNOW, I WAS GOING TO CHECK IN ON MY DIM-WITTED APPREN-TICE...
WELL.
NEVER MIND.
NO SENSE WASTING TIME ON THAT BLOCKHEAD.
THERE'S A LOT OF RESEARCH I WANT TO DO.
NOW, THEN...
...WHAT EXPERIMENT SHOULD I RUN NEXT?

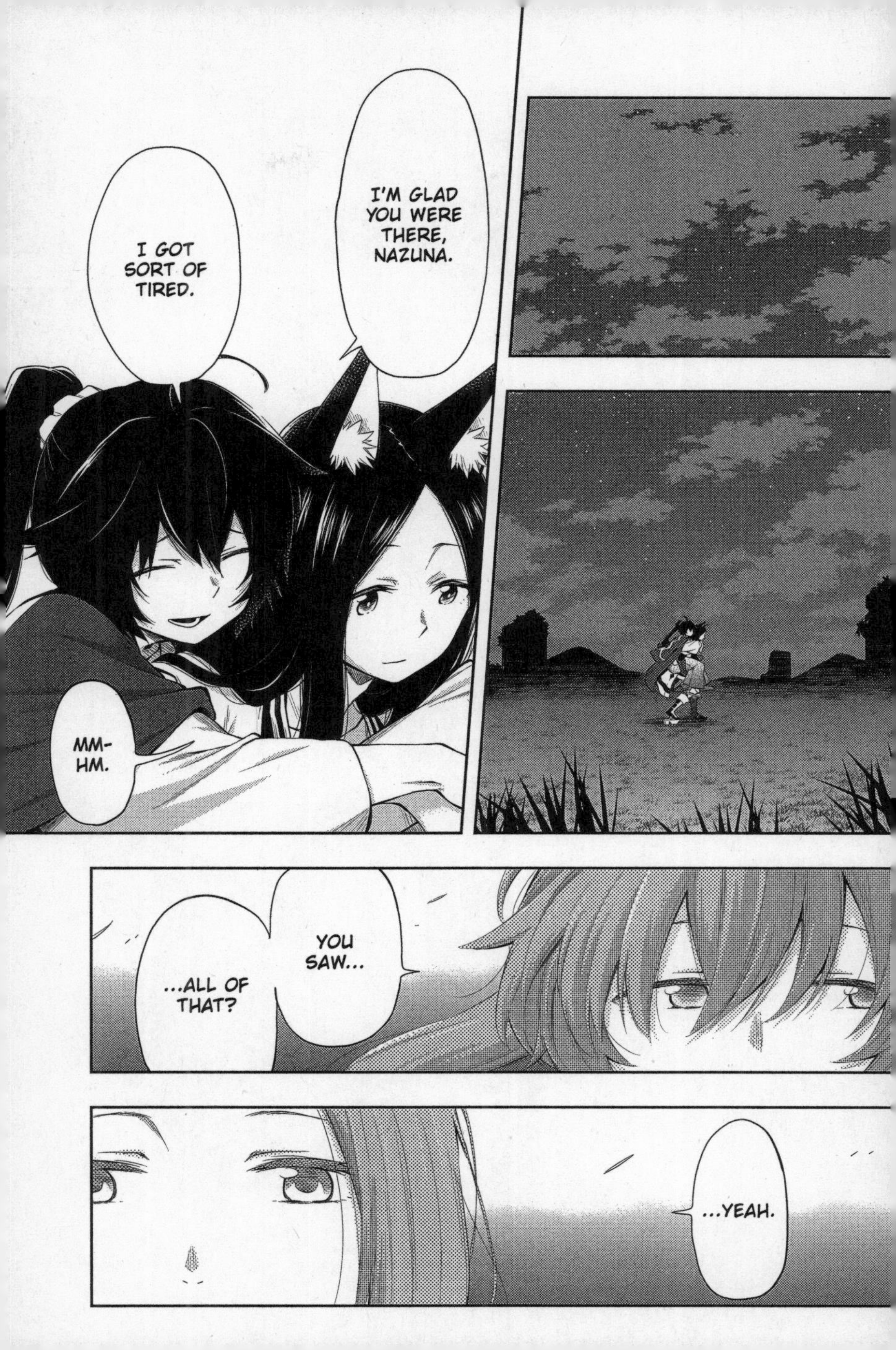
I'M GLAD YOU WERE THERE, NAZUNA.
I GOT SORT OF TIRED.
MM-HM.
YOU SAW...
...ALL OF THAT?
...YEAH.

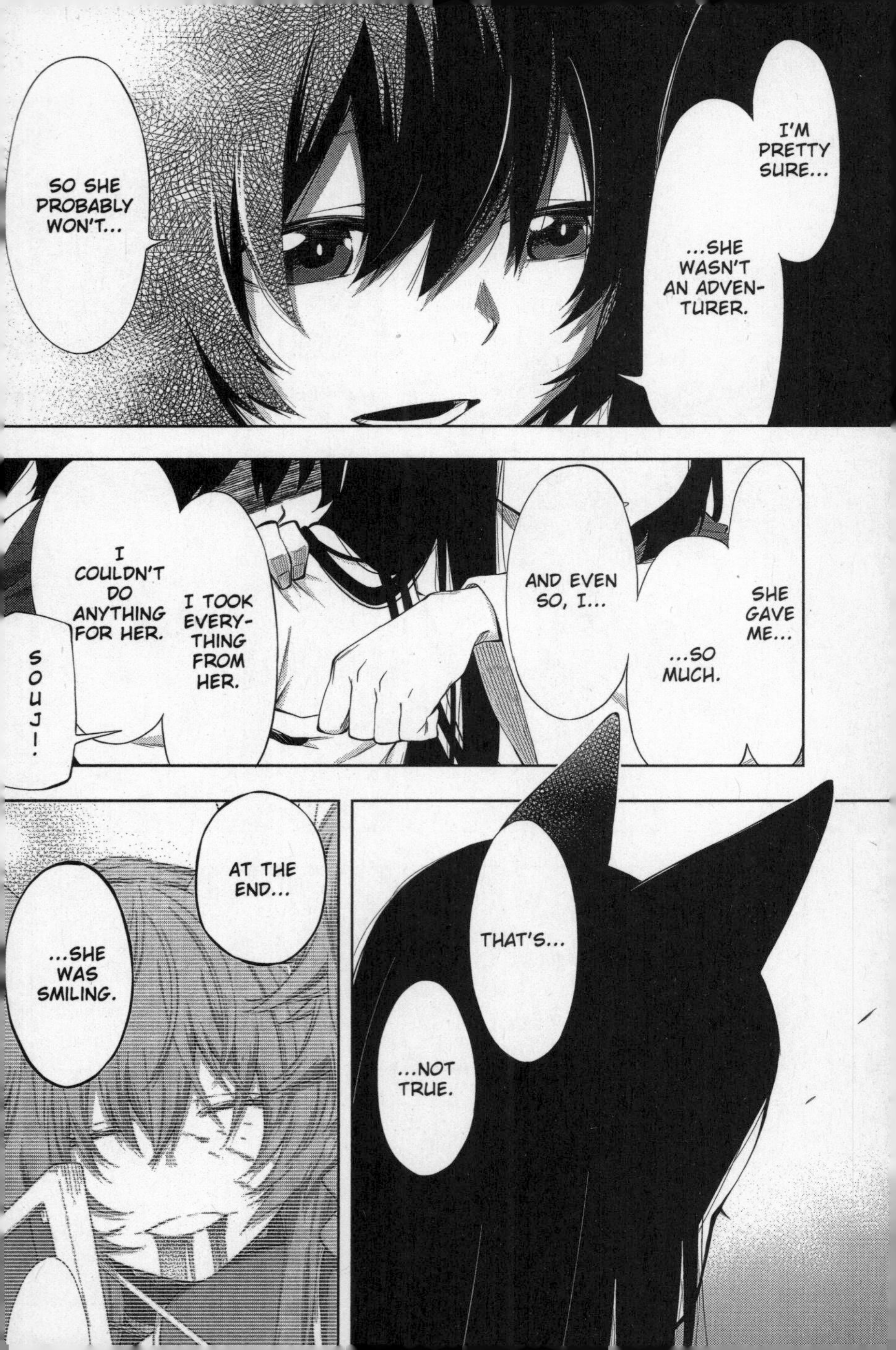
I'M PRETTY SURE...
...SHE WASN'T AN ADVEN-TURER.
SO SHE PROBABLY WON'T...
SHE GAVE ME...
...SO MUCH.
AND EVEN SO, I...
I TOOK EVERY-THING FROM HER.
I COULDN'T DO ANYTHING FOR HER.
SOUJI!
THAT'S...
...NOT TRUE.
AT THE END...
...SHE WAS SMILING.

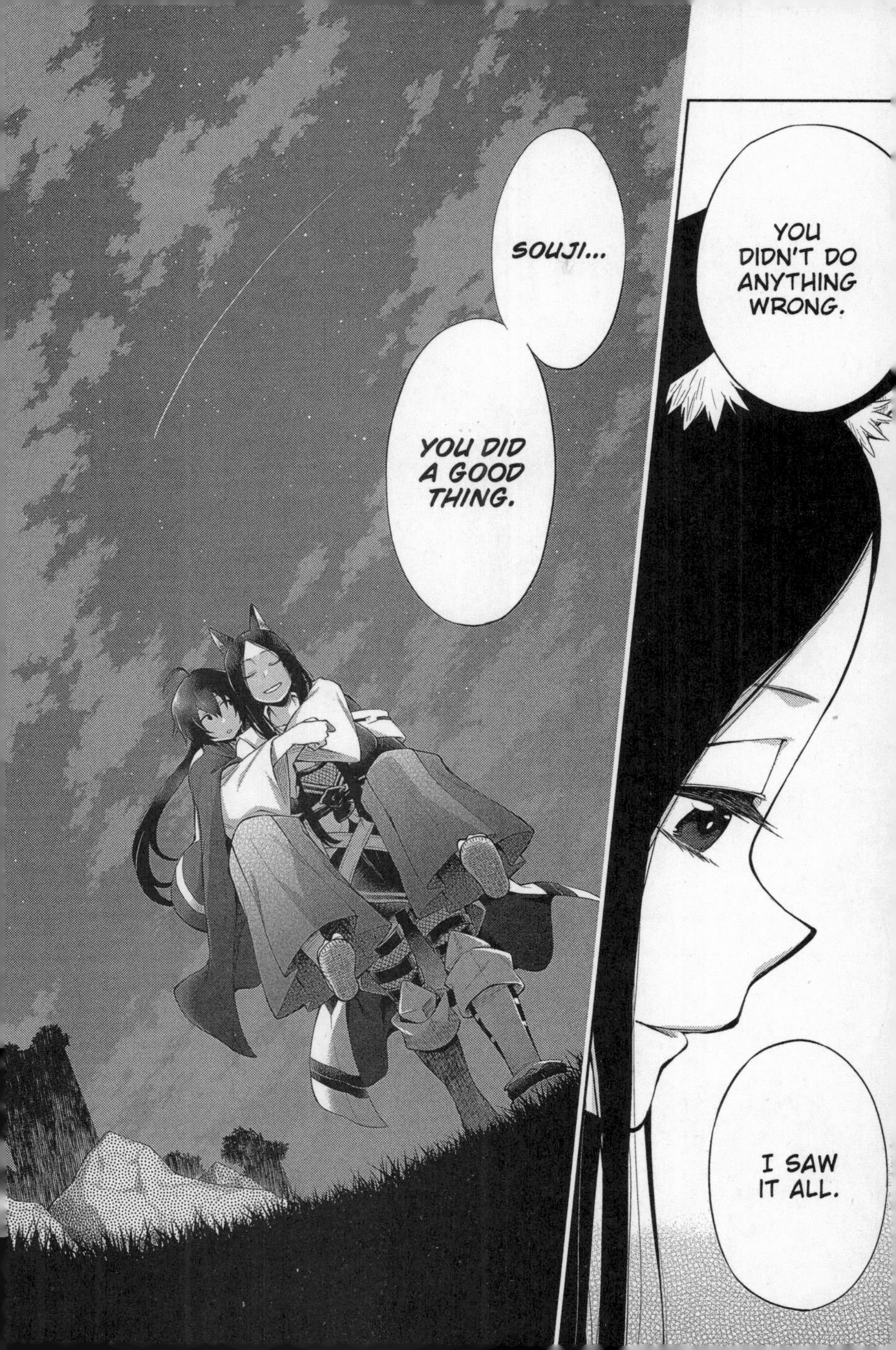
YOU DIDN'T DO ANYTHING WRONG.
I SAW IT ALL.
SOUJI...
YOU DID A GOOD THING.

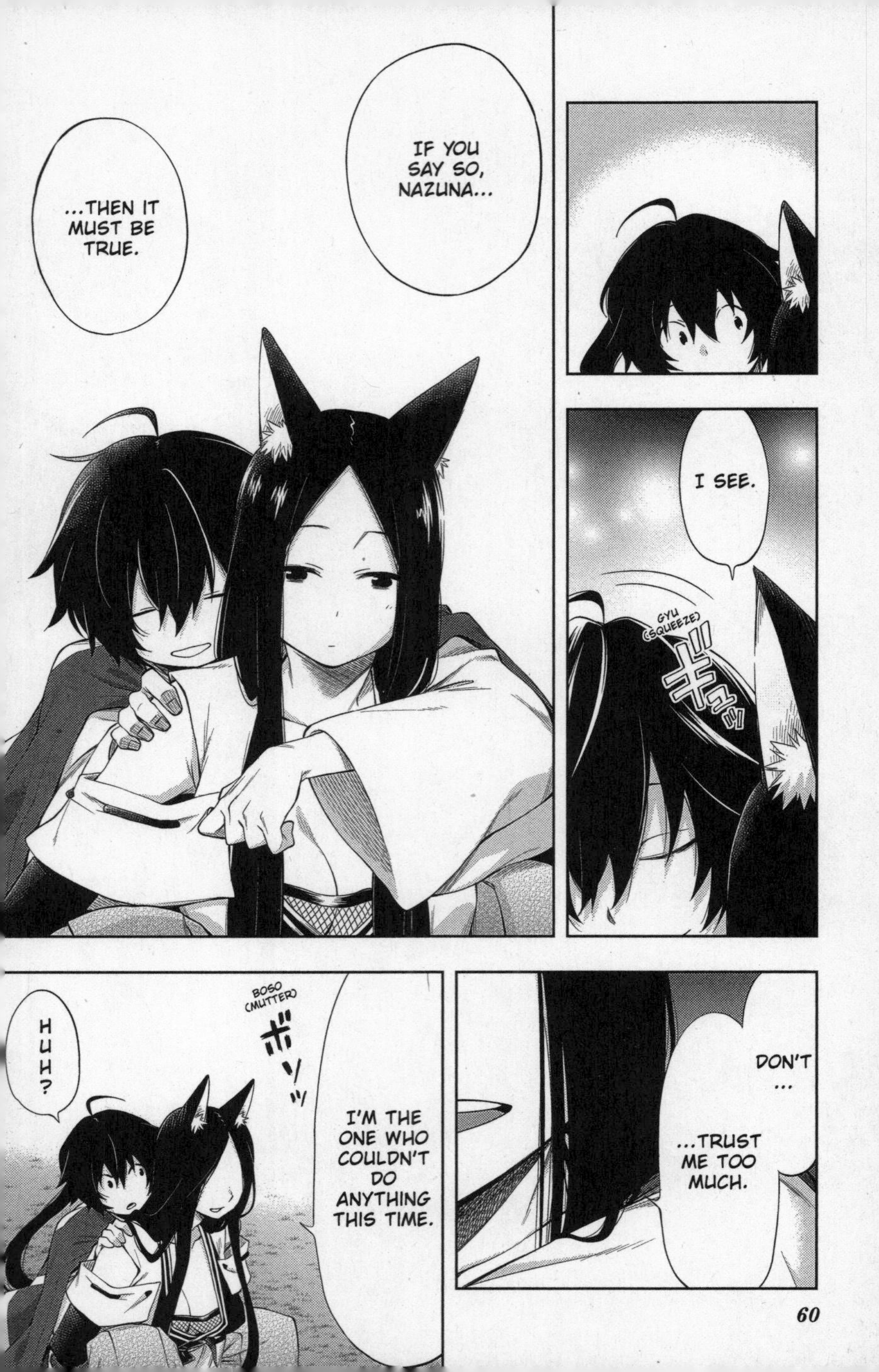
I SEE.
GYU (SQUEEZE)
IF YOU SAY SO, NAZUNA...
...THEN IT MUST BE TRUE.
DON'T ...
...TRUST ME TOO MUCH.
I'M THE ONE WHO COULDN'T DO ANYTHING THIS TIME.
BOSO (MUTTER)
HUH?

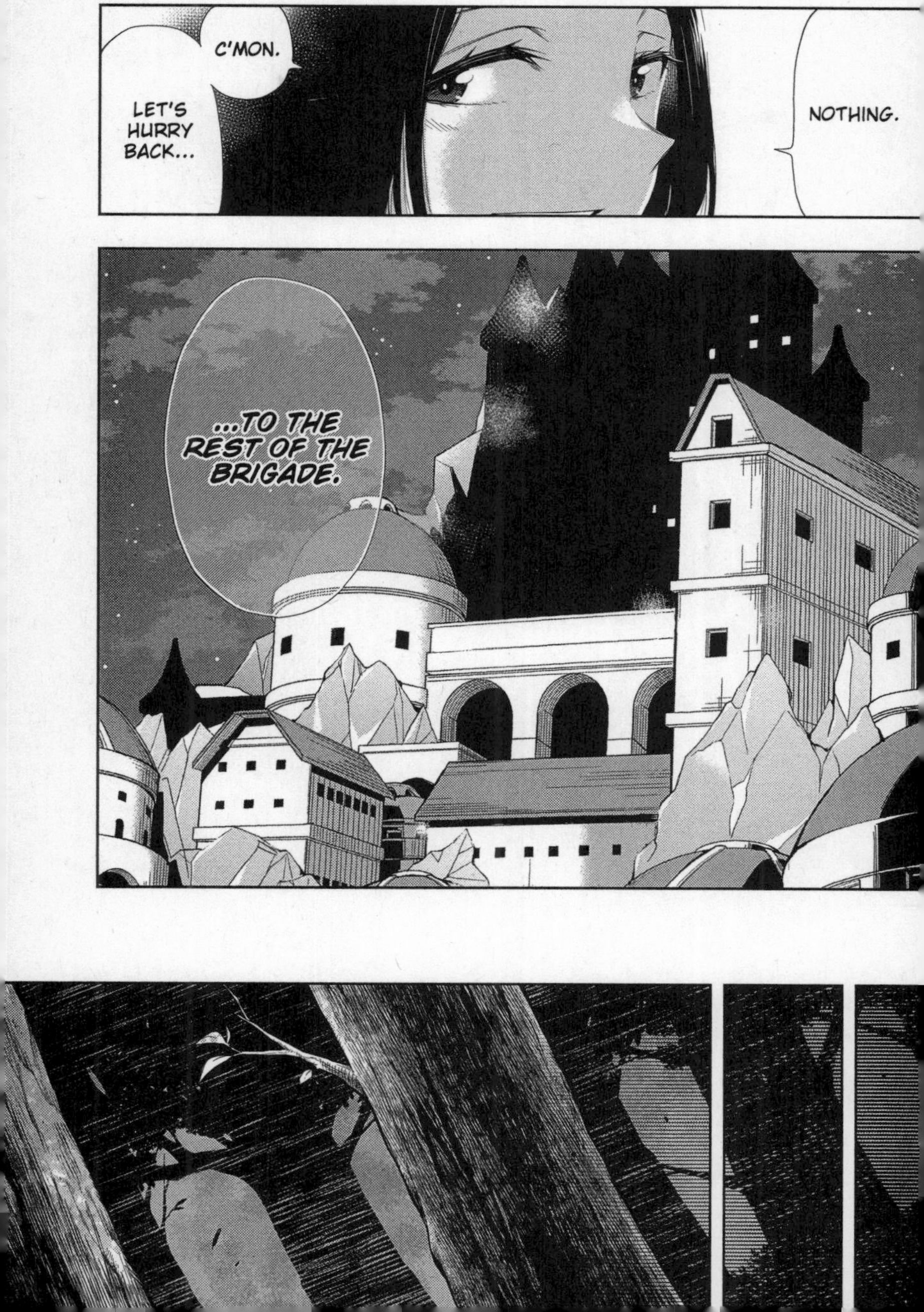
NOTHING.
C'MON.
LET'S HURRY BACK...
...TO THE REST OF THE BRIGADE.

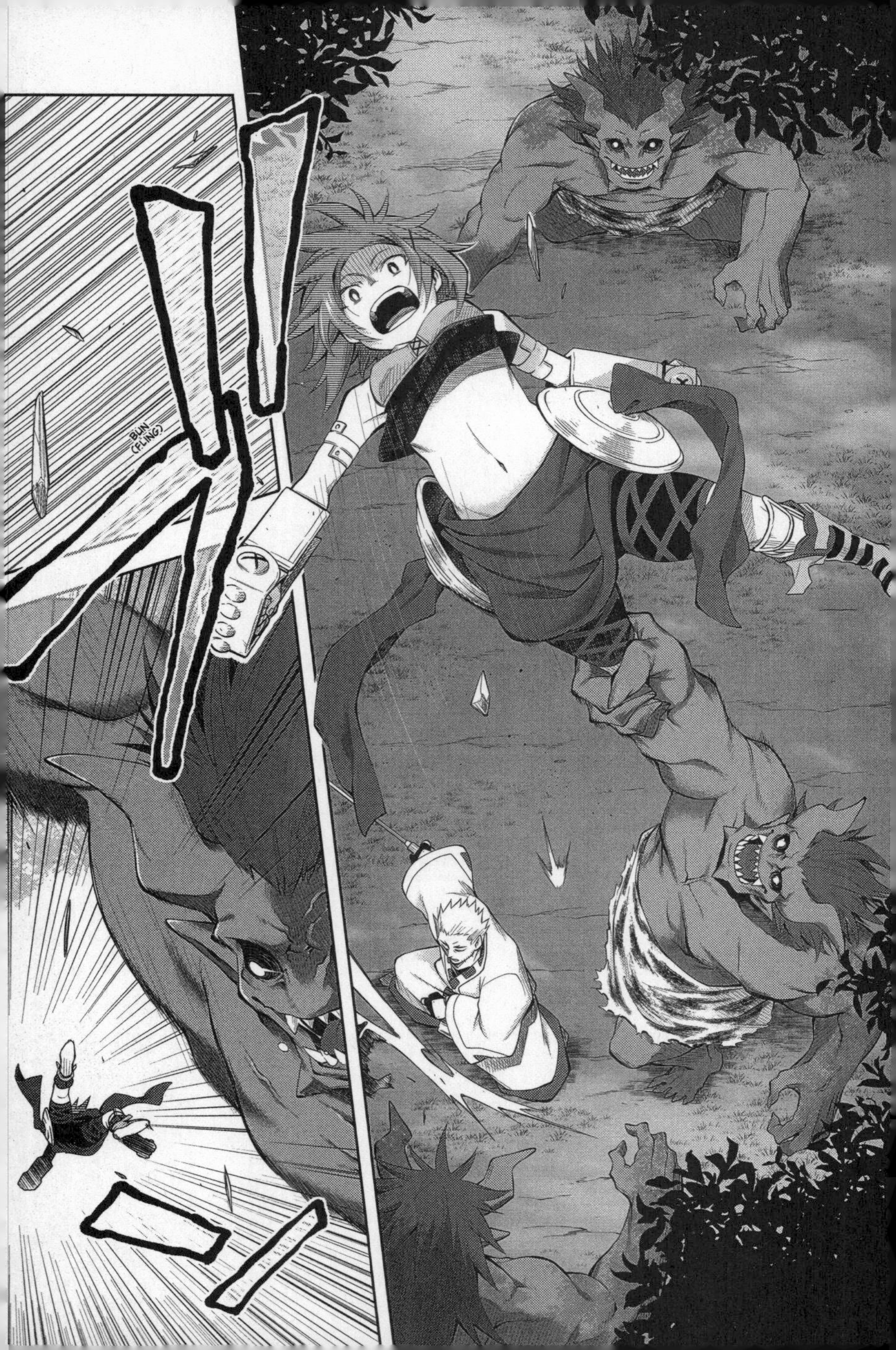
BUN
(FLING)

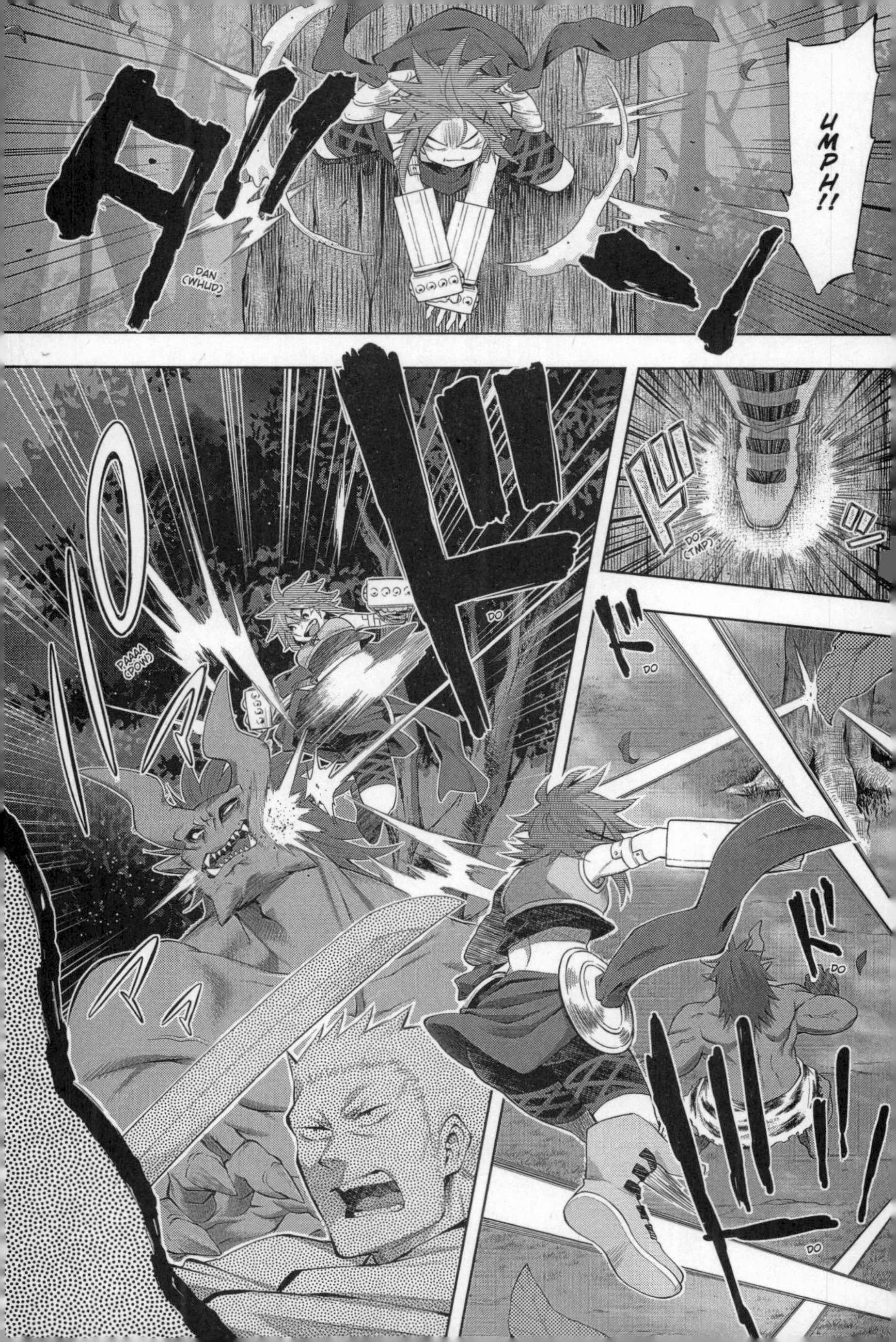
UMPH!!
DAN (WHUD)
DO (TMP)
DO
DO
DO
DO
PAAAA (PON)

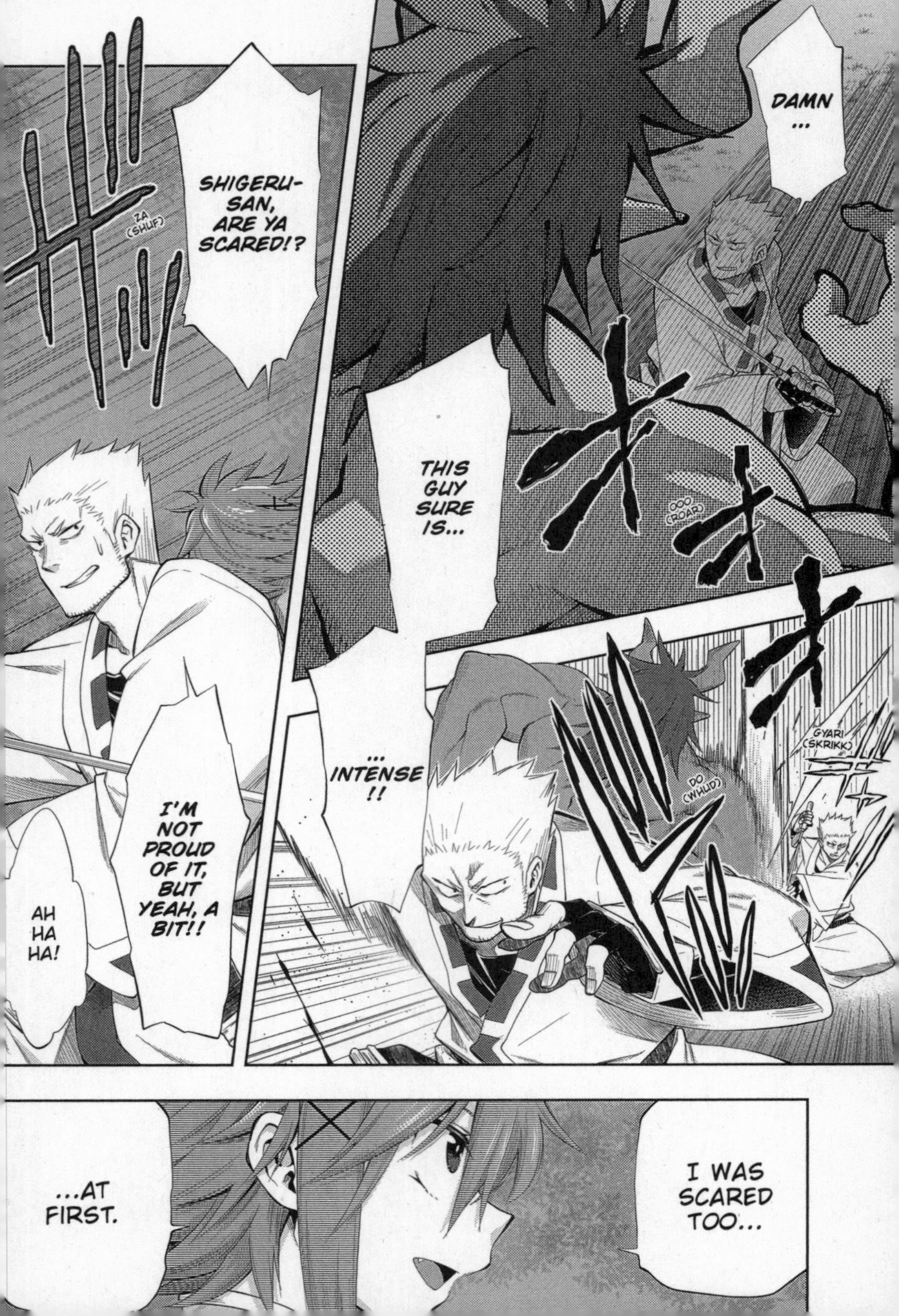
DAMN ...
THIS GUY SURE IS...
OOO (ROAR)
... INTENSE !!
GYARI (SKRIKK)
DO (WHUD)
ZA (SHUF)
SHIGERU-SAN, ARE YA SCARED!?
I'M NOT PROUD OF IT, BUT YEAH, A BIT!!
AH HA HA!
I WAS SCARED TOO...
...AT FIRST.

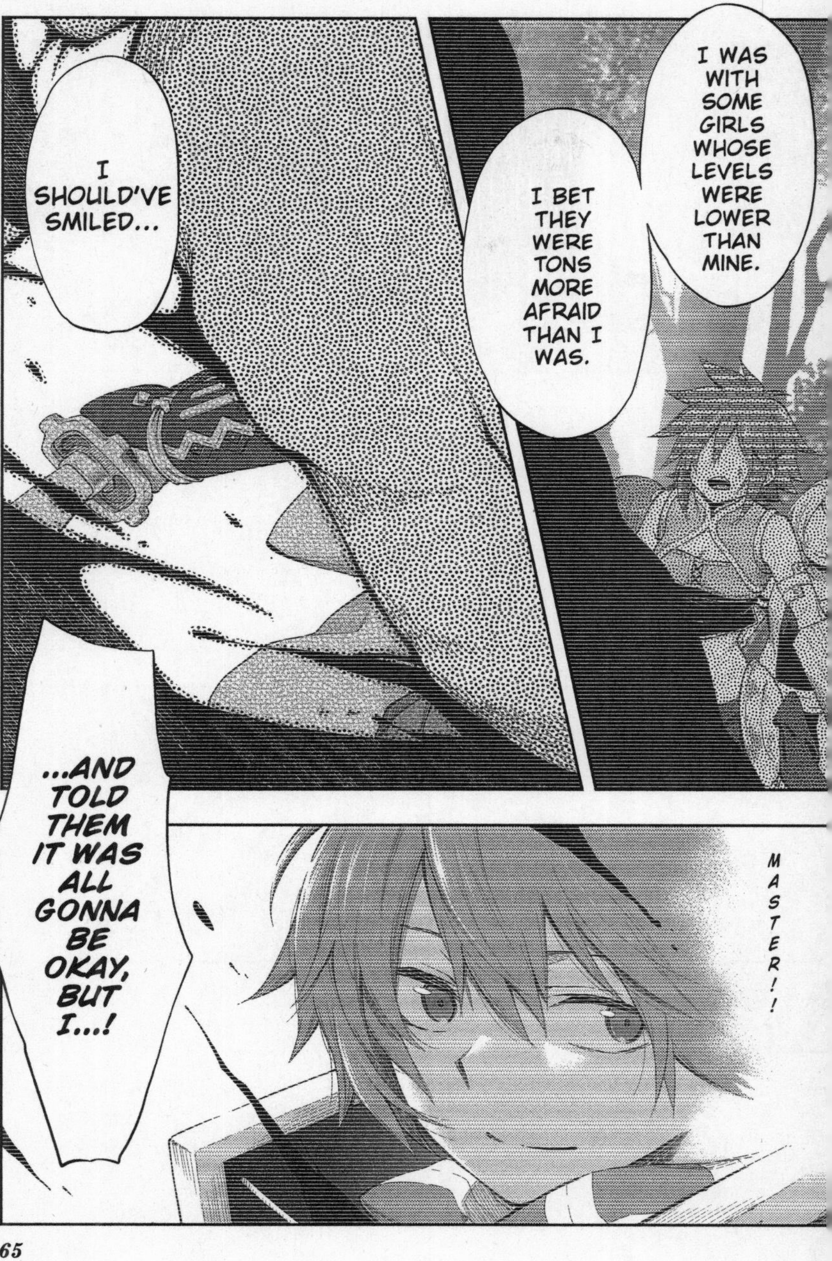
I WAS WITH SOME GIRLS WHOSE LEVELS WERE LOWER THAN MINE.
I BET THEY WERE TONS MORE AFRAID THAN I WAS.
I SHOULD'VE SMILED...
...AND TOLD THEM IT WAS ALL GONNA BE OKAY, BUT I...!
MASTER!!

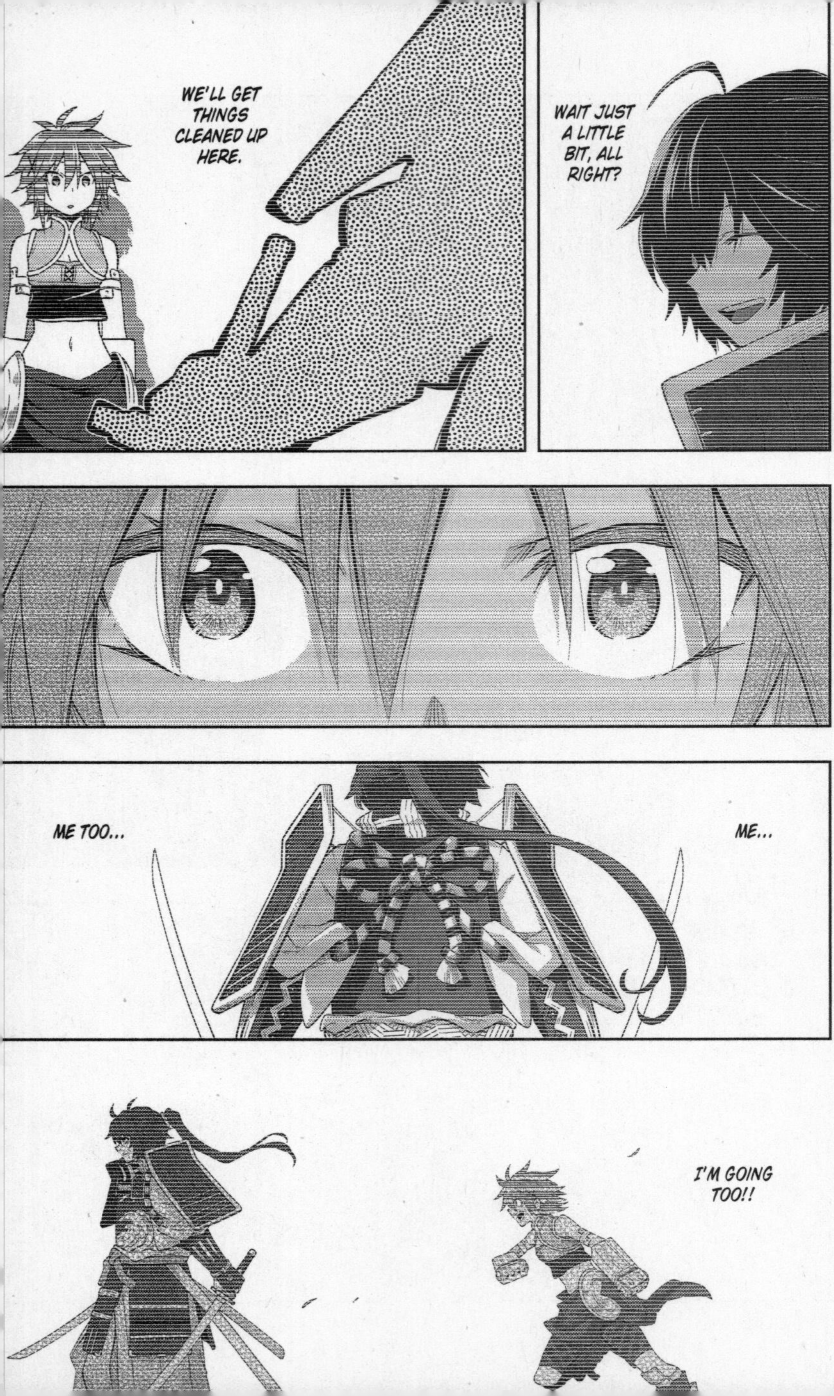
WAIT JUST A LITTLE BIT, ALL RIGHT?
WE'LL GET THINGS CLEANED UP HERE.
ME...
ME TOO...
I'M GOING TOO!!

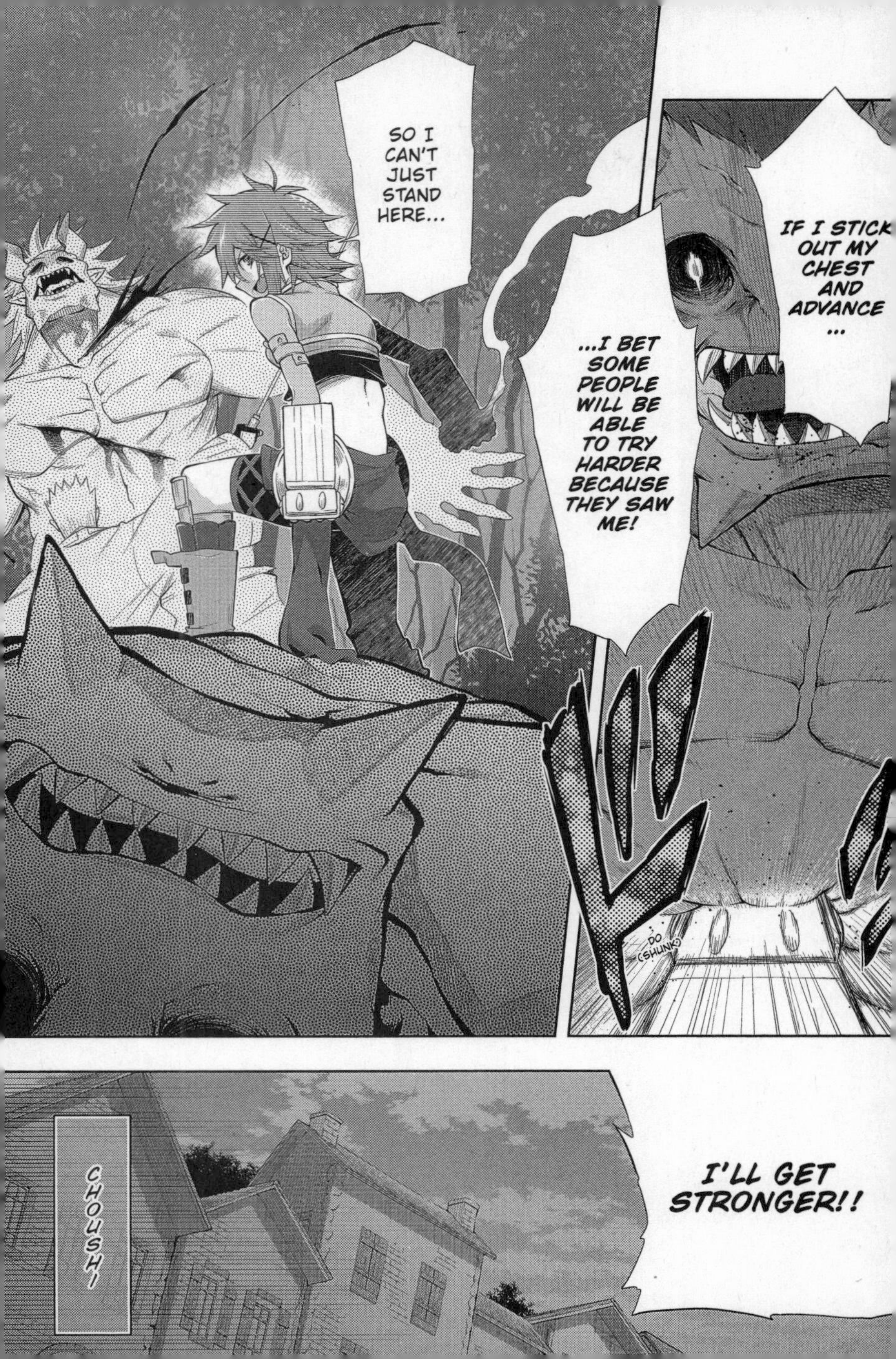
IF I STICK OUT MY CHEST AND ADVANCE ...
...I BET SOME PEOPLE WILL BE ABLE TO TRY HARDER BECAUSE THEY SAW ME!
DO (SHUNK)
SO I CAN'T JUST STAND HERE...
I'LL GET STRONGER!!
CHOUSHI

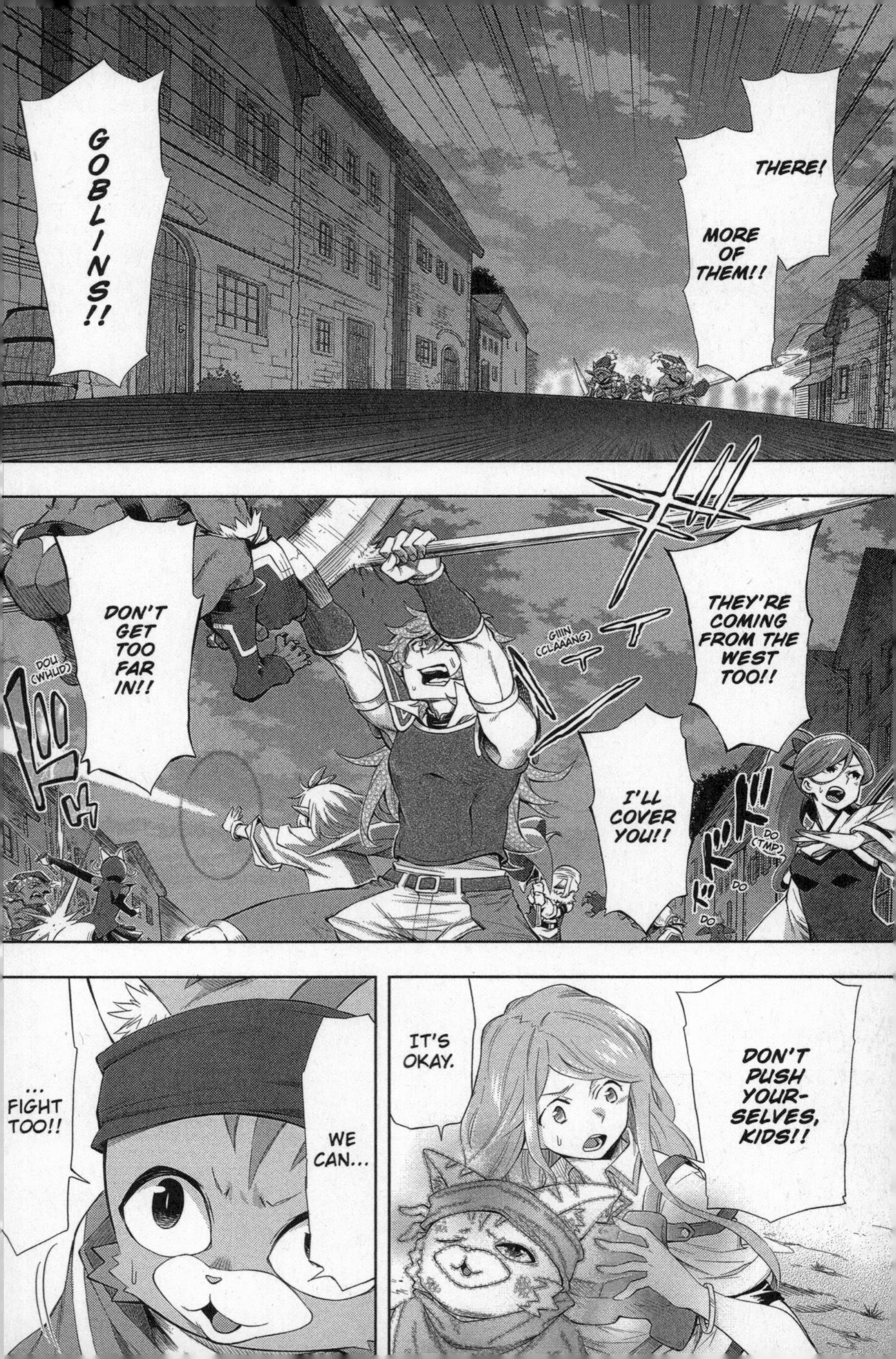
THERE!
MORE OF THEM!!
GOBLINS!!
THEY'RE COMING FROM THE WEST TOO!!
DO (TMP)
DO
DO
I'LL COVER YOU!!
GIIIN (CLAAANG)
DON'T GET TOO FAR IN!!
DOU (WHUD)
DON'T PUSH YOUR-SELVES, KIDS!!
IT'S OKAY.
WE CAN...
...FIGHT TOO!!

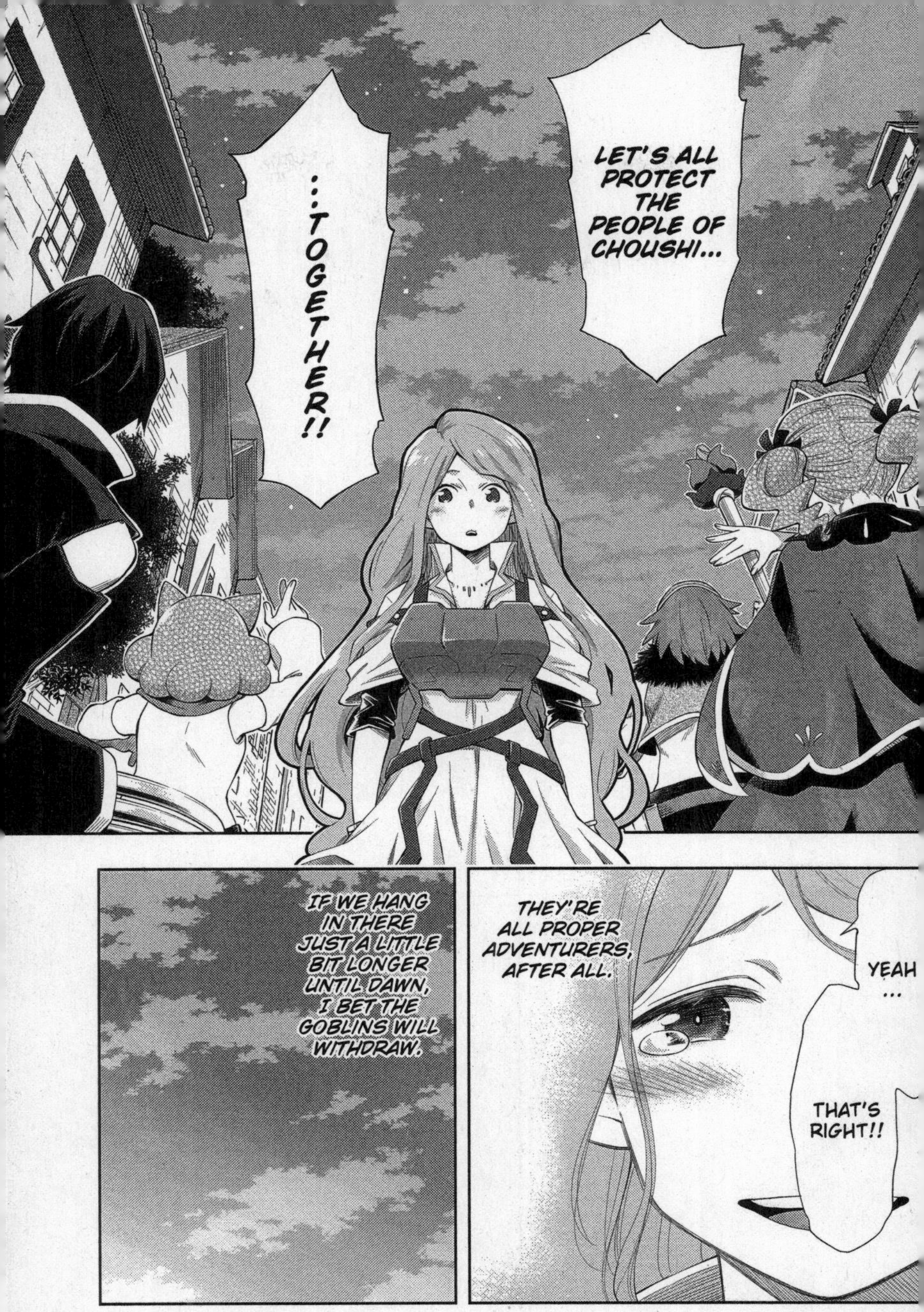
LET'S ALL PROTECT THE PEOPLE OF CHOUSHI...
...TOGETHER!!
YEAH...
THAT'S RIGHT!!
THEY'RE ALL PROPER ADVENTURERS, AFTER ALL.
IF WE HANG IN THERE JUST A LITTLE BIT LONGER UNTIL DAWN, I BET THE GOBLINS WILL WITHDRAW.

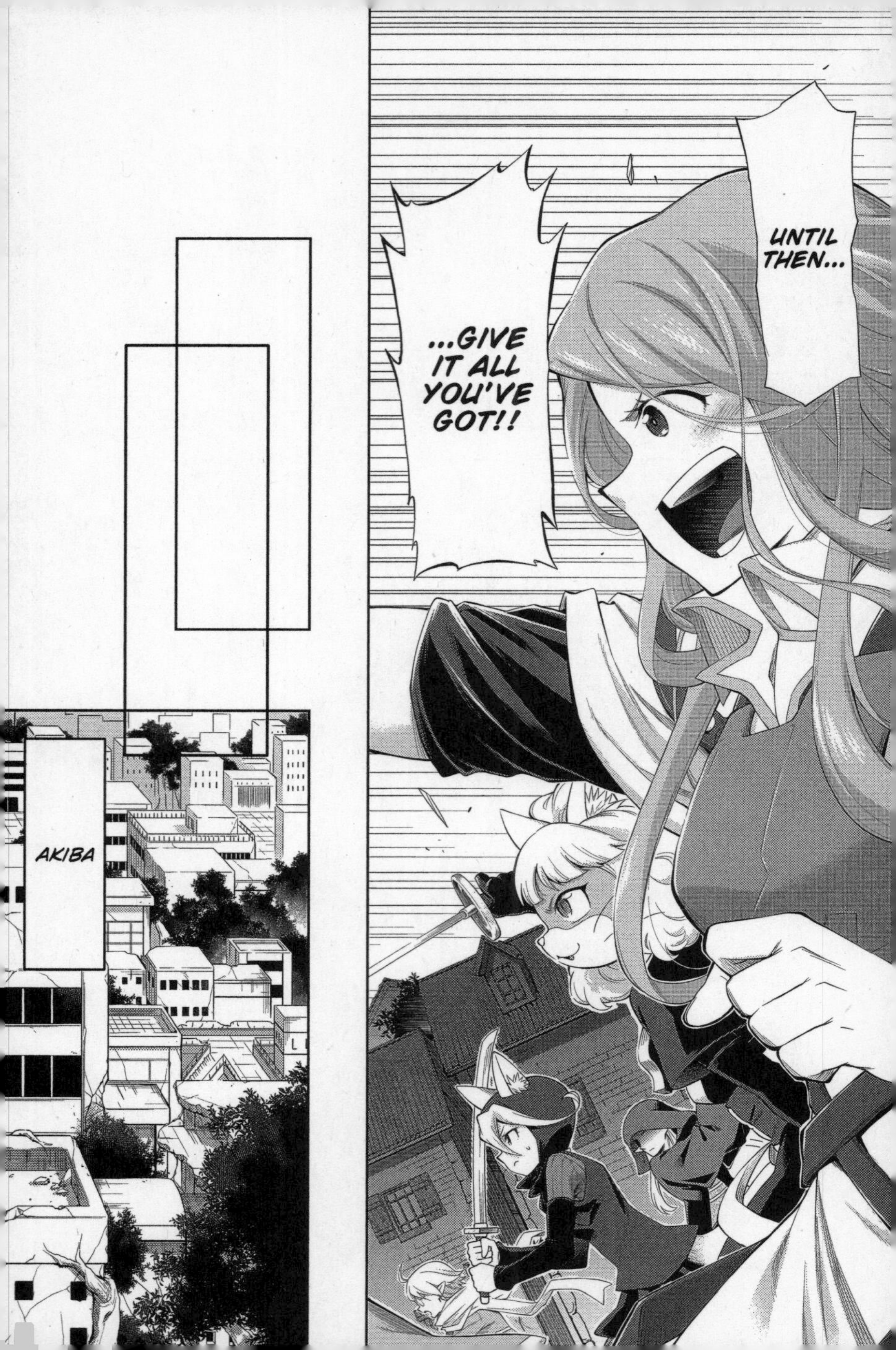
UNTIL THEN...
...GIVE IT ALL YOU'VE GOT!!
AKIBA

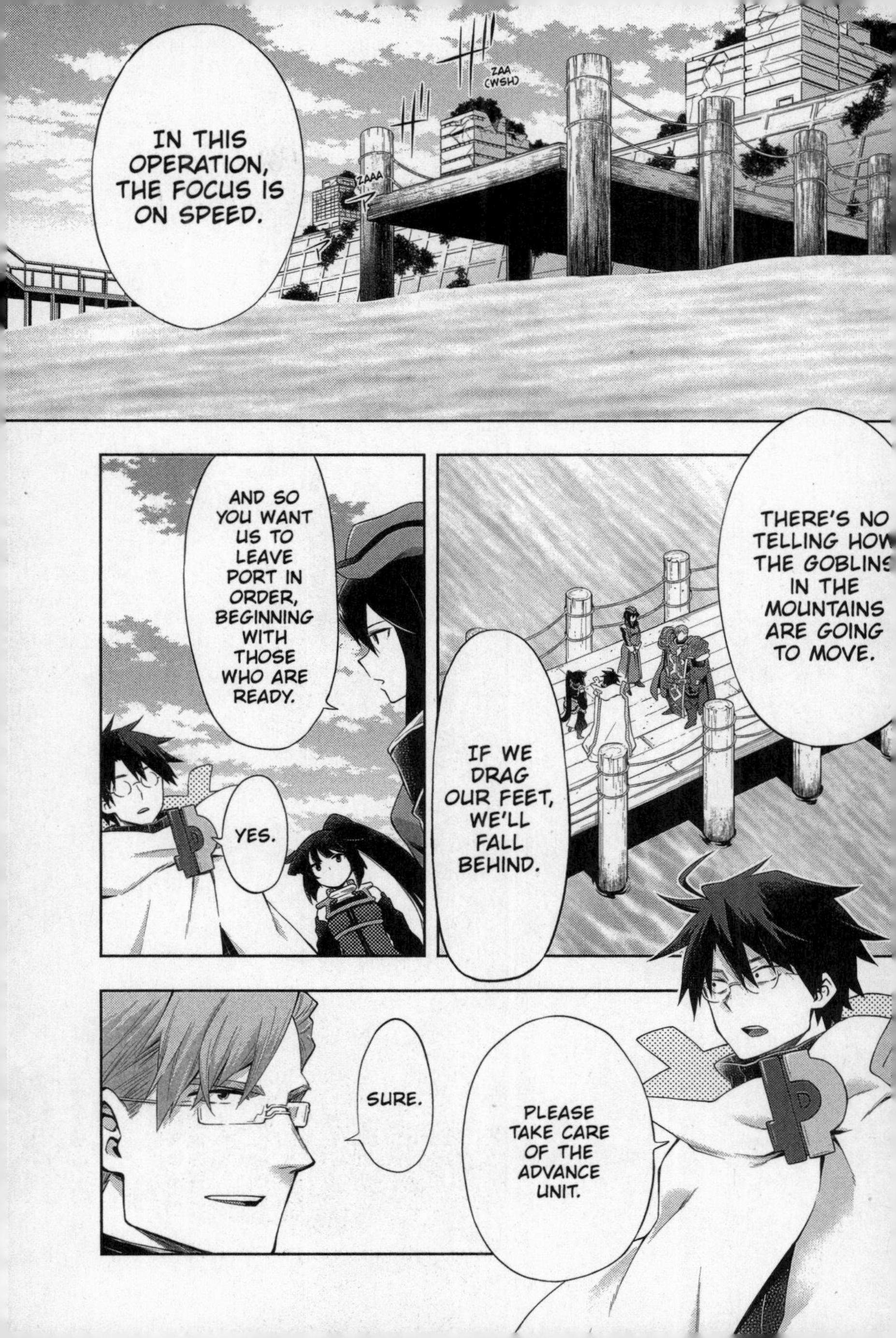
ZAA (WSH)
ZAAA
IN THIS OPERATION, THE FOCUS IS ON SPEED.
THERE'S NO TELLING HOW THE GOBLINS IN THE MOUNTAINS ARE GOING TO MOVE.
IF WE DRAG OUR FEET, WE'LL FALL BEHIND.
AND SO YOU WANT US TO LEAVE PORT IN ORDER, BEGINNING WITH THOSE WHO ARE READY.
YES.
PLEASE TAKE CARE OF THE ADVANCE UNIT.
SURE.

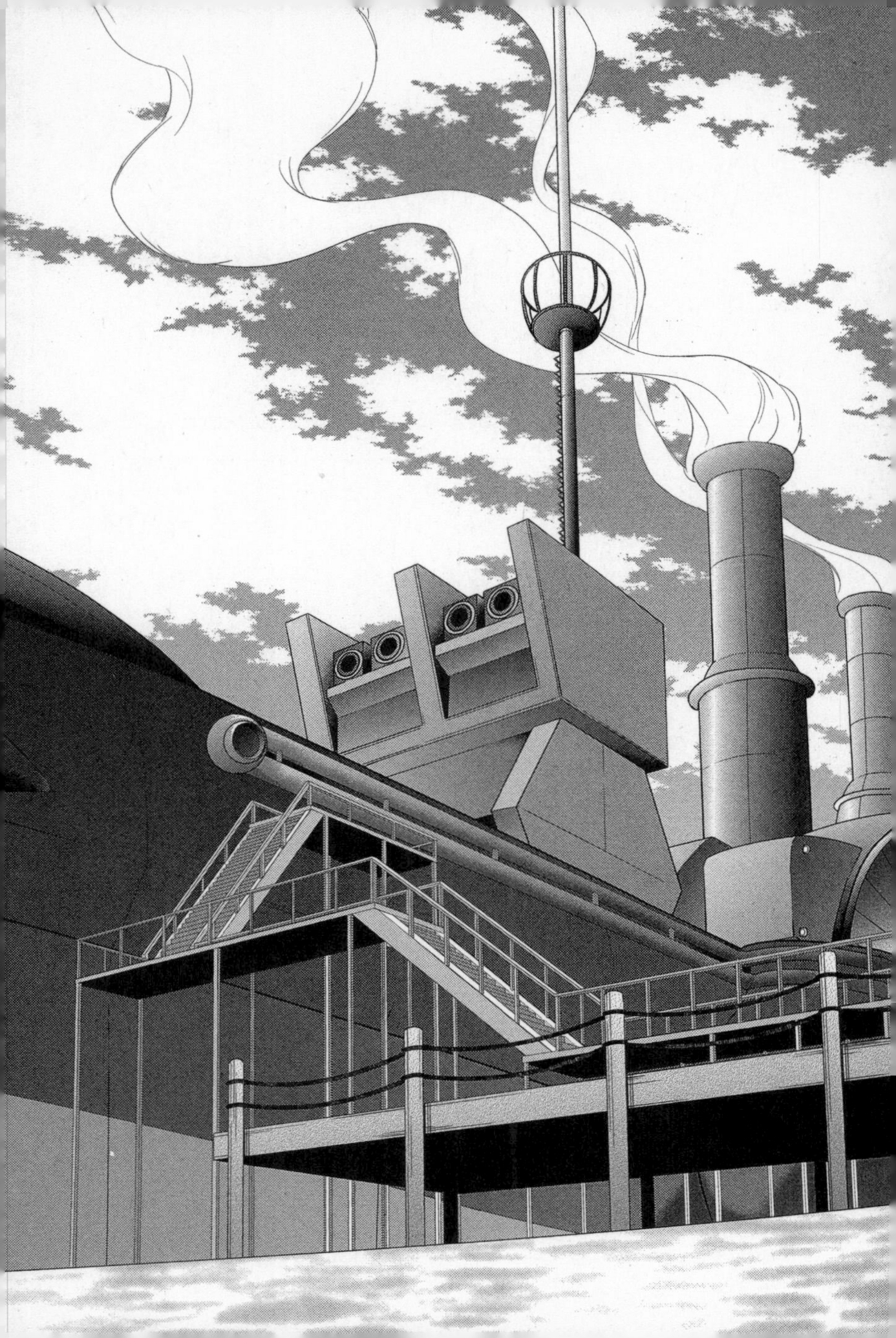

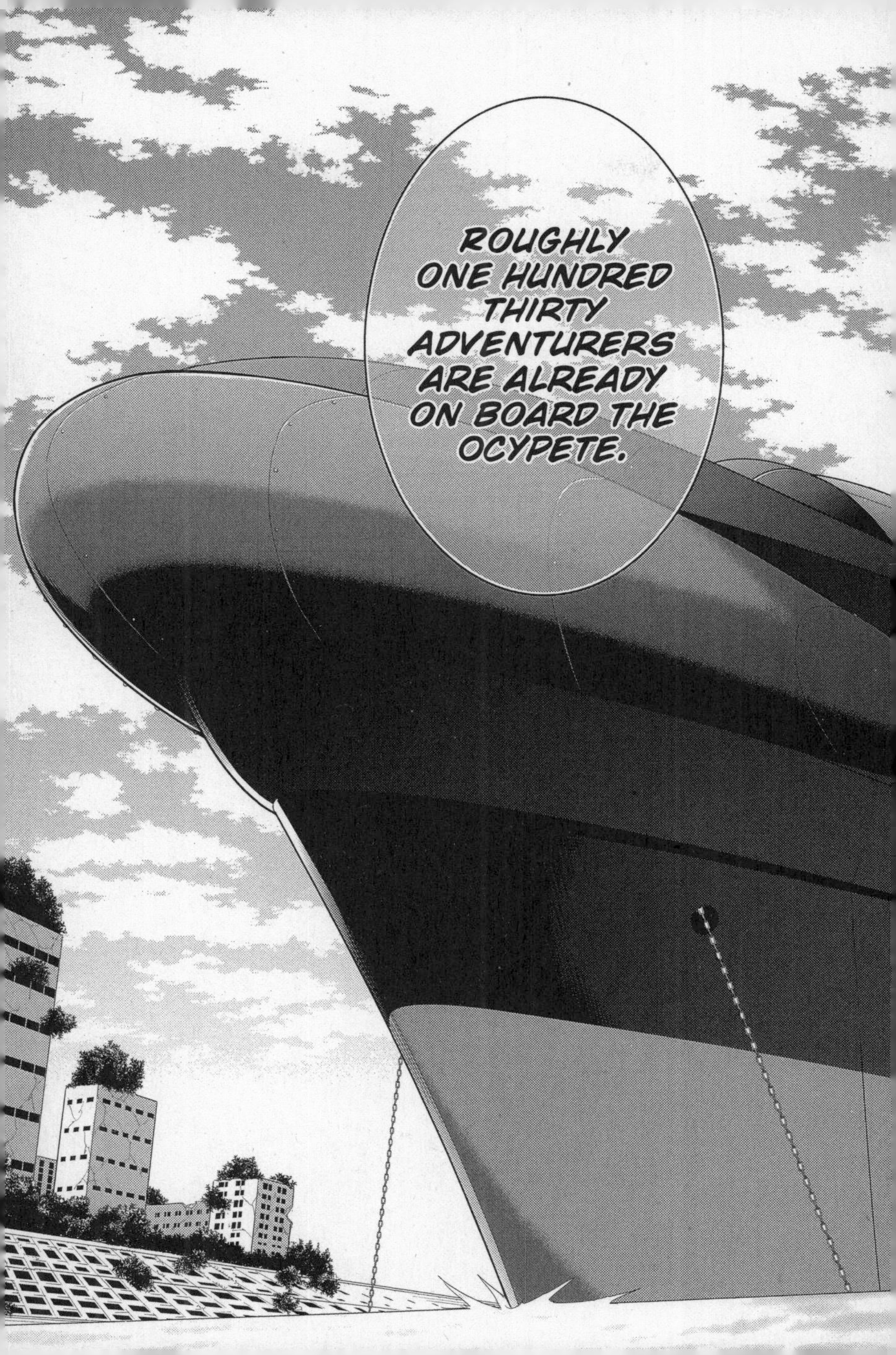
ROUGHLY ONE HUNDRED THIRTY ADVENTURERS ARE ALREADY ON BOARD THE OCYPETE.

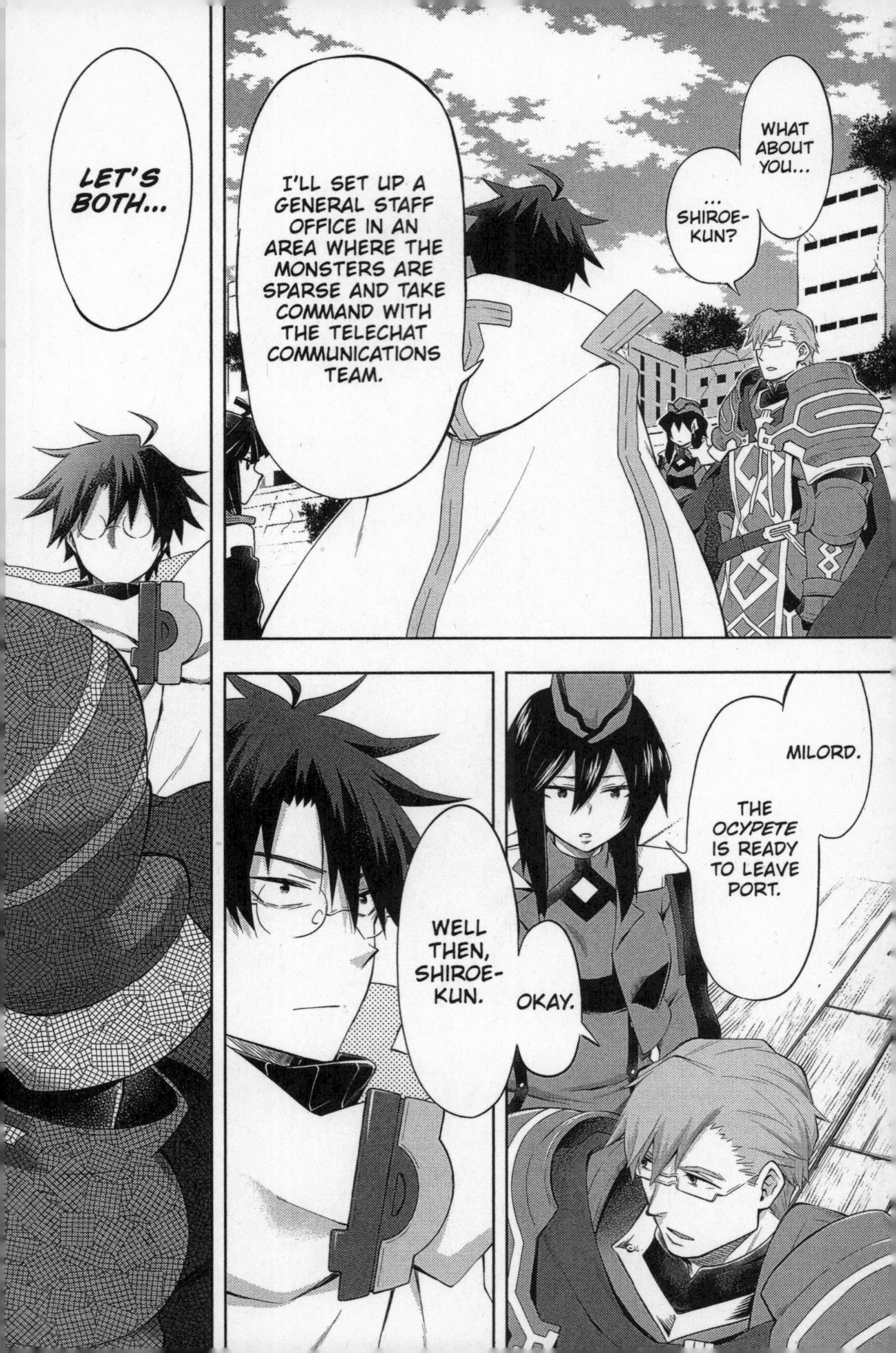

WHAT ABOUT YOU... ...SHIROE-KUN?
I'LL SET UP A GENERAL STAFF OFFICE IN AN AREA WHERE THE MONSTERS ARE SPARSE AND TAKE COMMAND WITH THE TELECHAT COMMUNICATIONS TEAM.
MILORD.
THE *OCYPETE* IS READY TO LEAVE PORT.
OKAY.
WELL THEN, SHIROE-KUN.
LET'S BOTH...

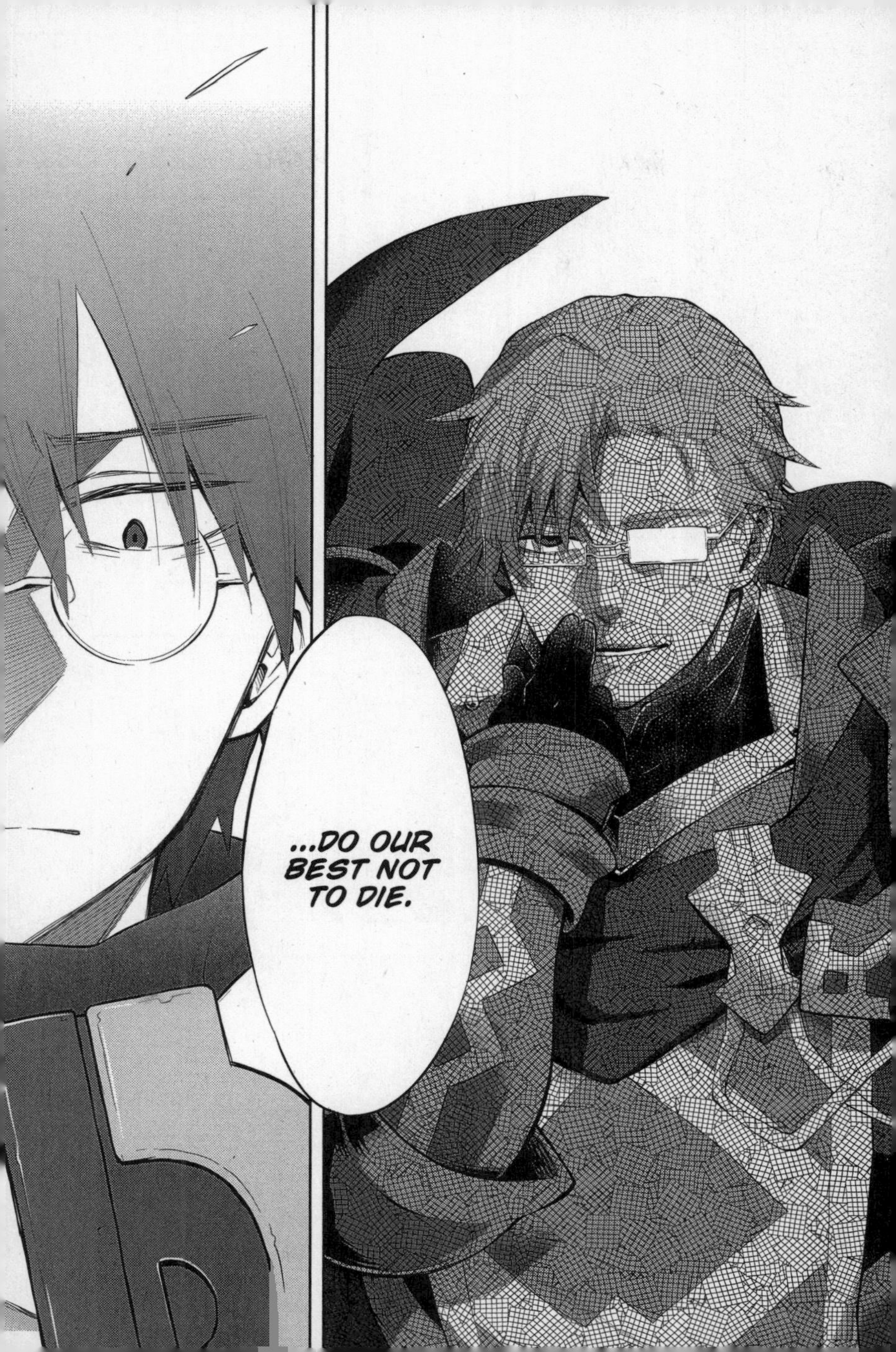
...DO OUR BEST NOT TO DIE.

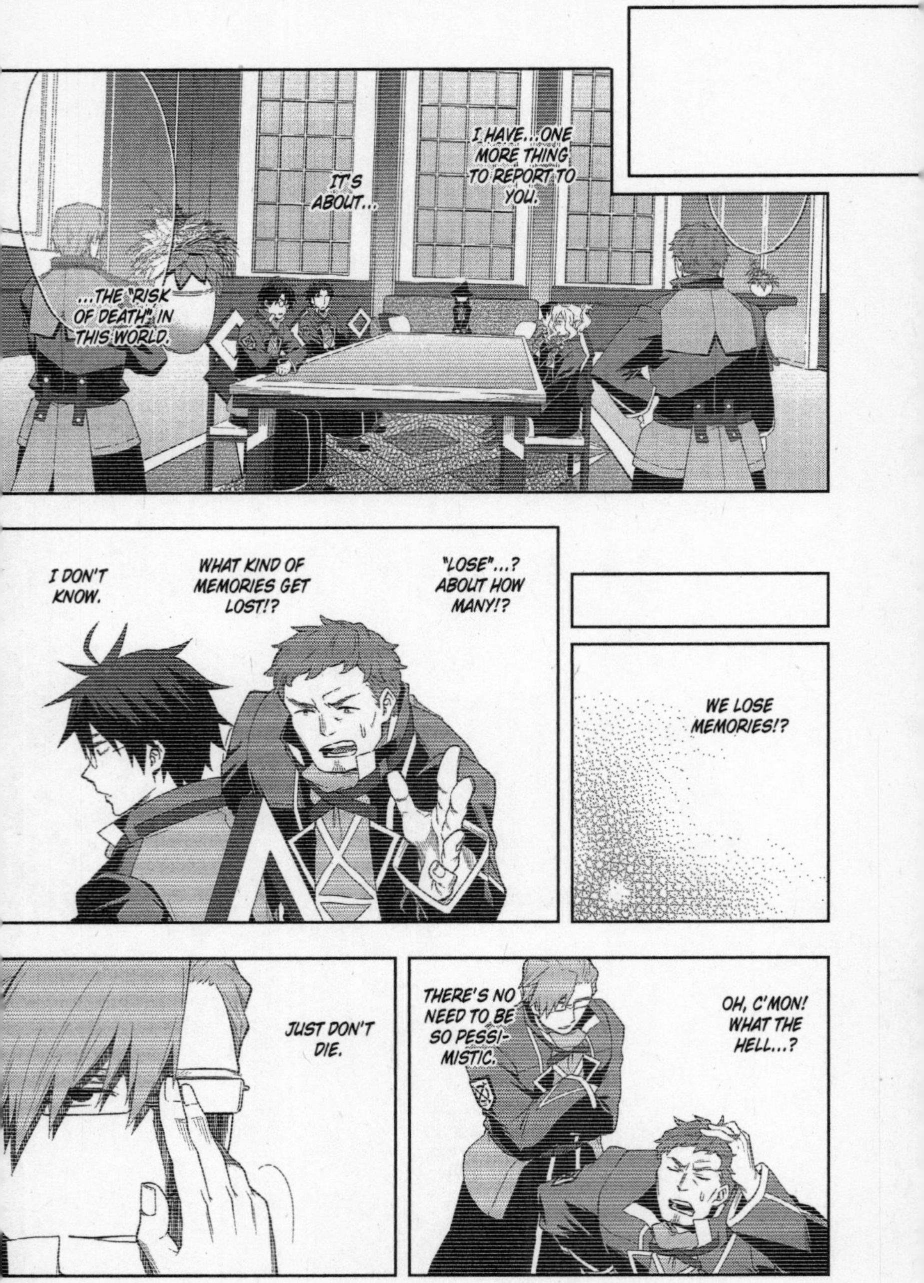
I HAVE...ONE MORE THING TO REPORT TO YOU.
IT'S ABOUT...
...THE "RISK OF DEATH" IN THIS WORLD.
WE LOSE MEMORIES!?
"LOSE"...? ABOUT HOW MANY!?
WHAT KIND OF MEMORIES GET LOST!?
I DON'T KNOW.
OH, C'MON! WHAT THE HELL...?
THERE'S NO NEED TO BE SO PESSI-MISTIC.
JUST DON'T DIE.

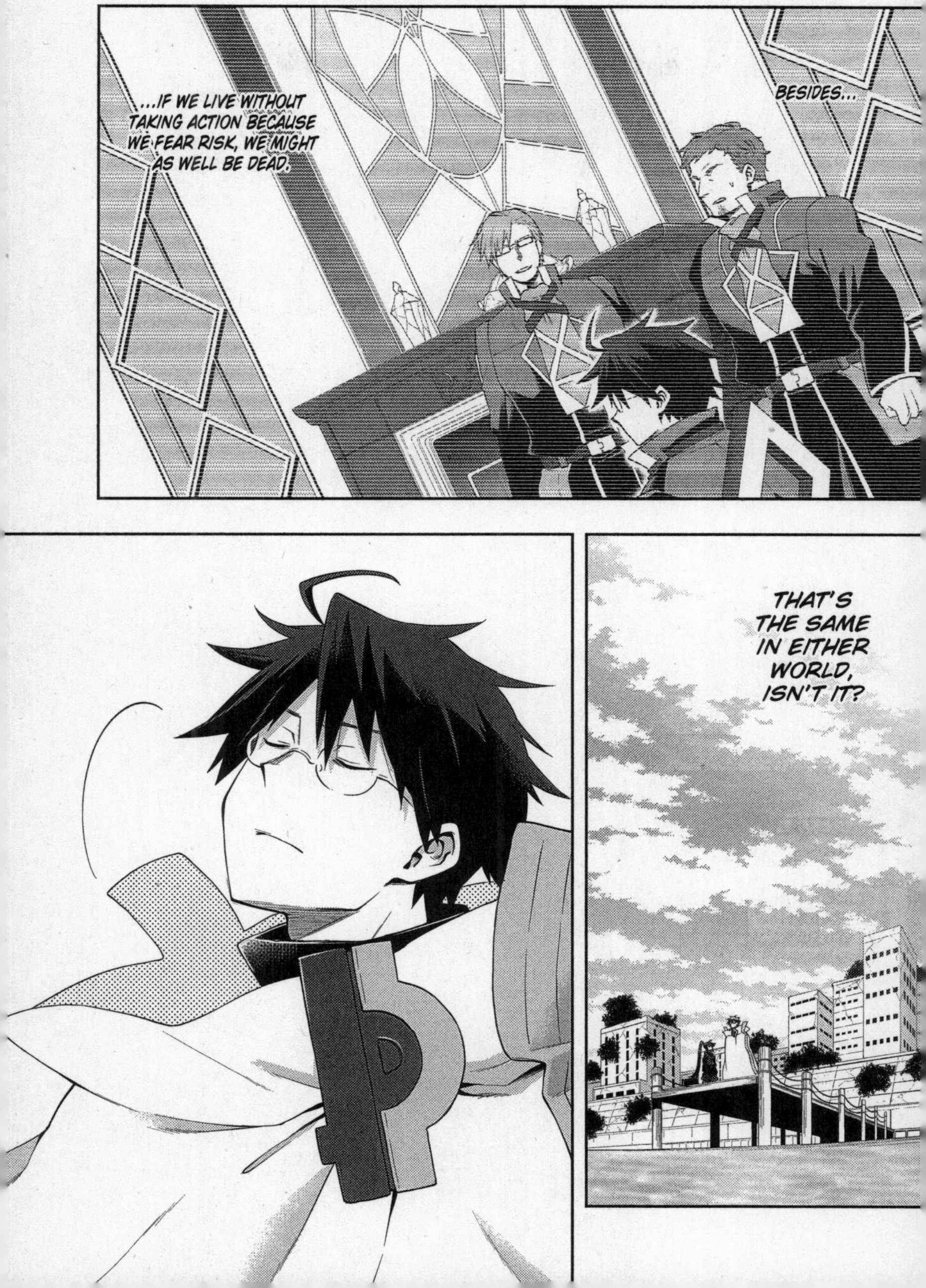
BESIDES...
...IF WE LIVE WITHOUT TAKING ACTION BECAUSE WE FEAR RISK, WE MIGHT AS WELL BE DEAD.
THAT'S THE SAME IN EITHER WORLD, ISN'T IT?

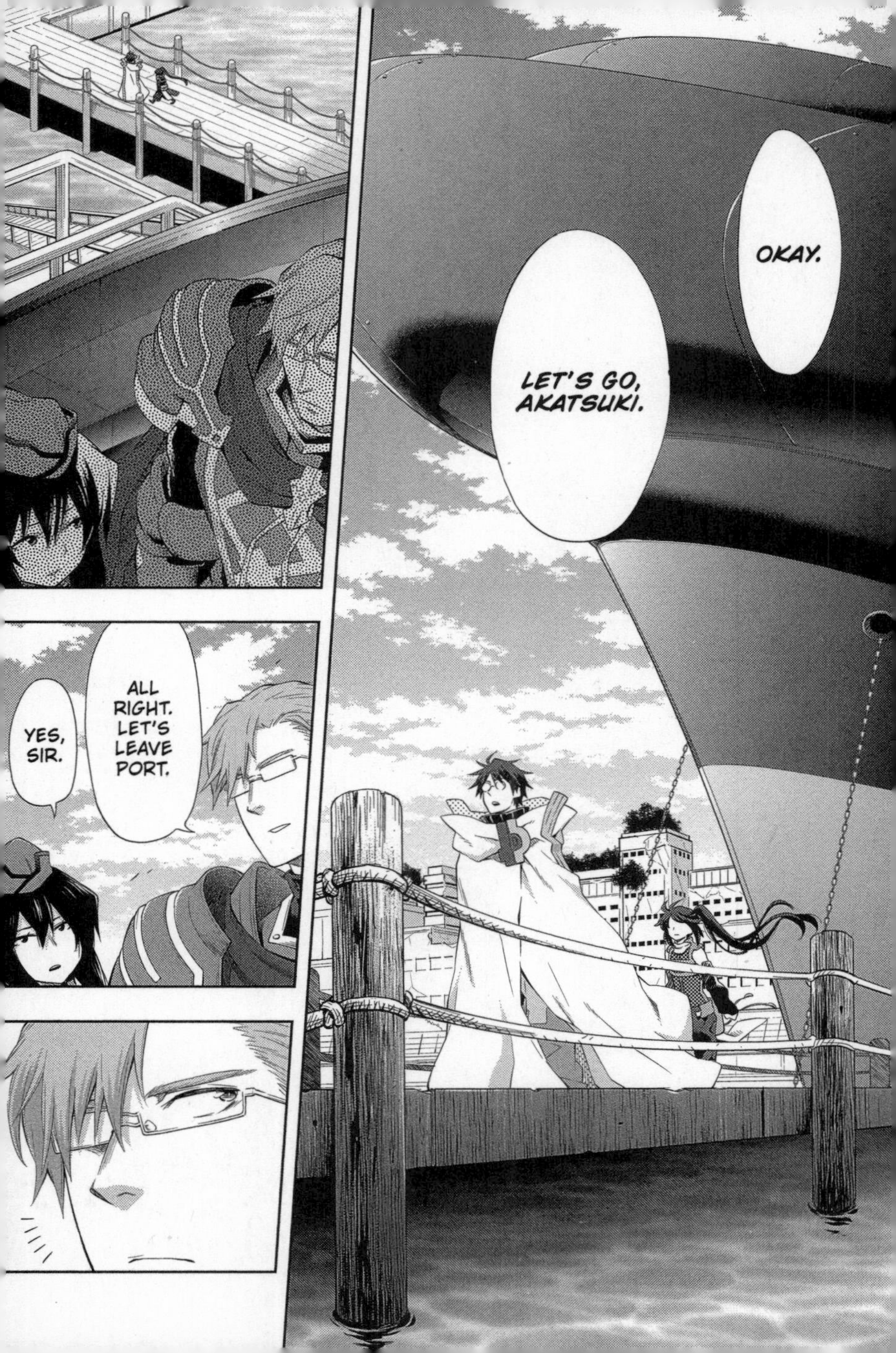
OKAY.
LET'S GO, AKATSUKI.
ALL RIGHT. LET'S LEAVE PORT.
YES, SIR.

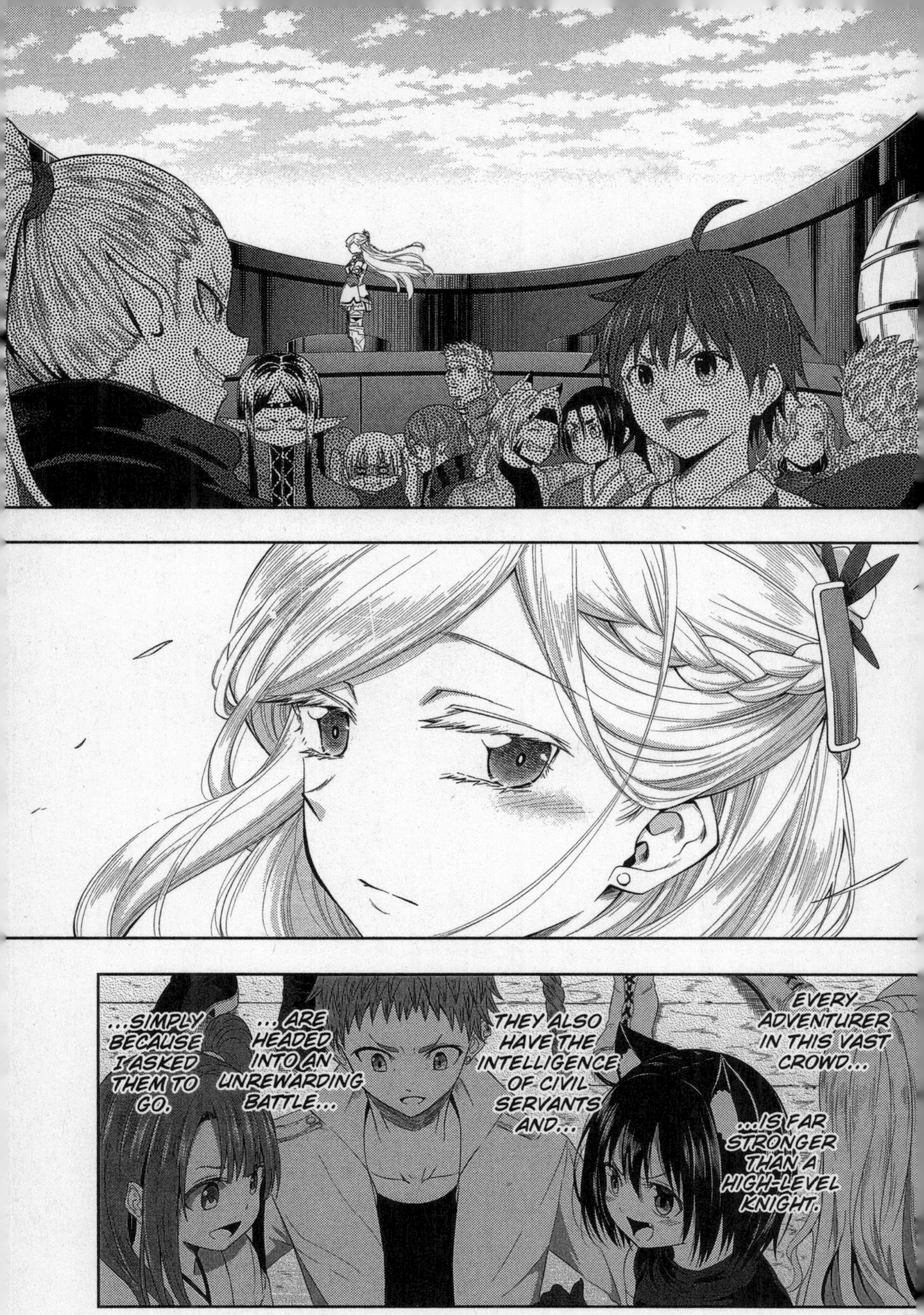
EVERY ADVENTURER IN THIS VAST CROWD...
...IS FAR STRONGER THAN A HIGH-LEVEL KNIGHT.
THEY ALSO HAVE THE INTELLIGENCE OF CIVIL SERVANTS AND...
...ARE HEADED INTO AN UNREWARDING BATTLE...
...SIMPLY BECAUSE I ASKED THEM TO GO.

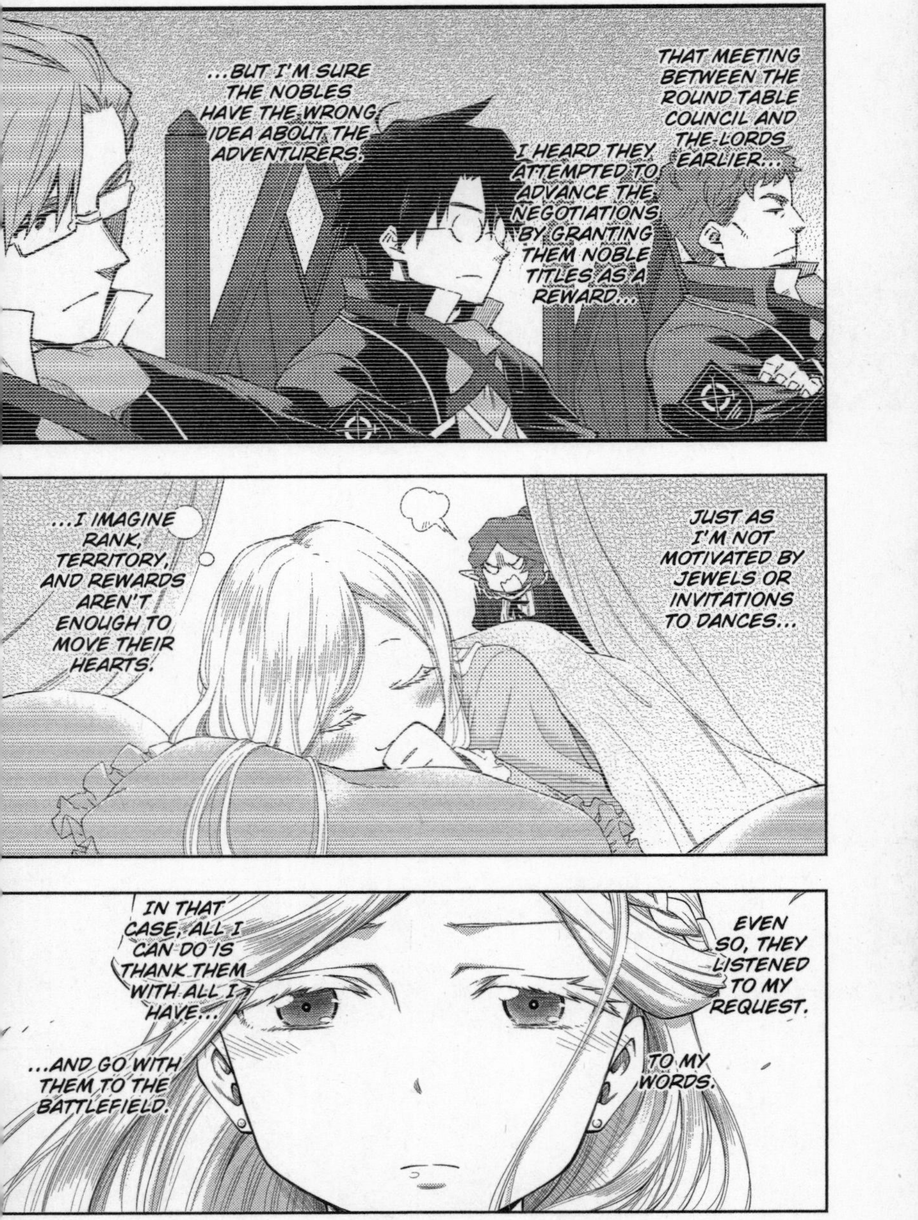
THAT MEETING BETWEEN THE ROUND TABLE COUNCIL AND THE LORDS EARLIER...
I HEARD THEY ATTEMPTED TO ADVANCE THE NEGOTIATIONS BY GRANTING THEM NOBLE TITLES AS A REWARD...
...BUT I'M SURE THE NOBLES HAVE THE WRONG IDEA ABOUT THE ADVENTURERS.
JUST AS I'M NOT MOTIVATED BY JEWELS OR INVITATIONS TO DANCES...
...I IMAGINE RANK, TERRITORY, AND REWARDS AREN'T ENOUGH TO MOVE THEIR HEARTS.
EVEN SO, THEY LISTENED TO MY REQUEST.
TO MY WORDS.
IN THAT CASE, ALL I CAN DO IS THANK THEM WITH ALL I HAVE...
...AND GO WITH THEM TO THE BATTLEFIELD.

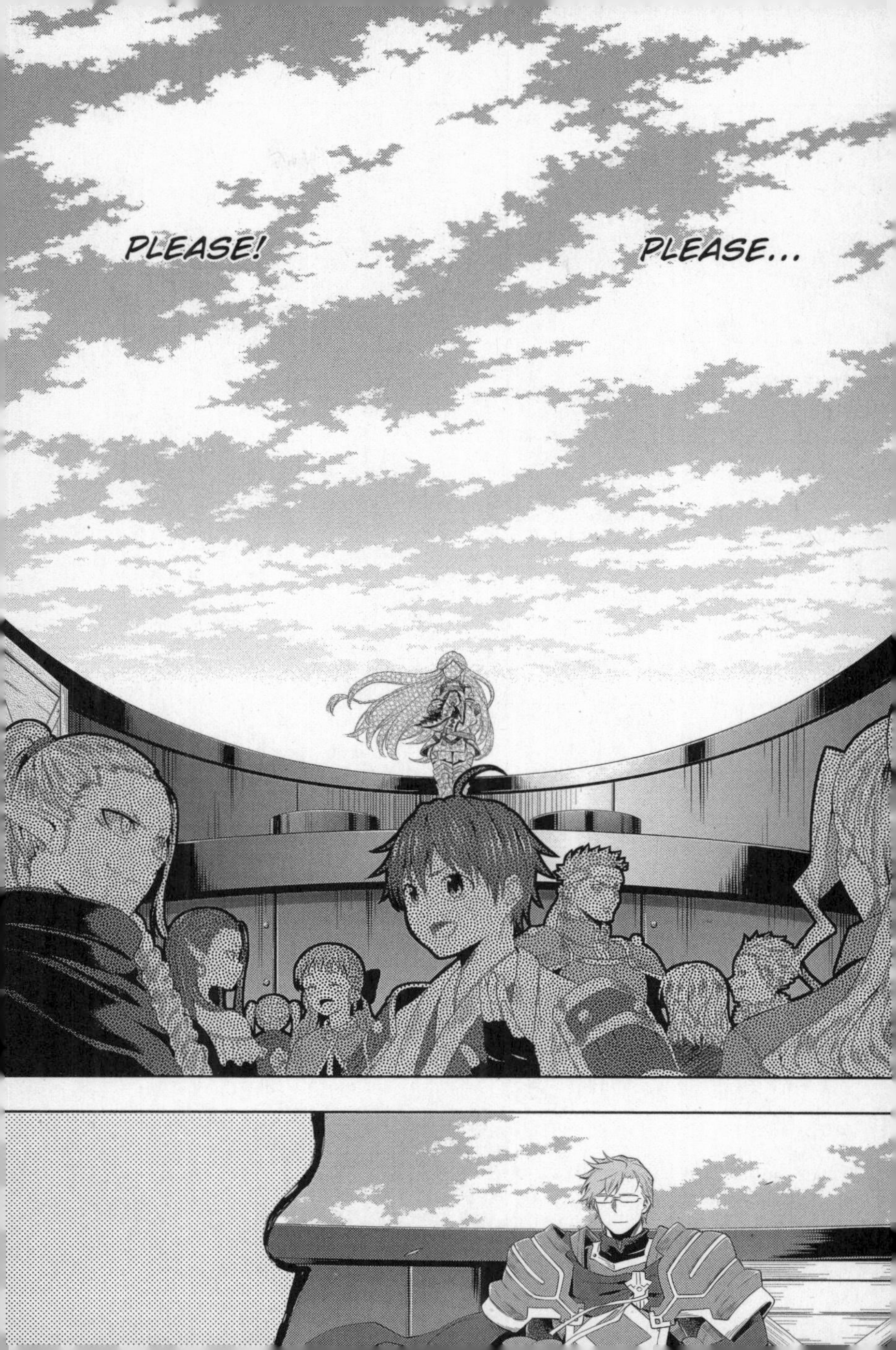
PLEASE...
PLEASE!

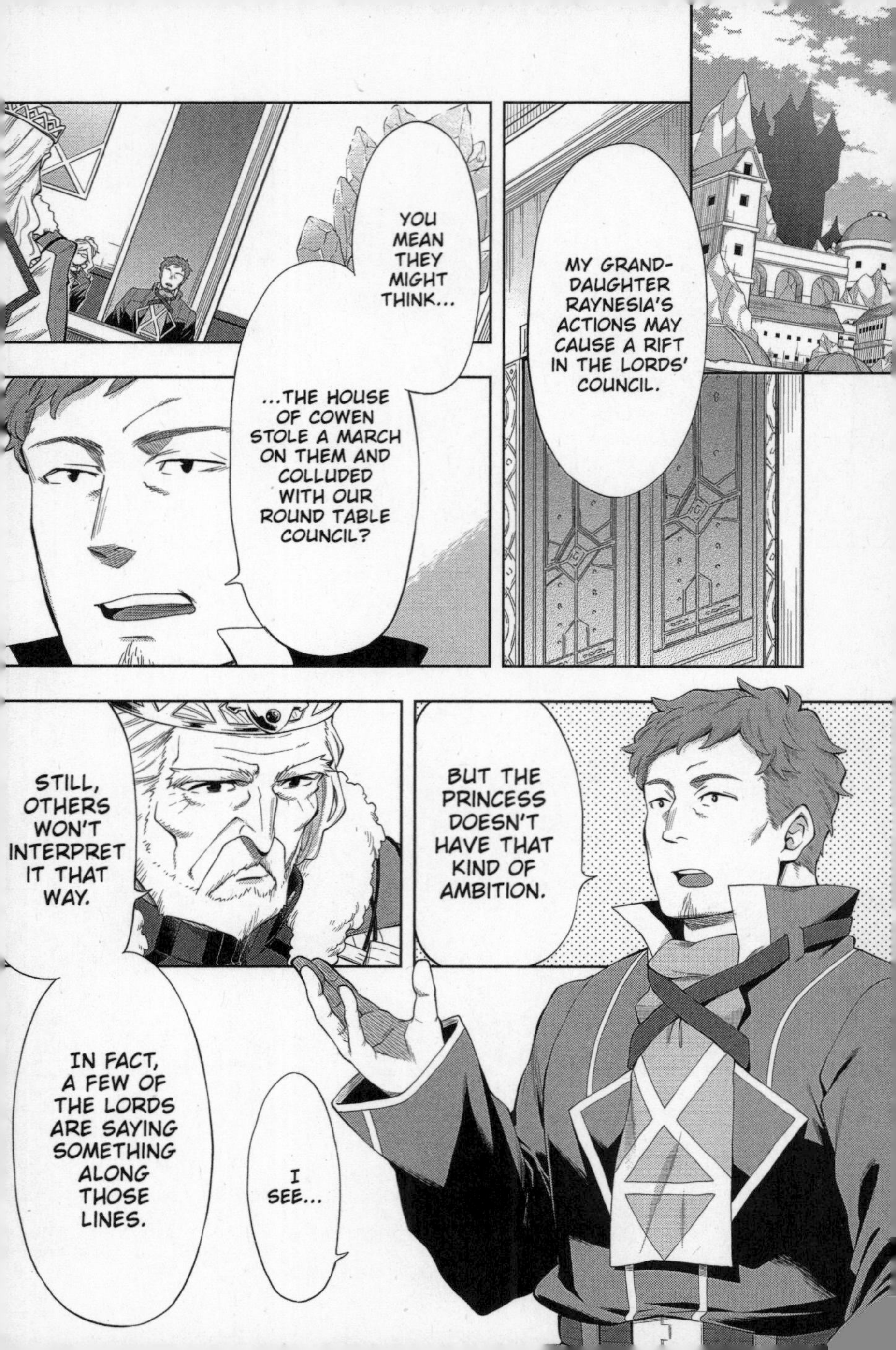
MY GRAND-DAUGHTER RAYNESIA'S ACTIONS MAY CAUSE A RIFT IN THE LORDS' COUNCIL.
YOU MEAN THEY MIGHT THINK...
...THE HOUSE OF COWEN STOLE A MARCH ON THEM AND COLLUDED WITH OUR ROUND TABLE COUNCIL?
BUT THE PRINCESS DOESN'T HAVE THAT KIND OF AMBITION.
STILL, OTHERS WON'T INTERPRET IT THAT WAY.
IN FACT, A FEW OF THE LORDS ARE SAYING SOMETHING ALONG THOSE LINES.
I SEE...

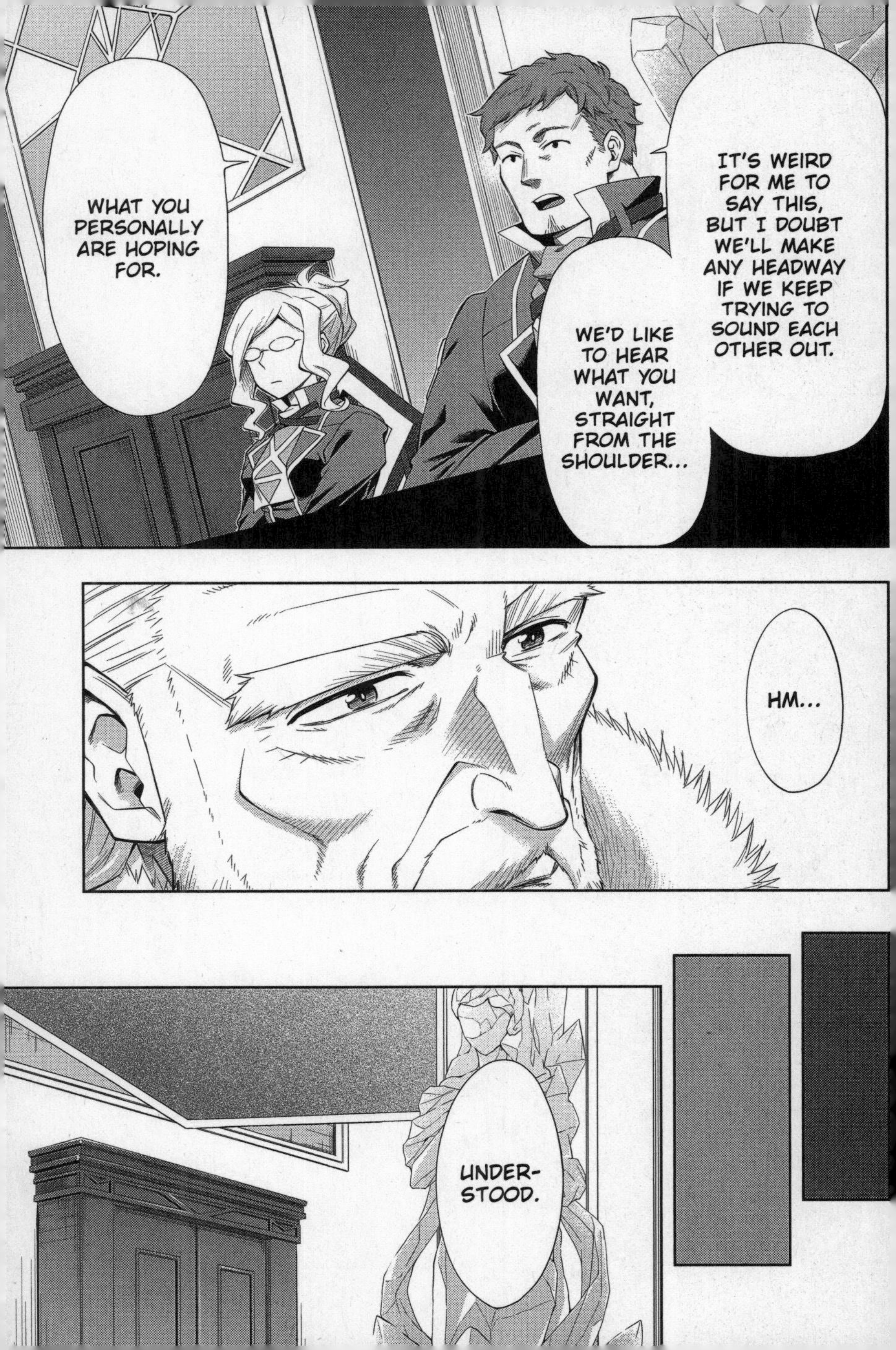
IT'S WEIRD FOR ME TO SAY THIS, BUT I DOUBT WE'LL MAKE ANY HEADWAY IF WE KEEP TRYING TO SOUND EACH OTHER OUT.
WE'D LIKE TO HEAR WHAT YOU WANT, STRAIGHT FROM THE SHOULDER...
WHAT YOU PERSONALLY ARE HOPING FOR.
HM...
UNDER-STOOD.

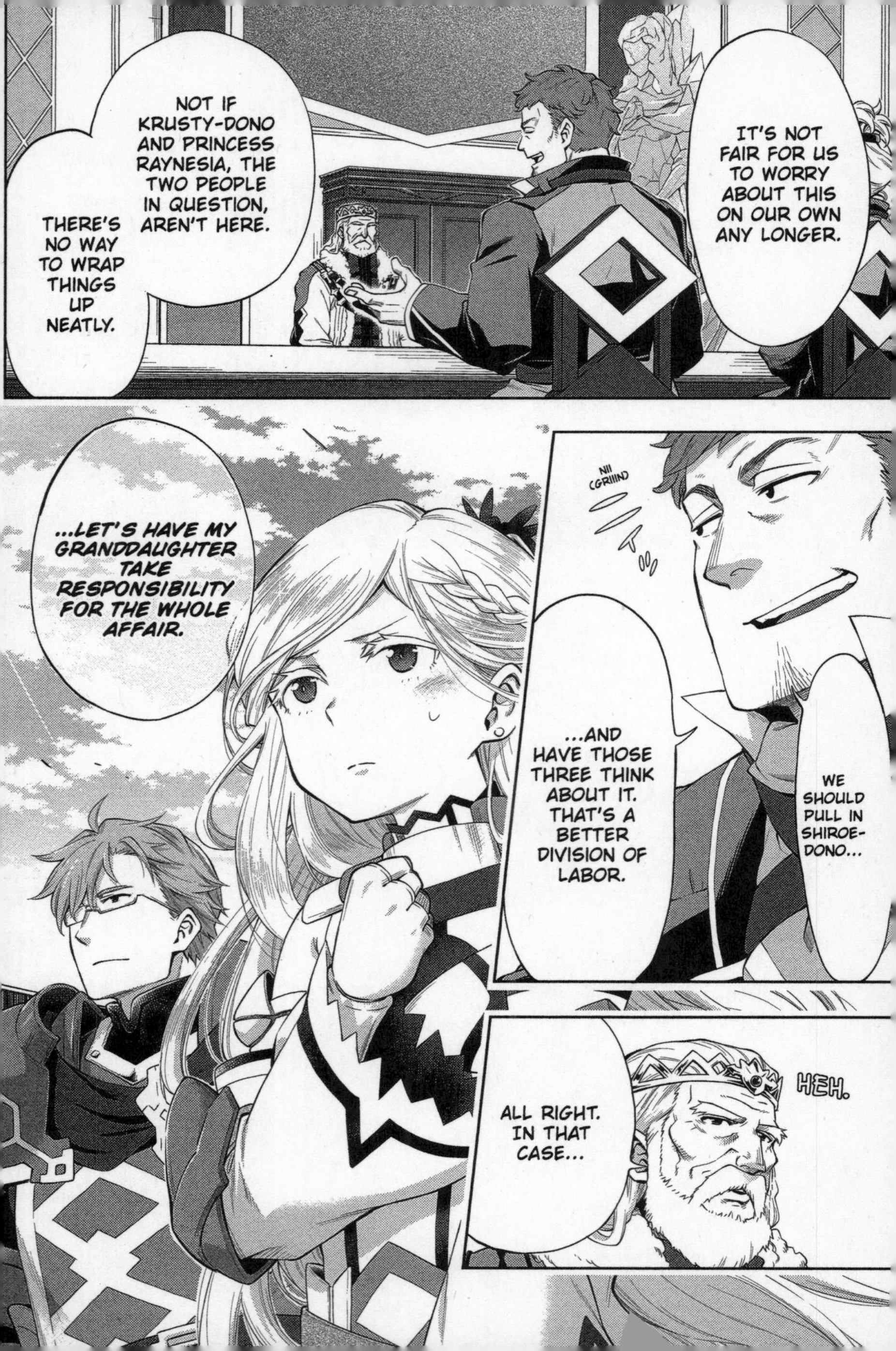
IT'S NOT FAIR FOR US TO WORRY ABOUT THIS ON OUR OWN ANY LONGER.
NOT IF KRUSTY-DONO AND PRINCESS RAYNESIA, THE TWO PEOPLE IN QUESTION, AREN'T HERE.
THERE'S NO WAY TO WRAP THINGS UP NEATLY.
NII (GRIIIN)
WE SHOULD PULL IN SHIROE-DONO...
...AND HAVE THOSE THREE THINK ABOUT IT. THAT'S A BETTER DIVISION OF LABOR.
HEH.
ALL RIGHT. IN THAT CASE...
...LET'S HAVE MY GRANDDAUGHTER TAKE RESPONSIBILITY FOR THE WHOLE AFFAIR.

LOG HORIZON

THE WEST WIND BRIGADE

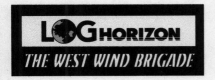

LOG HORIZON

THE WEST WIND BRIGADE

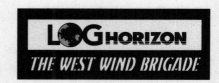

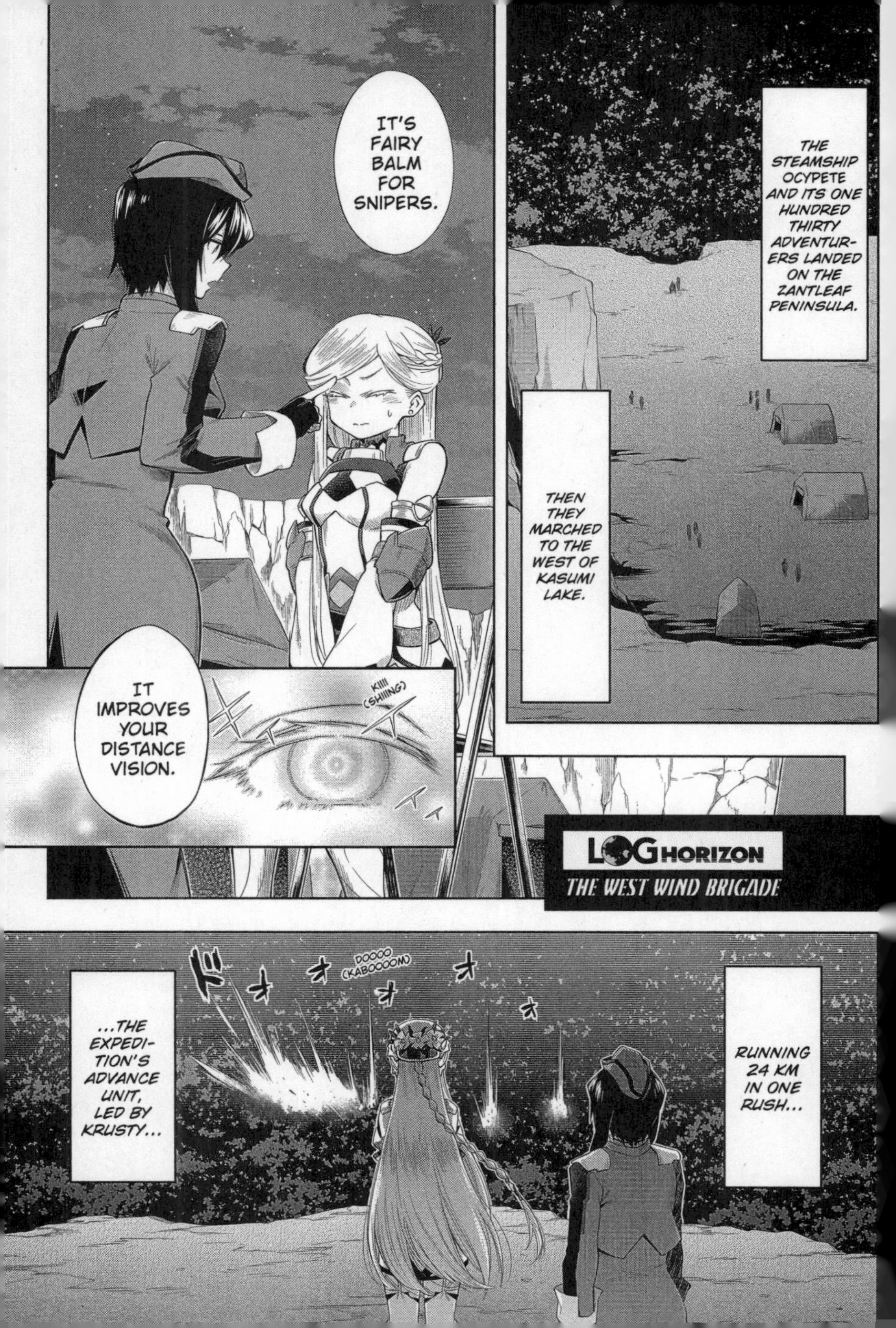
THE STEAMSHIP OCYPETE AND ITS ONE HUNDRED THIRTY ADVENTURERS LANDED ON THE ZANTLEAF PENINSULA.
THEN THEY MARCHED TO THE WEST OF KASUMI LAKE.
IT'S FAIRY BALM FOR SNIPERS.
KIIII (SHIIING)
IT IMPROVES YOUR DISTANCE VISION.
LOG HORIZON
THE WEST WIND BRIGADE
RUNNING 24 KM IN ONE RUSH...
DOOOO (KABOOOOM)
...THE EXPEDITION'S ADVANCE UNIT, LED BY KRUSTY...

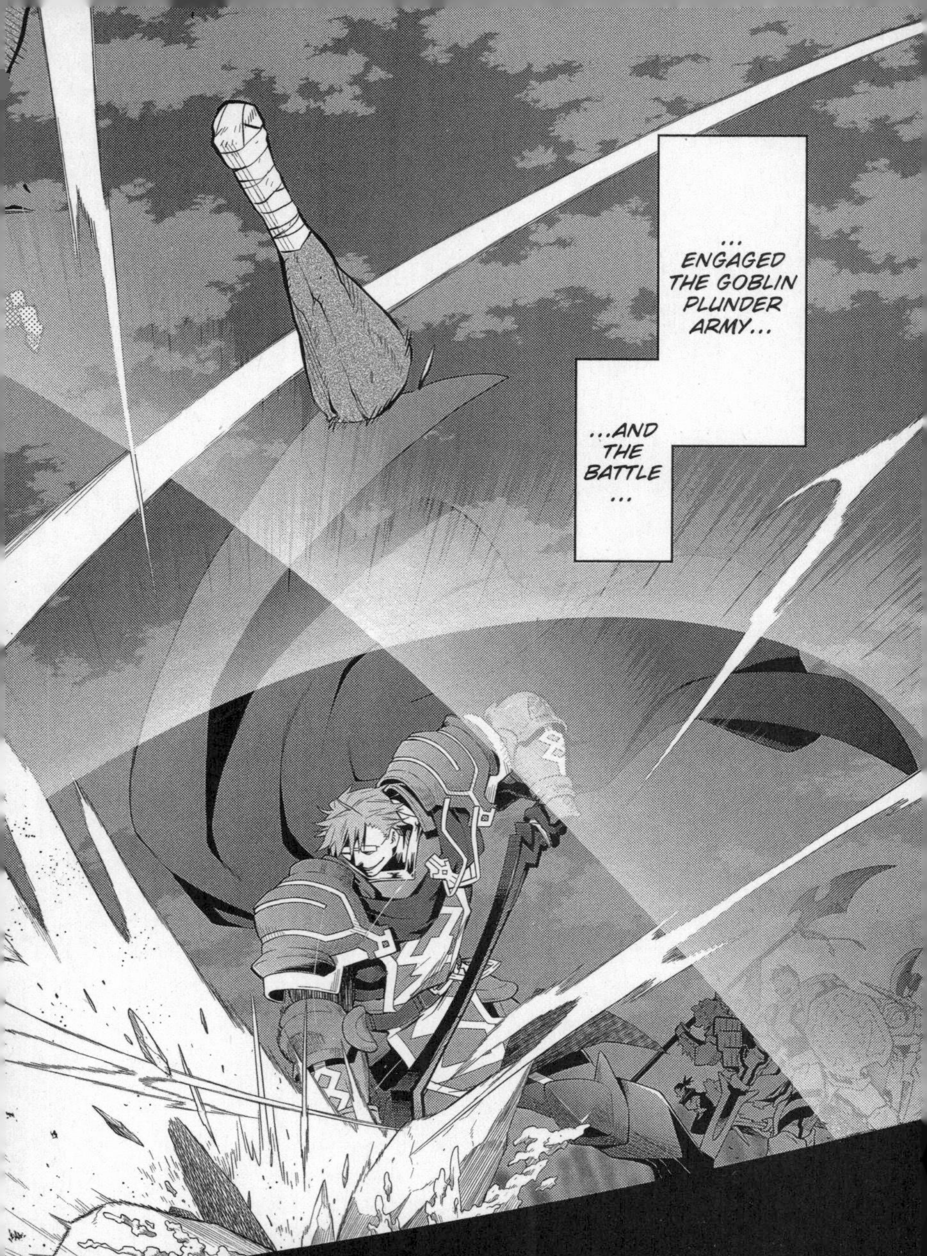
...ENGAGED THE GOBLIN PLUNDER ARMY...
...AND THE BATTLE...

CHAPTER: 45 Charge

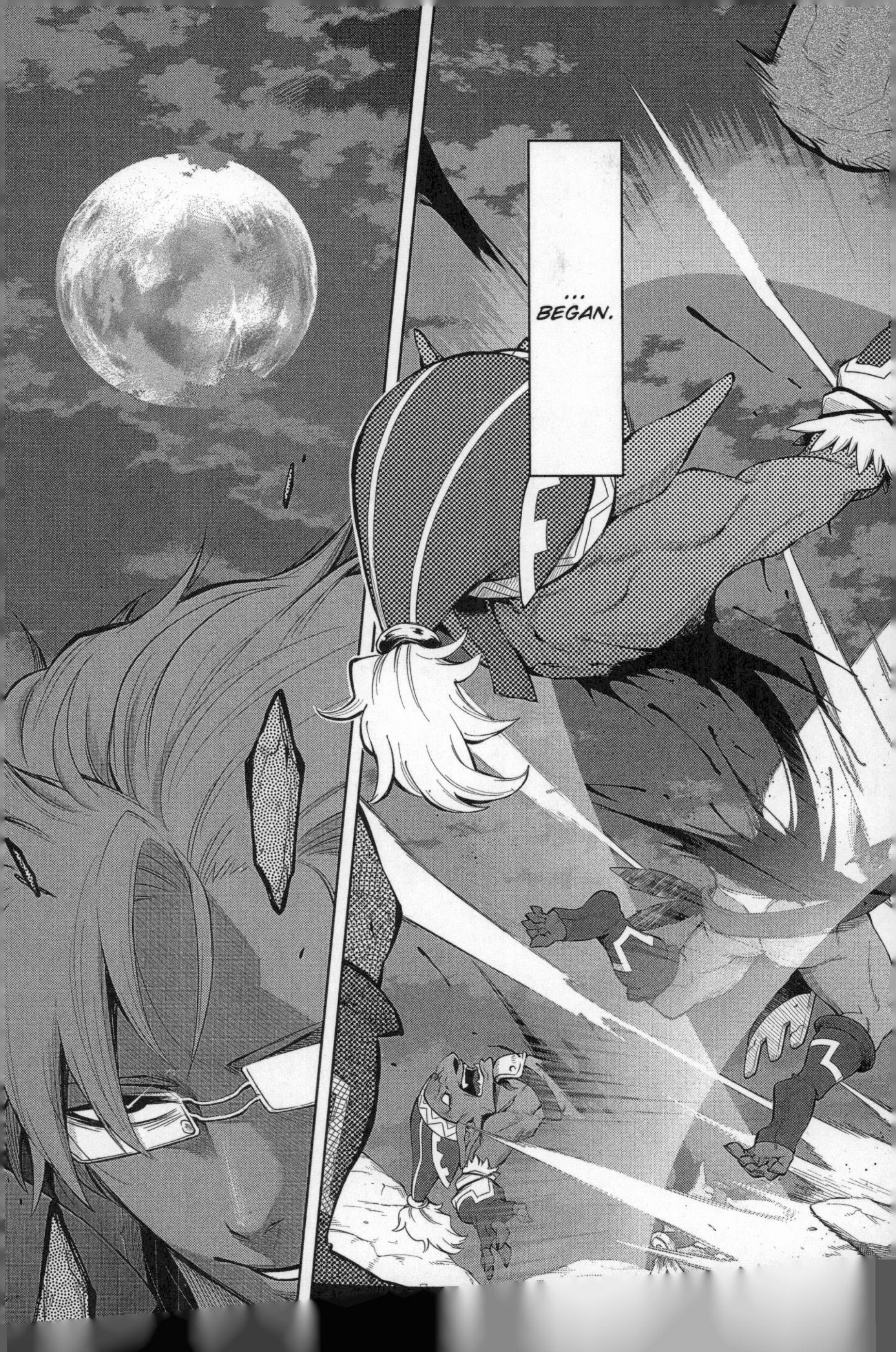
...BEGAN.

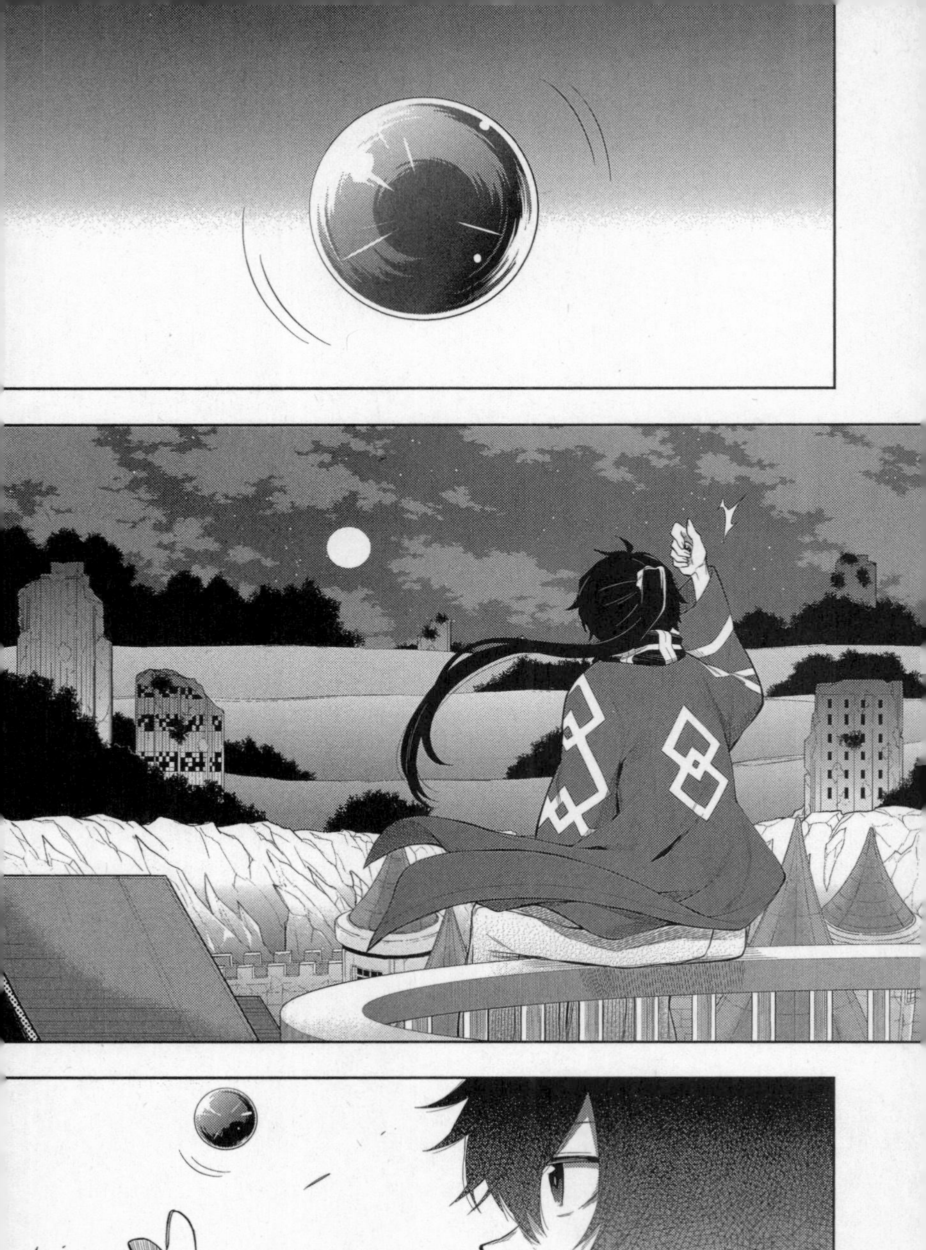

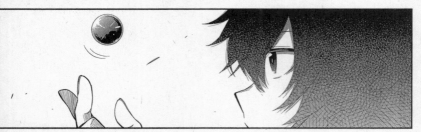

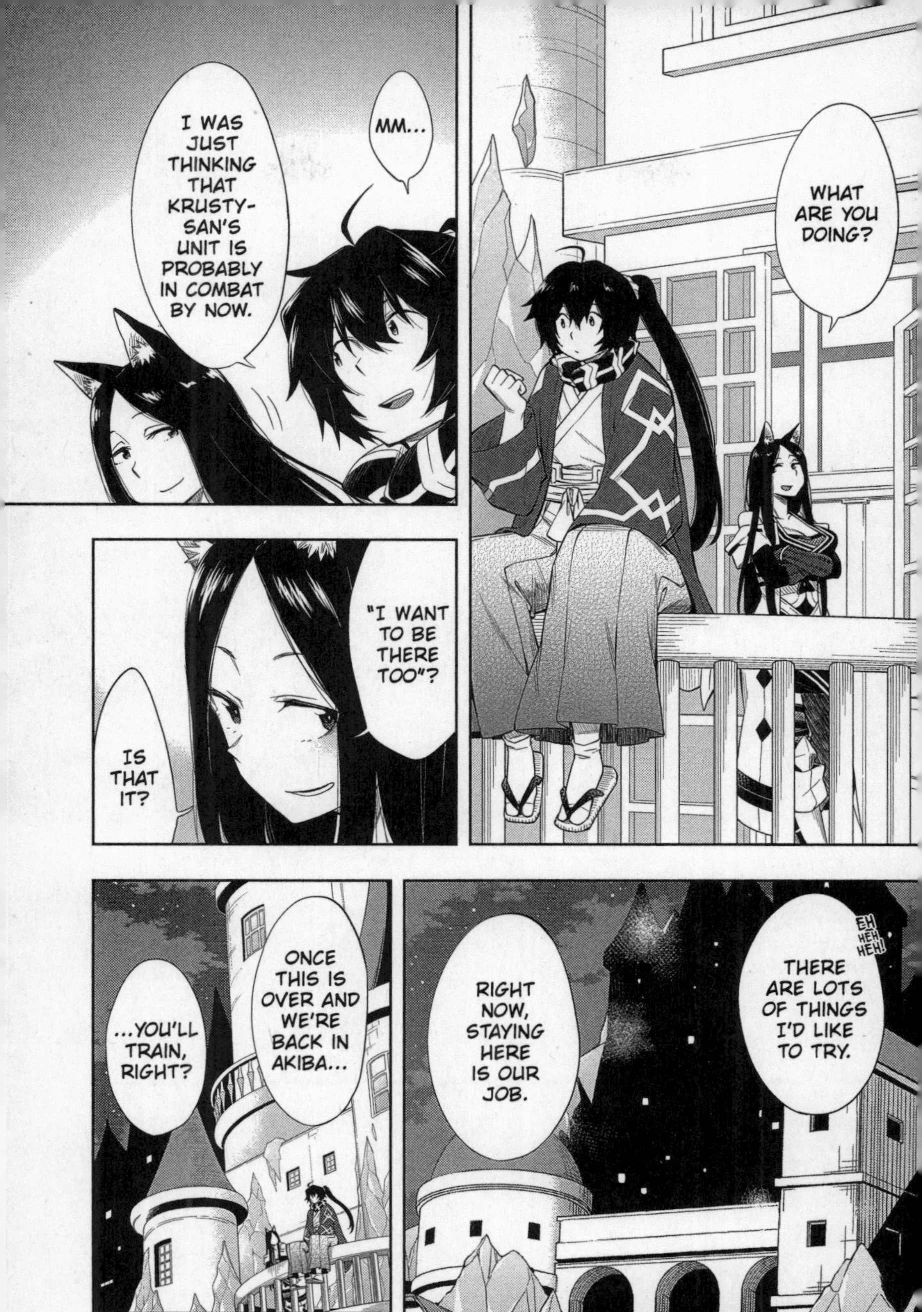
WHAT ARE YOU DOING?
MM...
I WAS JUST THINKING THAT KRUSTY-SAN'S UNIT IS PROBABLY IN COMBAT BY NOW.
"I WANT TO BE THERE TOO"?
IS THAT IT?
EH HEH HEH!
THERE ARE LOTS OF THINGS I'D LIKE TO TRY.
RIGHT NOW, STAYING HERE IS OUR JOB.
ONCE THIS IS OVER AND WE'RE BACK IN AKIBA...
...YOU'LL TRAIN, RIGHT?

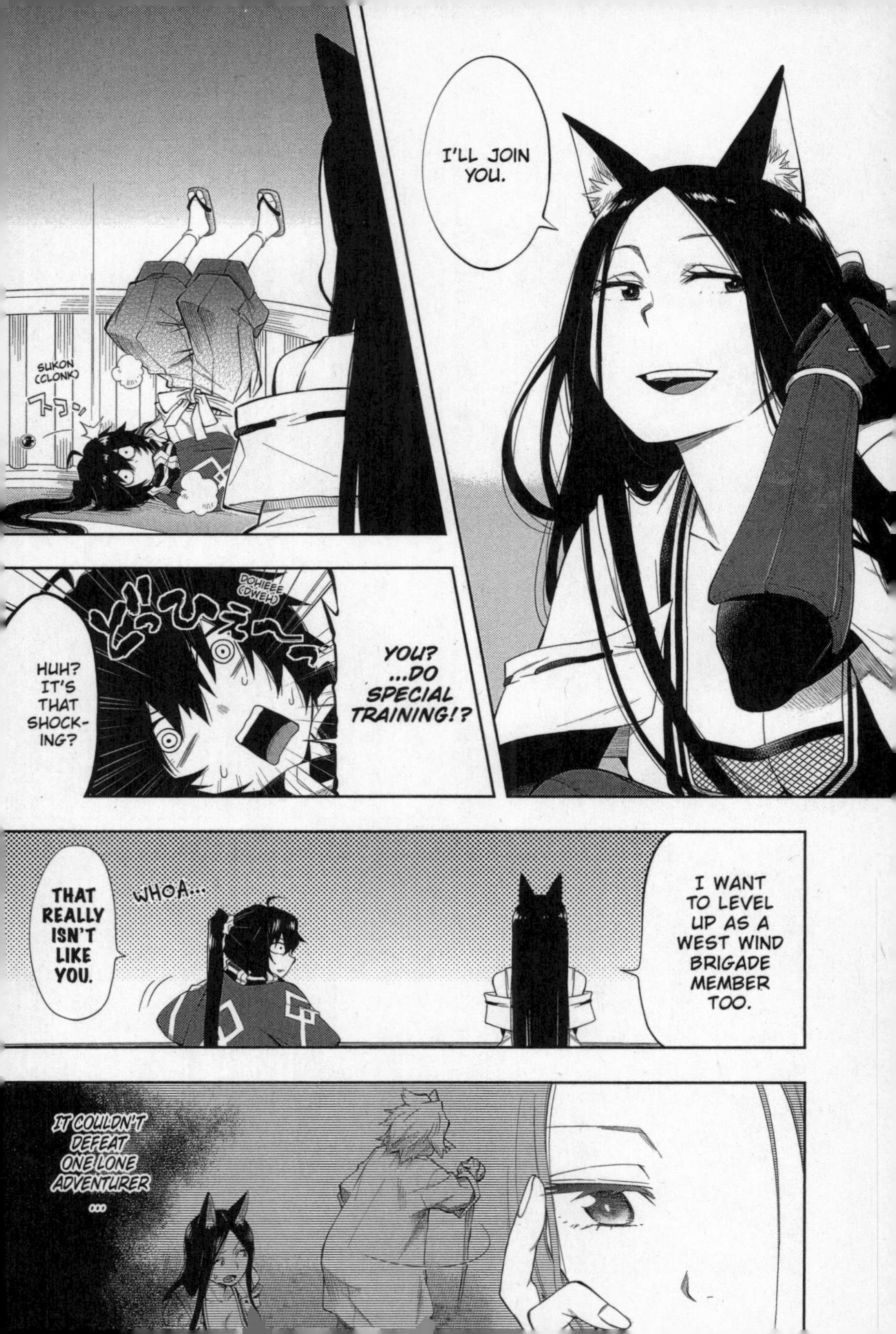
I'LL JOIN YOU.
SUKON (CLONK)
YOU? ...DO SPECIAL TRAINING!?
DOHIEEE (DWEH)
HUH? IT'S THAT SHOCKING?
I WANT TO LEVEL UP AS A WEST WIND BRIGADE MEMBER TOO.
WHOA...
THAT REALLY ISN'T LIKE YOU.
IT COULDN'T DEFEAT ONE LONE ADVENTURER ...

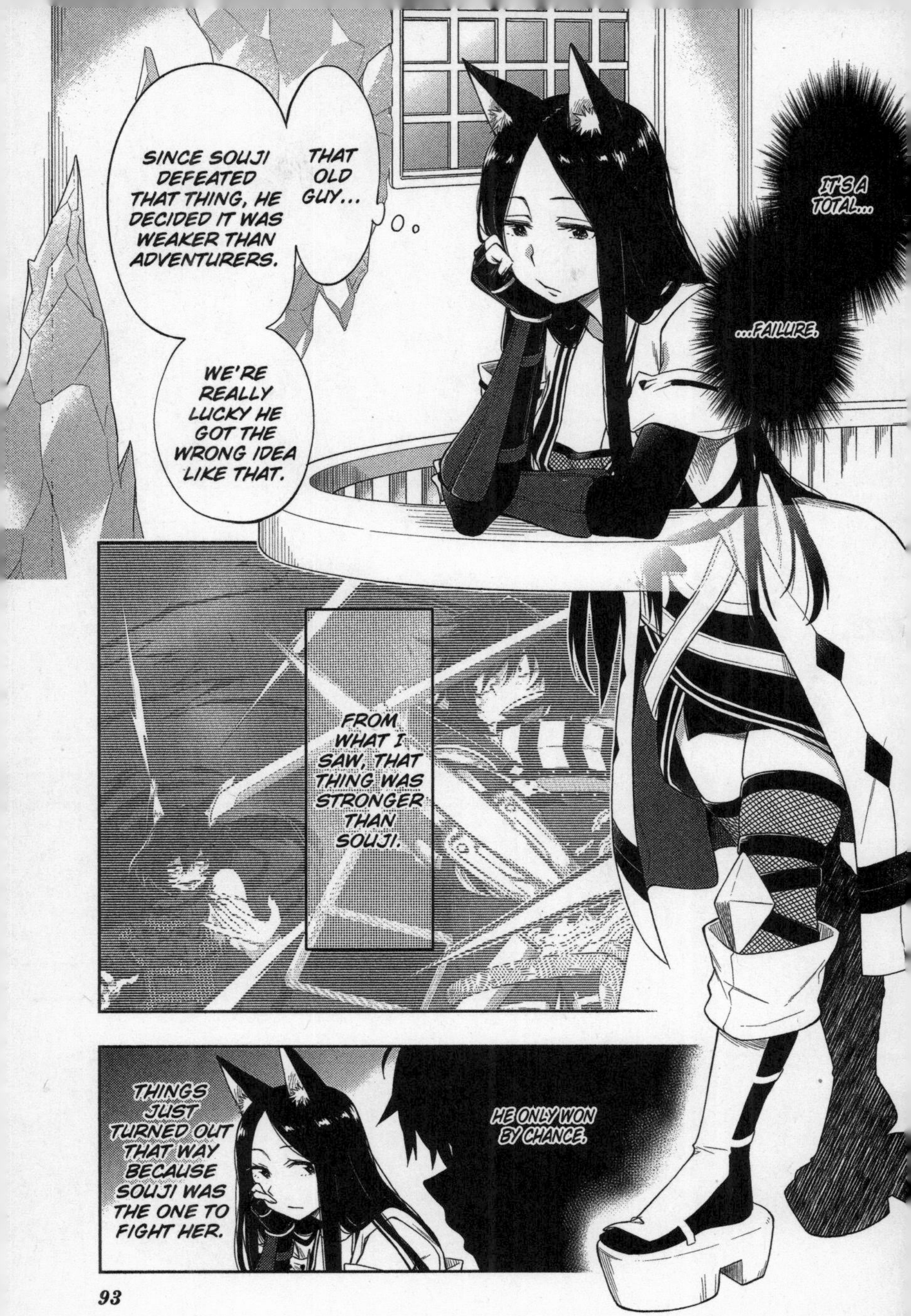
THAT OLD GUY...
SINCE SOUJI DEFEATED THAT THING, HE DECIDED IT WAS WEAKER THAN ADVENTURERS.
WE'RE REALLY LUCKY HE GOT THE WRONG IDEA LIKE THAT.
FROM WHAT I SAW, THAT THING WAS STRONGER THAN SOUJI.
HE ONLY WON BY CHANCE.
THINGS JUST TURNED OUT THAT WAY BECAUSE SOUJI WAS THE ONE TO FIGHT HER.
IT'S A TOTAL...
...FAILURE.

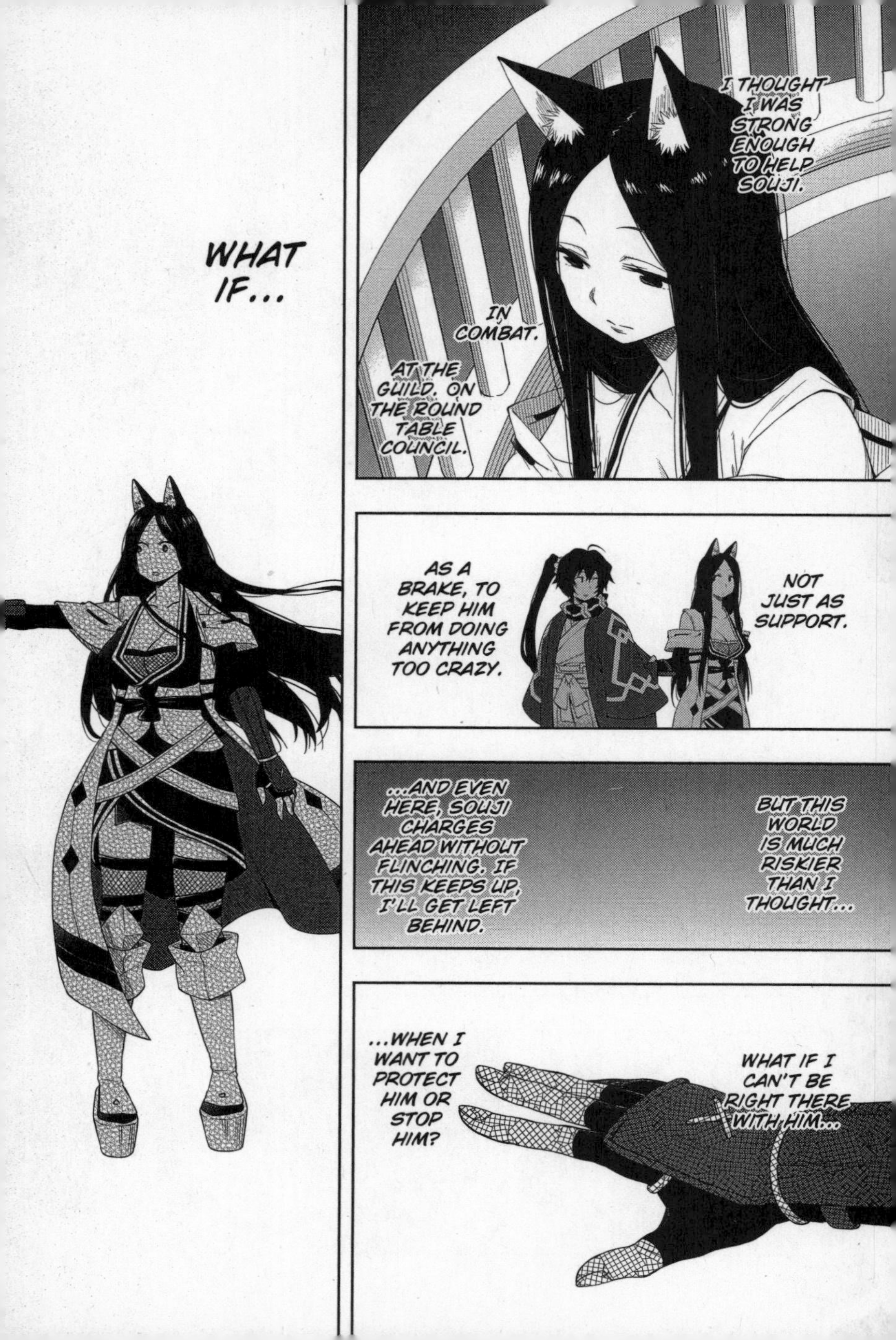
I THOUGHT I WAS STRONG ENOUGH TO HELP SOUJI.
IN COMBAT.
AT THE GUILD. ON THE ROUND TABLE COUNCIL.
NOT JUST AS SUPPORT.
AS A BRAKE, TO KEEP HIM FROM DOING ANYTHING TOO CRAZY.
BUT THIS WORLD IS MUCH RISKIER THAN I THOUGHT...
...AND EVEN HERE, SOUJI CHARGES AHEAD WITHOUT FLINCHING. IF THIS KEEPS UP, I'LL GET LEFT BEHIND.
WHAT IF I CAN'T BE RIGHT THERE WITH HIM...
...WHEN I WANT TO PROTECT HIM OR STOP HIM?
WHAT IF...

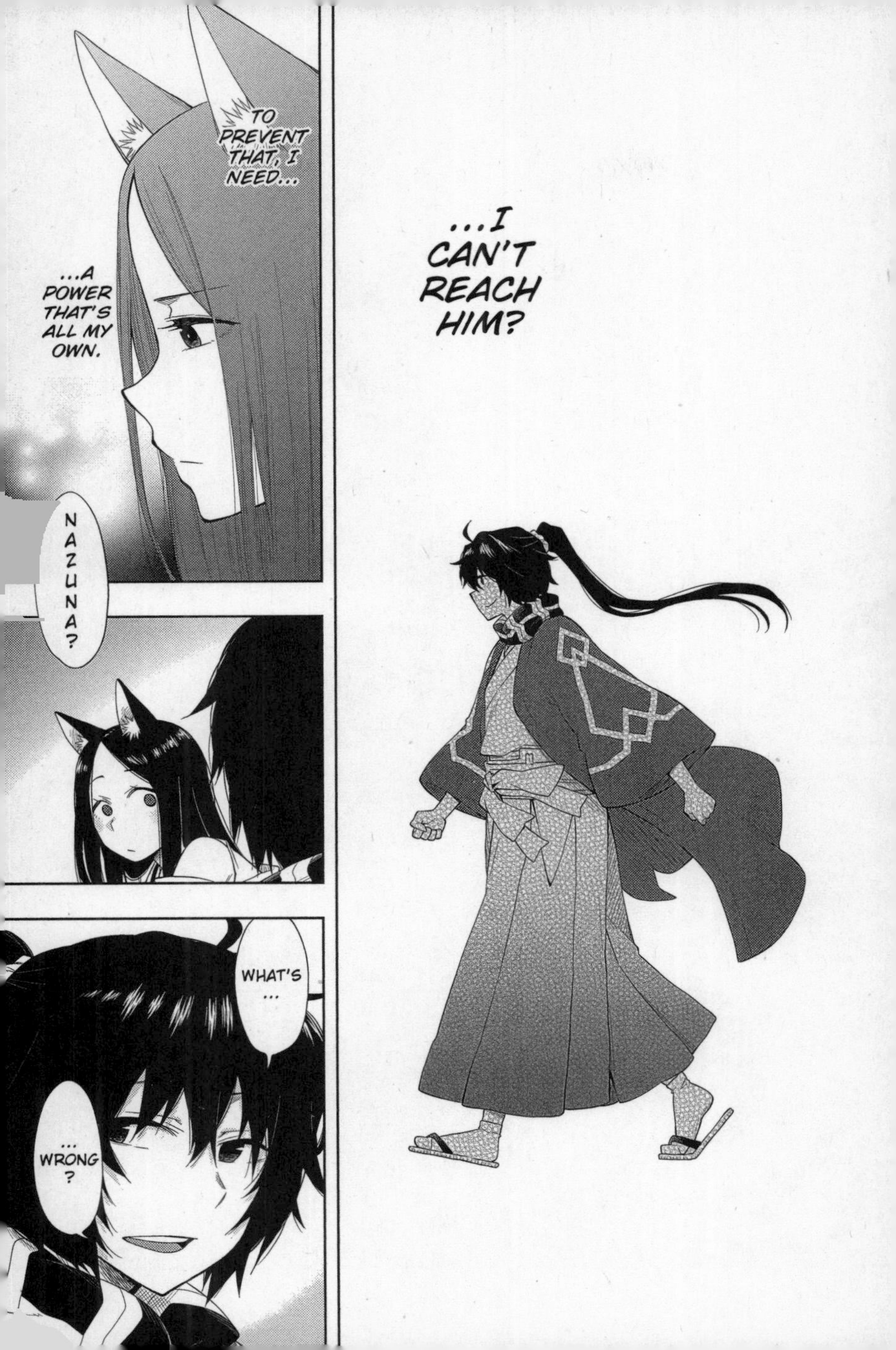
...I CAN'T REACH HIM?
TO PREVENT THAT, I NEED...
...A POWER THAT'S ALL MY OWN.
NAZUNA?
WHAT'S...
...WRONG?

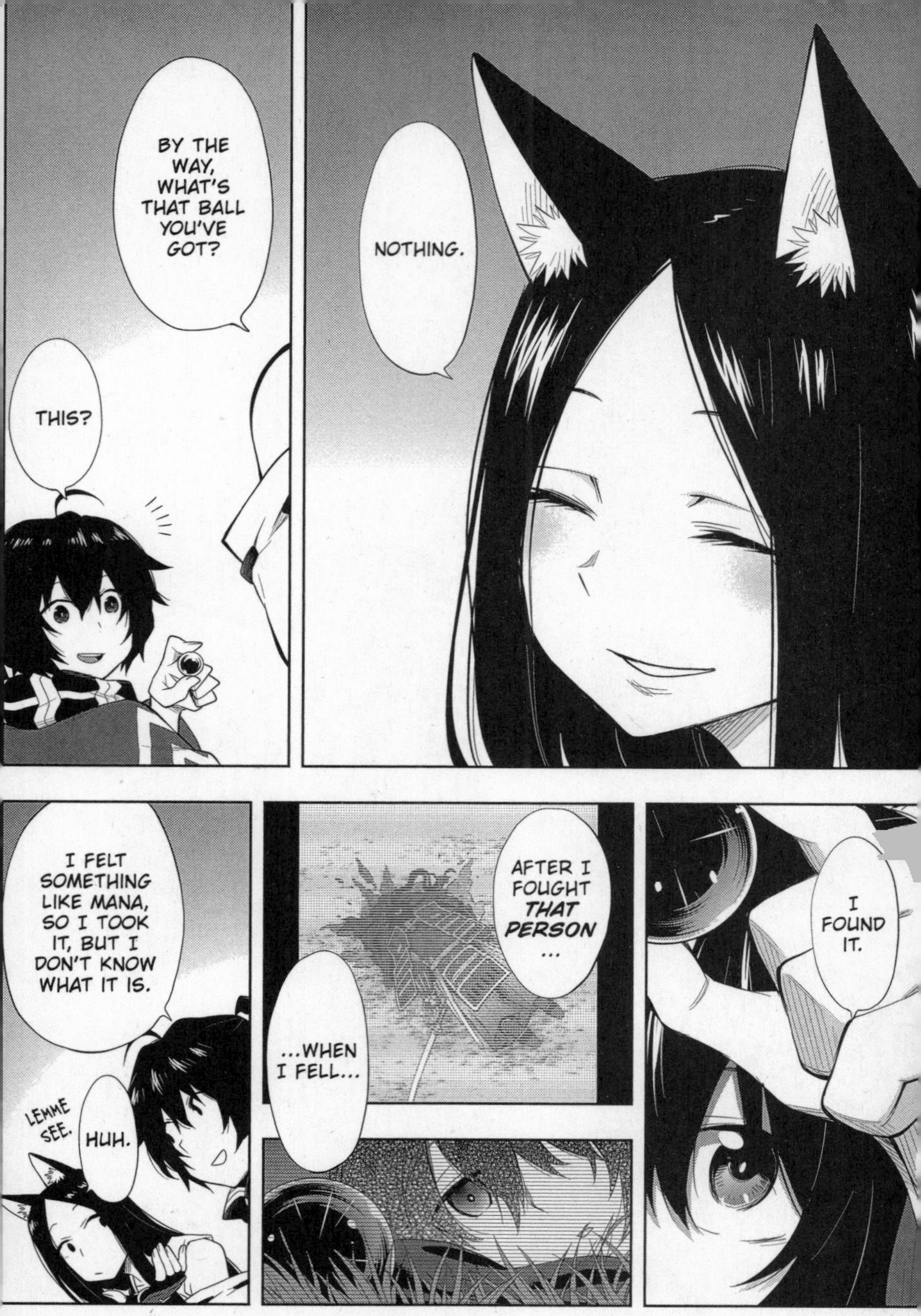
NOTHING.
BY THE WAY, WHAT'S THAT BALL YOU'VE GOT?
THIS?
I FOUND IT.
AFTER I FOUGHT *THAT PERSON*...
...WHEN I FELL...
I FELT SOMETHING LIKE MANA, SO I TOOK IT, BUT I DON'T KNOW WHAT IT IS.
HUH.
LEMME SEE.

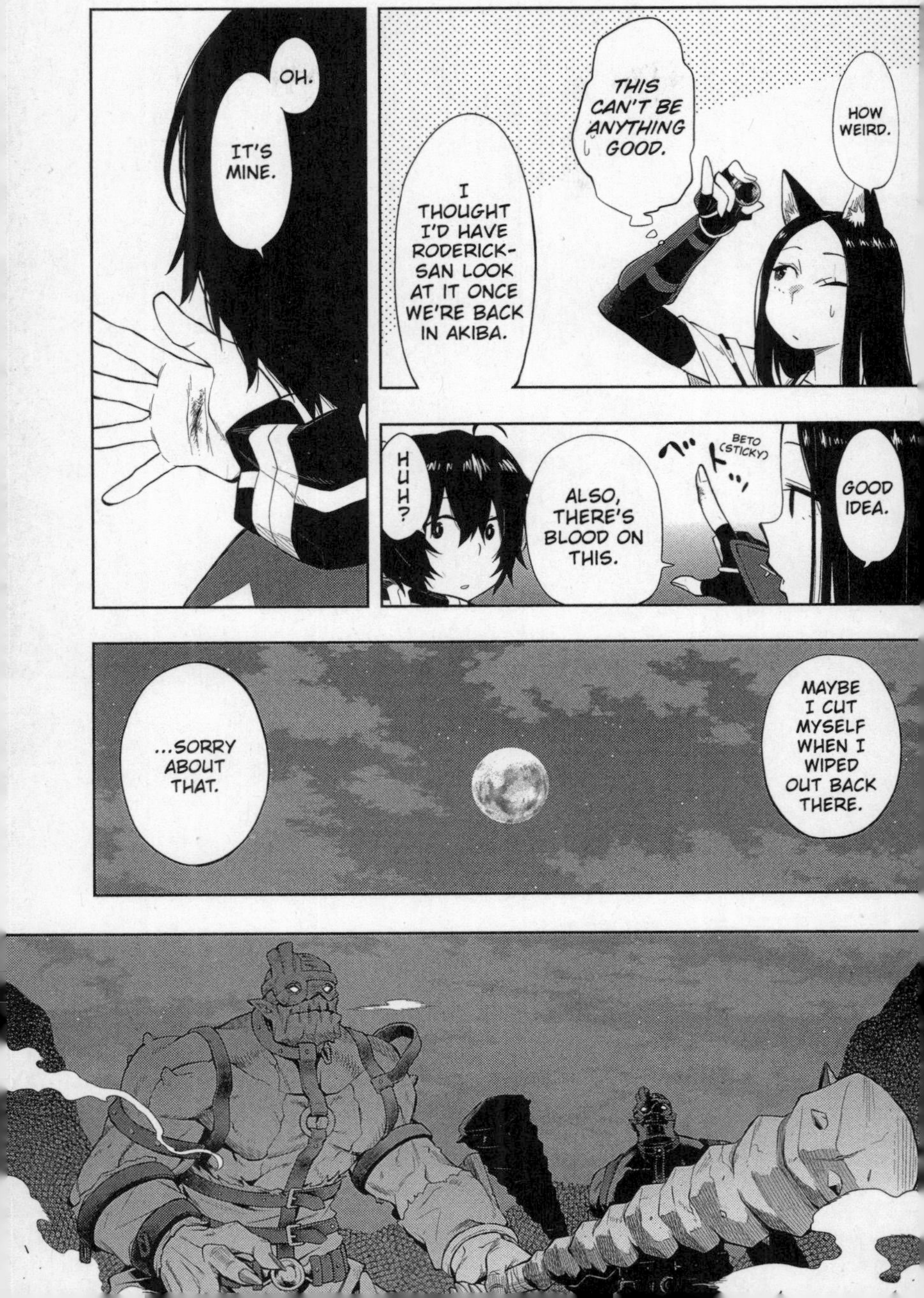
HOW WEIRD.
THIS CAN'T BE ANYTHING GOOD.
I THOUGHT I'D HAVE RODERICK-SAN LOOK AT IT ONCE WE'RE BACK IN AKIBA.
GOOD IDEA.
BETO (STICKY)
ALSO, THERE'S BLOOD ON THIS.
HUH?
OH.
IT'S MINE.
MAYBE I CUT MYSELF WHEN I WIPED OUT BACK THERE.
...SORRY ABOUT THAT.

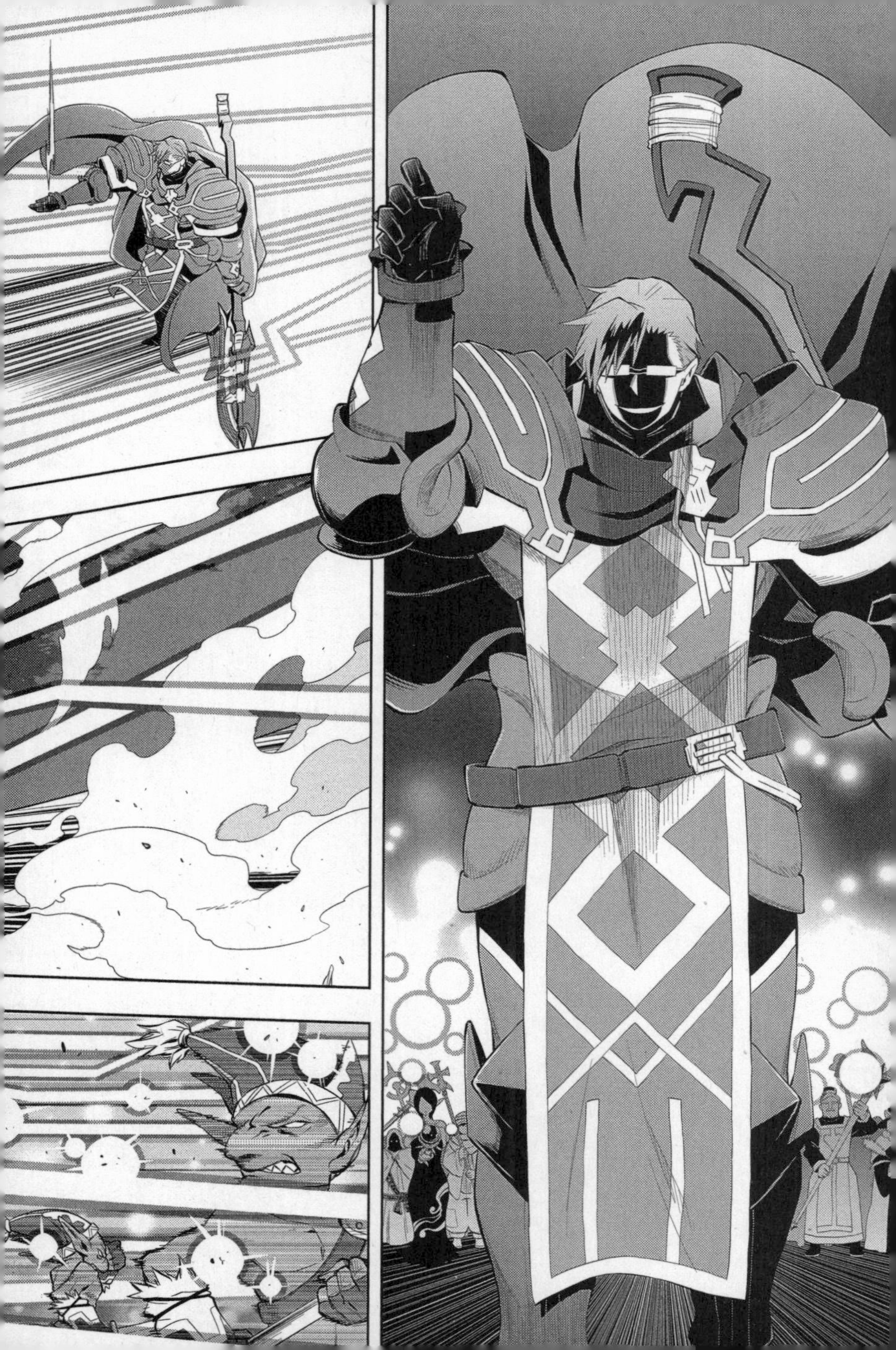

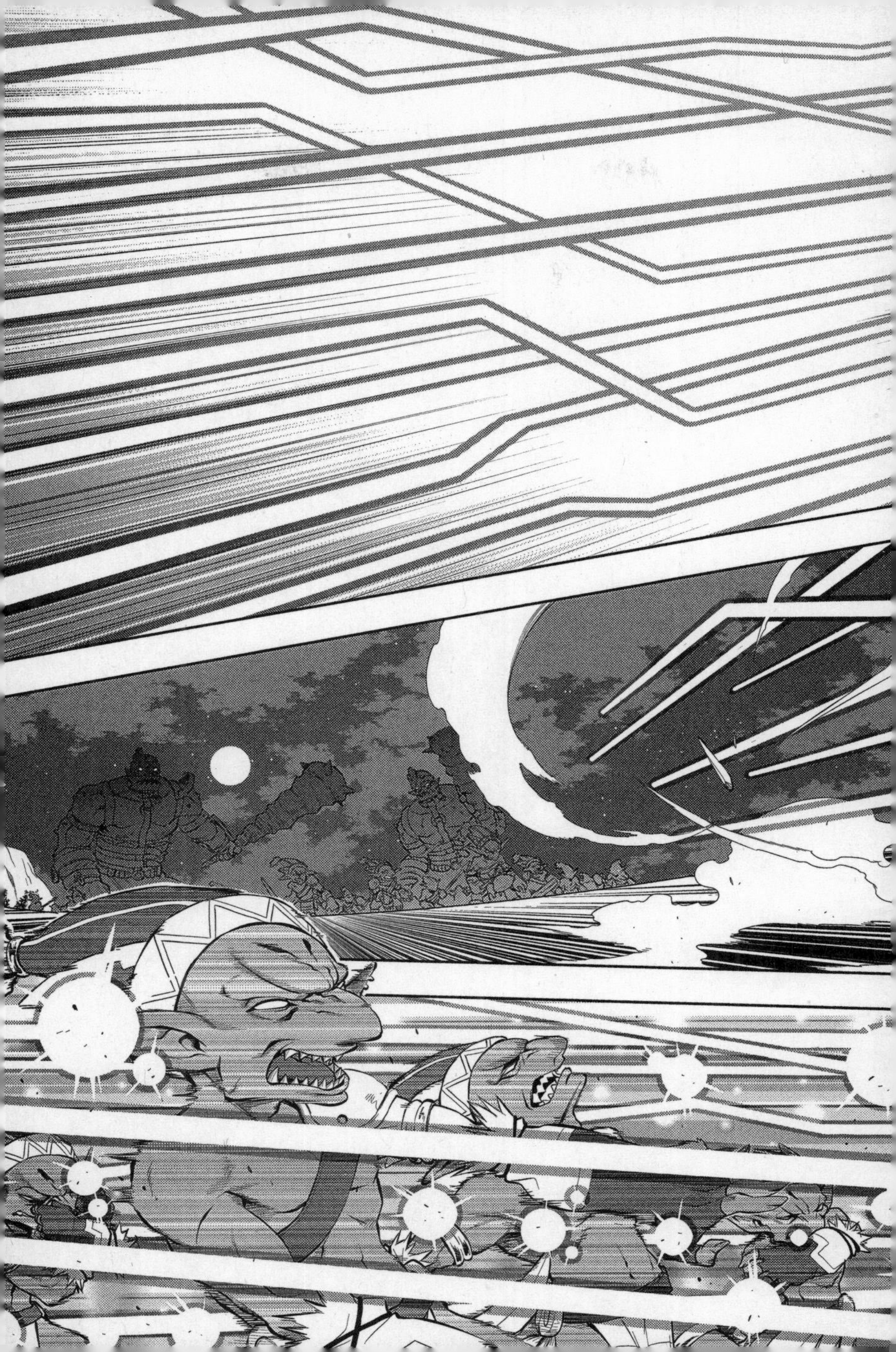

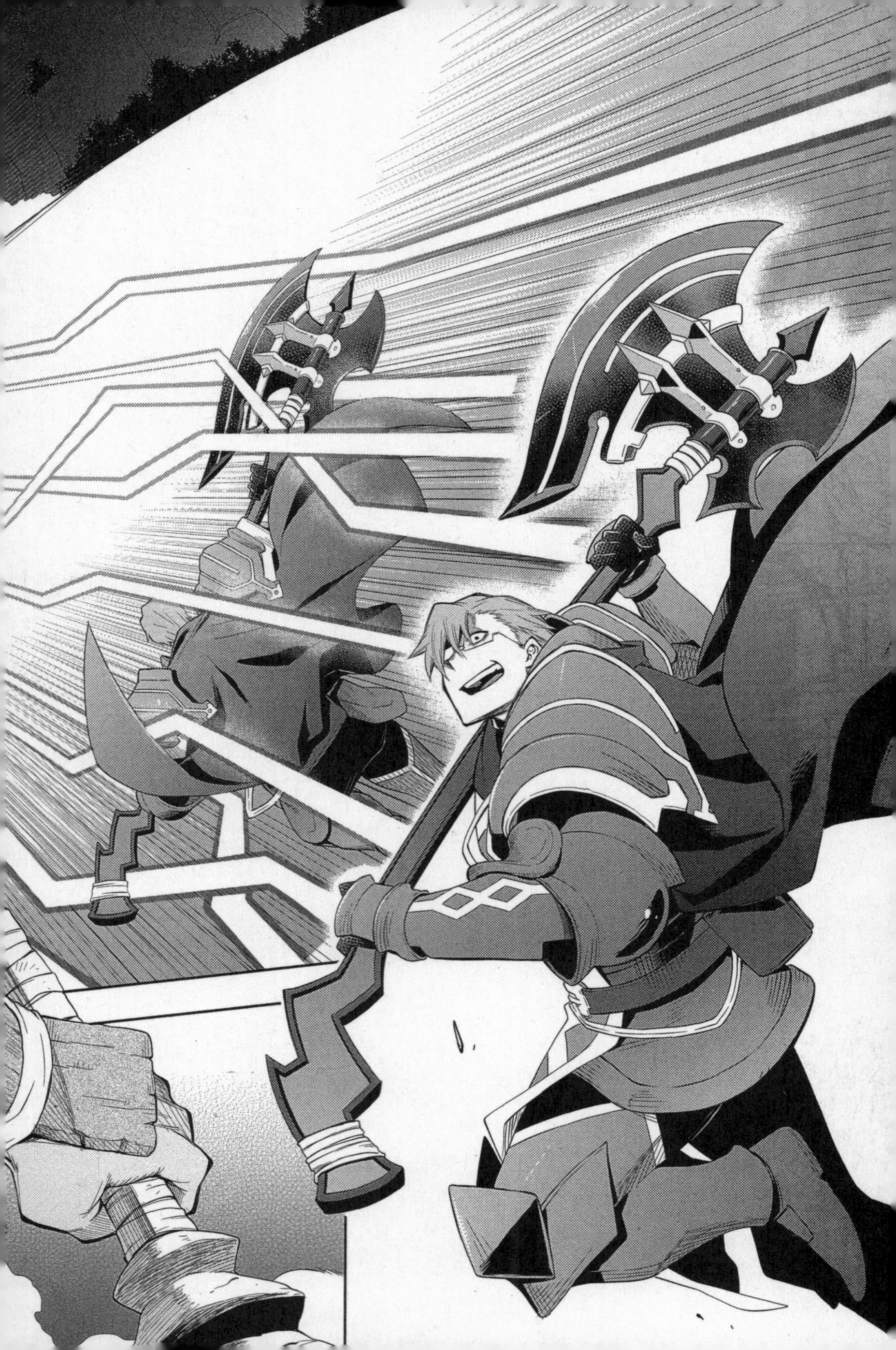

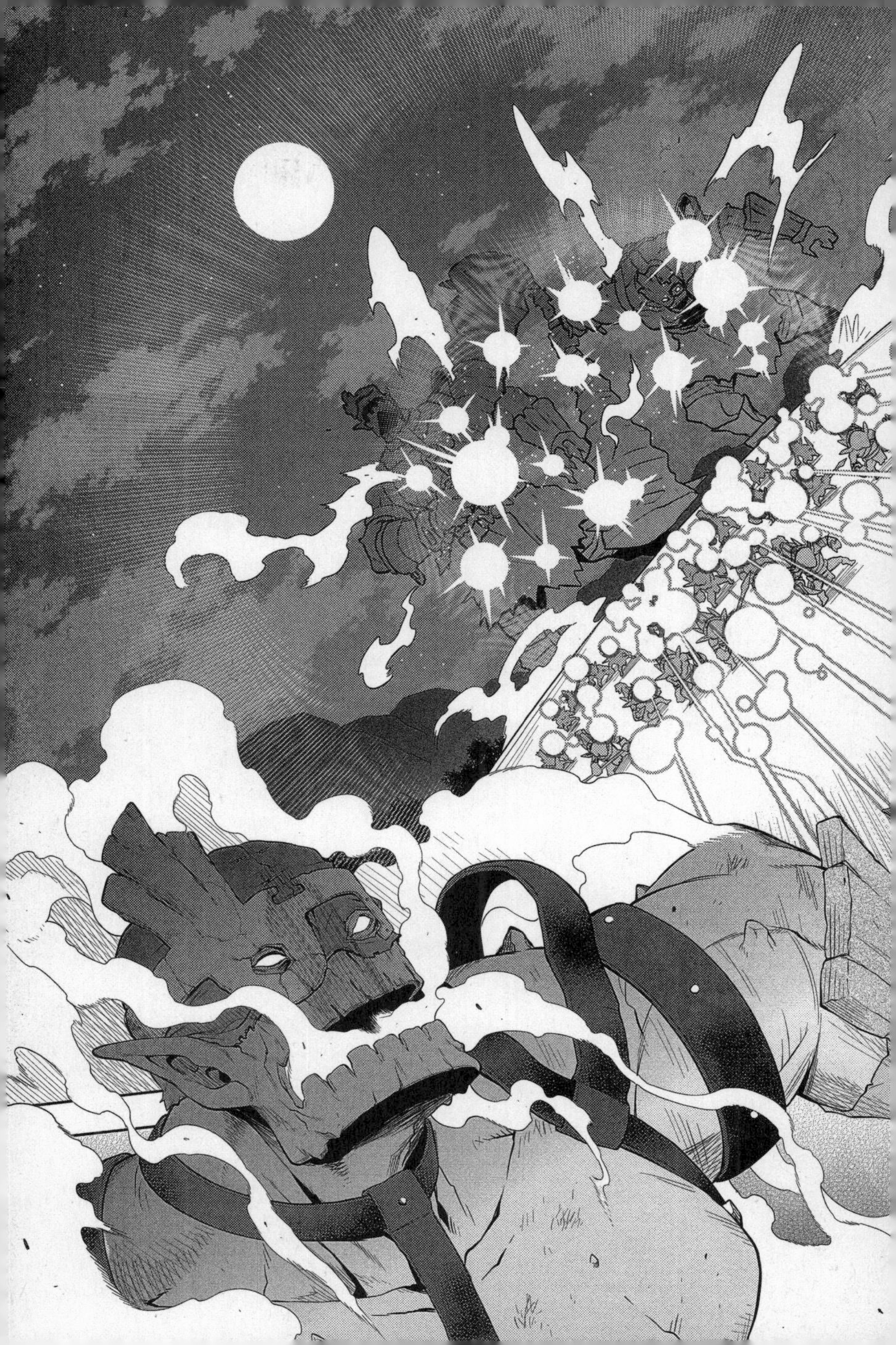

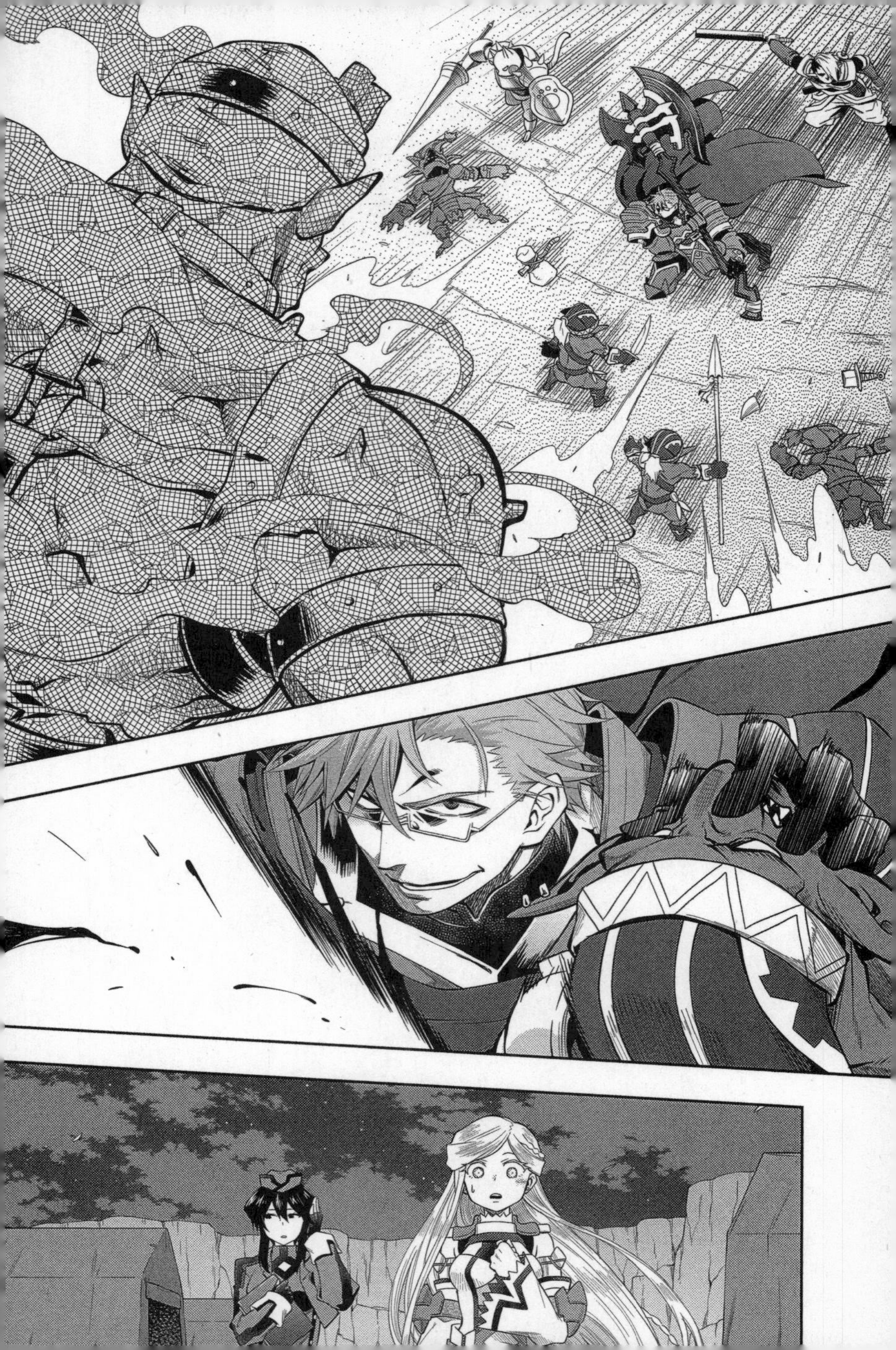

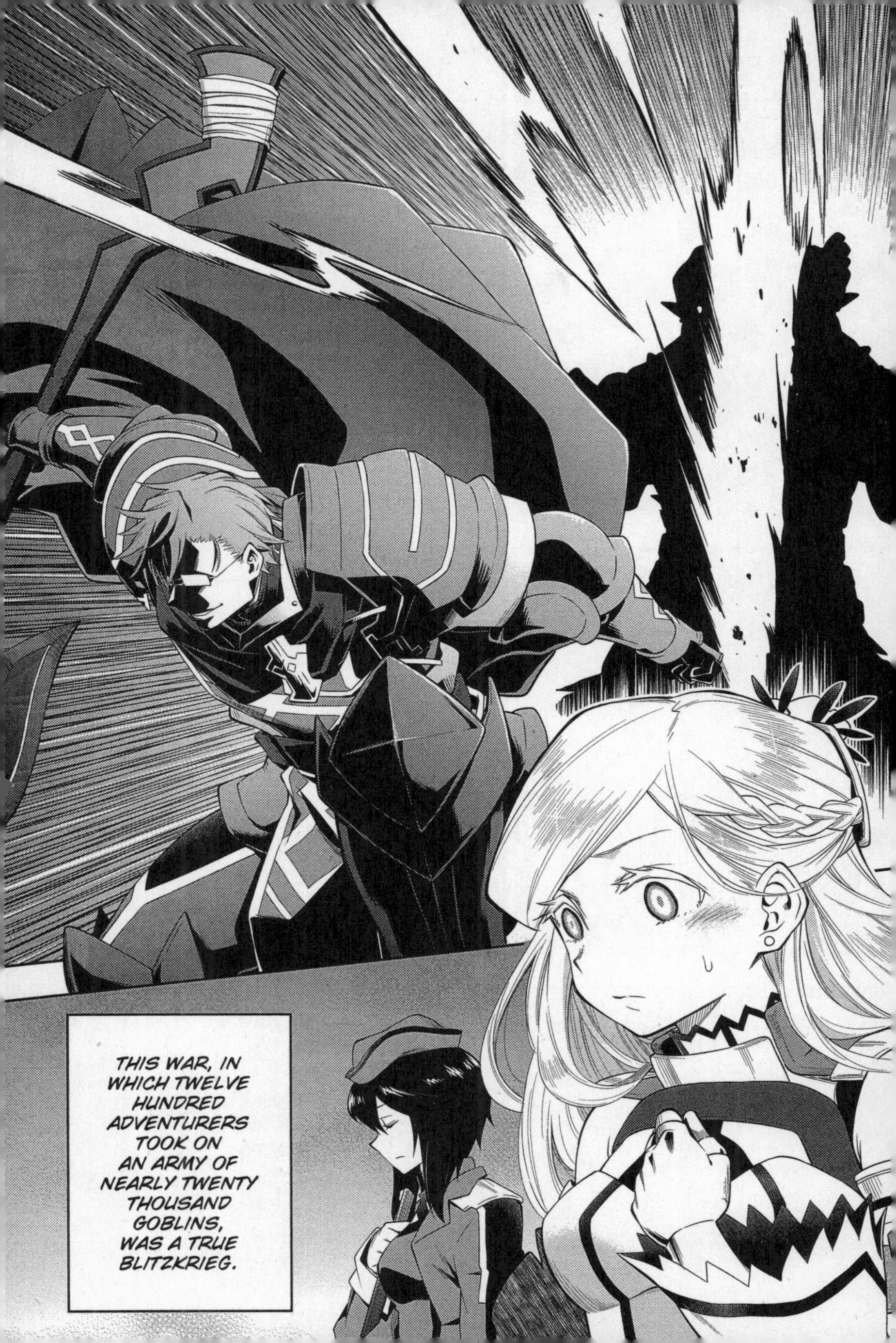
THIS WAR, IN WHICH TWELVE HUNDRED ADVENTURERS TOOK ON AN ARMY OF NEARLY TWENTY THOUSAND GOBLINS, WAS A TRUE BLITZKRIEG.

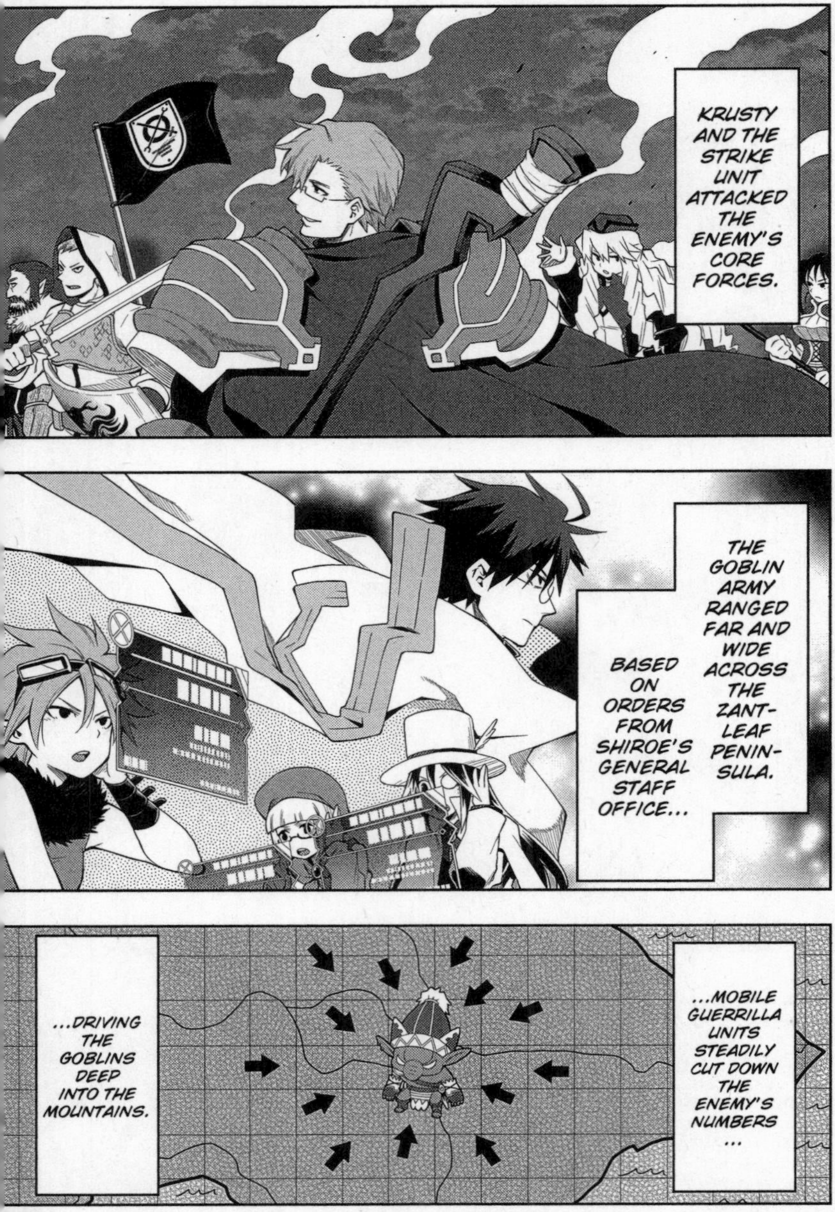
KRUSTY AND THE STRIKE UNIT ATTACKED THE ENEMY'S CORE FORCES.
THE GOBLIN ARMY RANGED FAR AND WIDE ACROSS THE ZANT-LEAF PENIN-SULA.
BASED ON ORDERS FROM SHIROE'S GENERAL STAFF OFFICE...
...MOBILE GUERRILLA UNITS STEADILY CUT DOWN THE ENEMY'S NUMBERS ...
...DRIVING THE GOBLINS DEEP INTO THE MOUNTAINS.

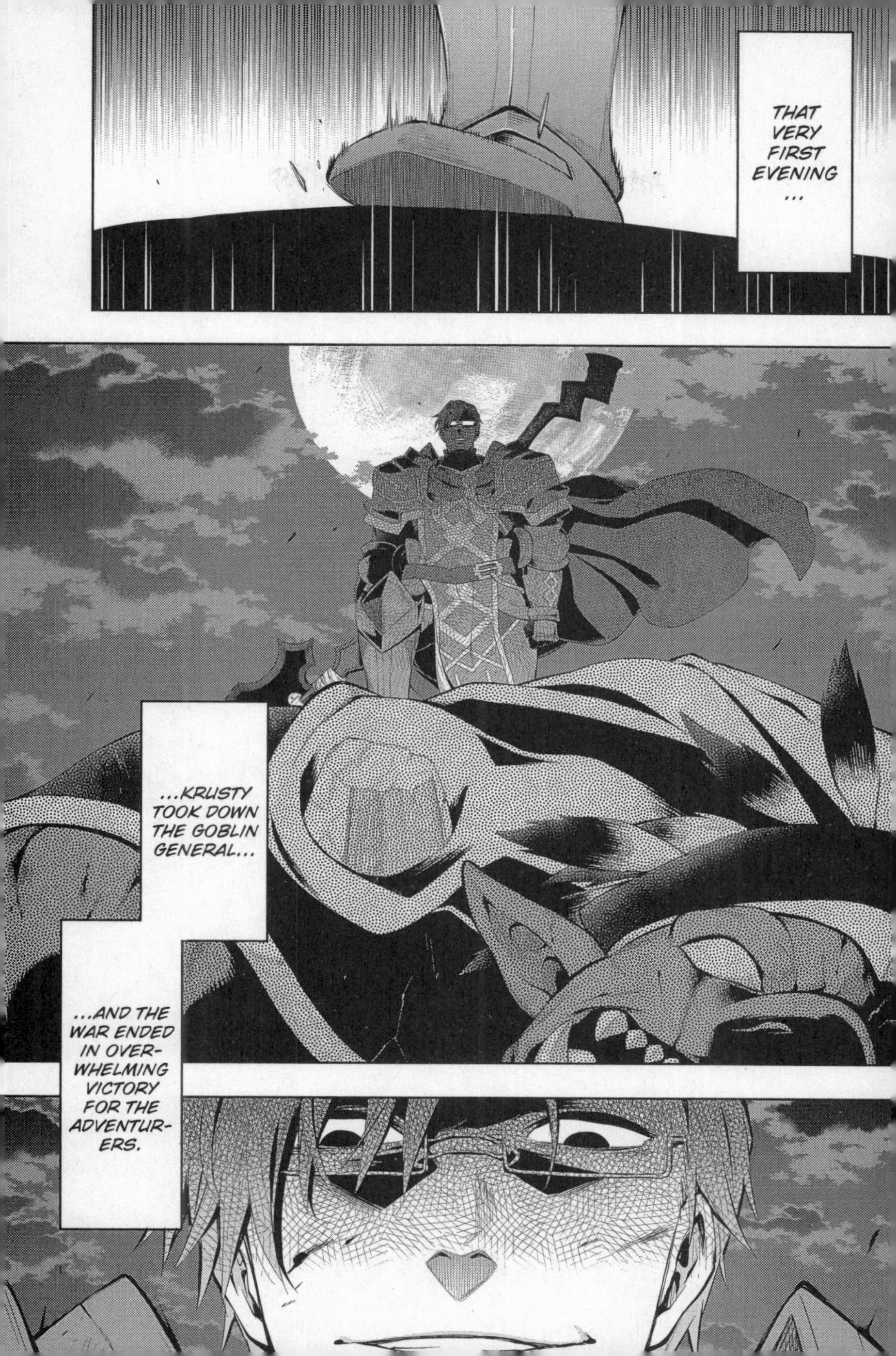
THAT VERY FIRST EVENING...
...KRUSTY TOOK DOWN THE GOBLIN GENERAL...
...AND THE WAR ENDED IN OVER-WHELMING VICTORY FOR THE ADVENTUR-ERS.

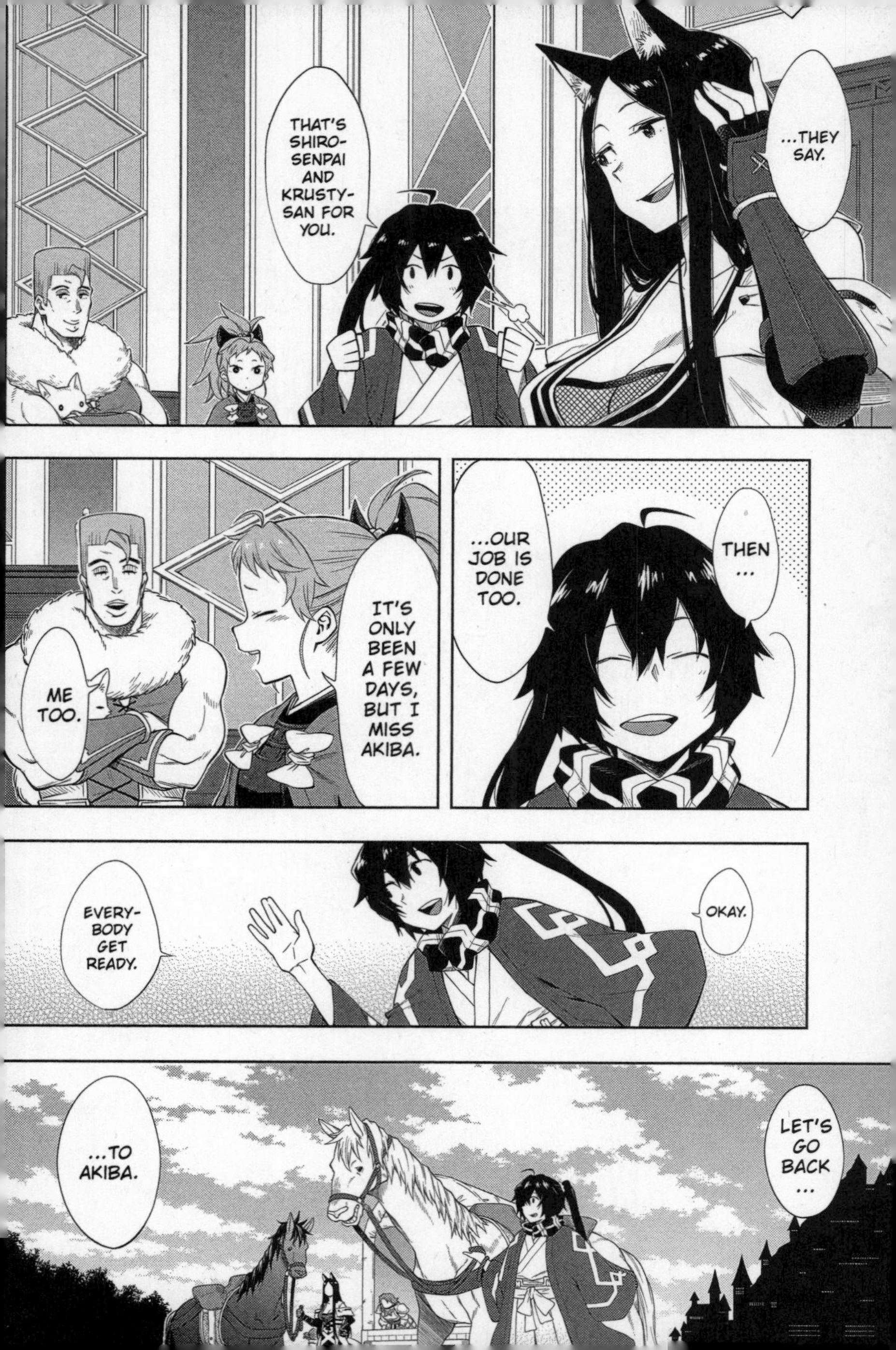
...THEY SAY.
THAT'S SHIRO-SENPAI AND KRUSTY-SAN FOR YOU.
THEN...
...OUR JOB IS DONE TOO.
IT'S ONLY BEEN A FEW DAYS, BUT I MISS AKIBA.
ME TOO.
OKAY.
EVERYBODY GET READY.
LET'S GO BACK...
...TO AKIBA.

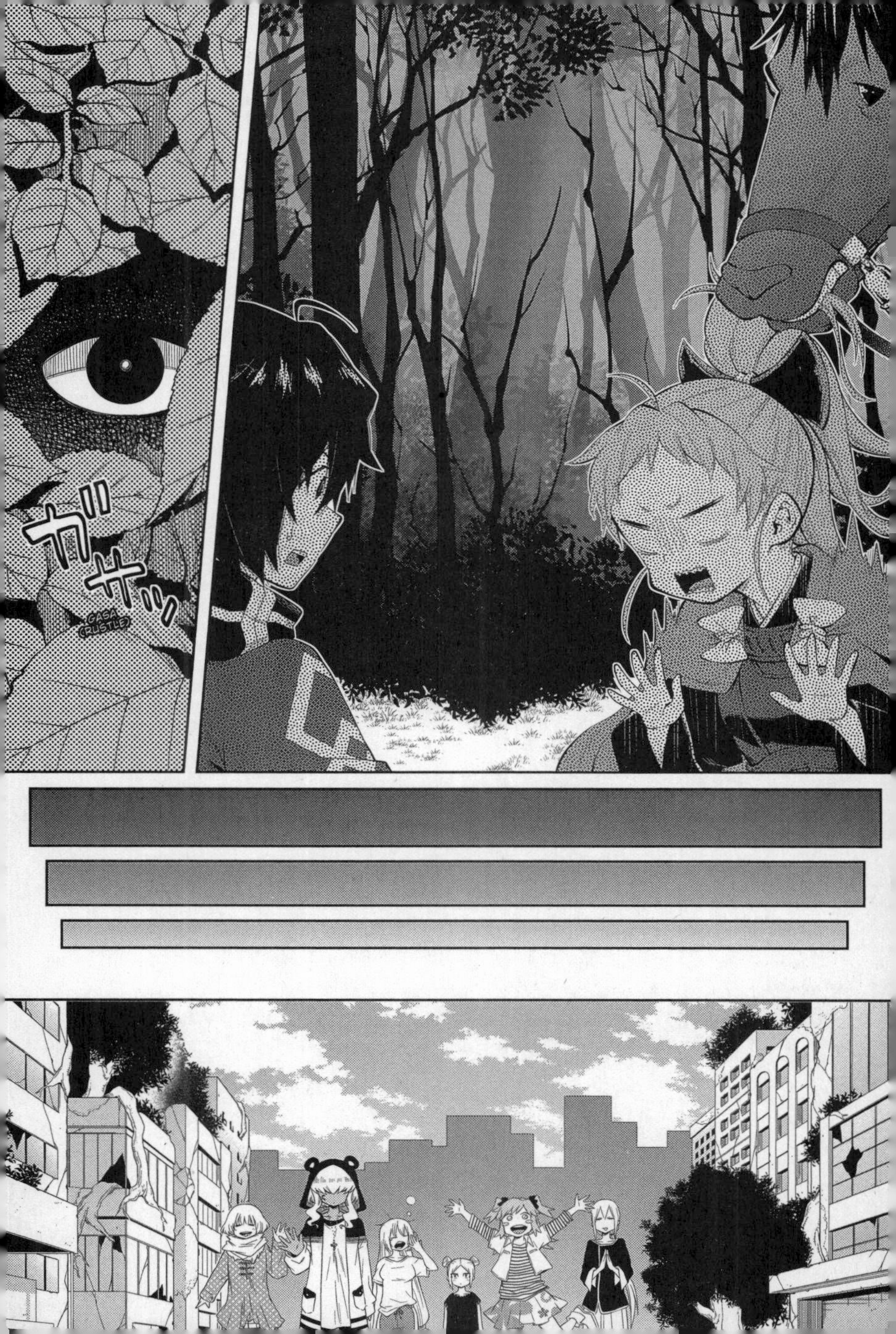
ガサッ
GASA (RUSTLE)

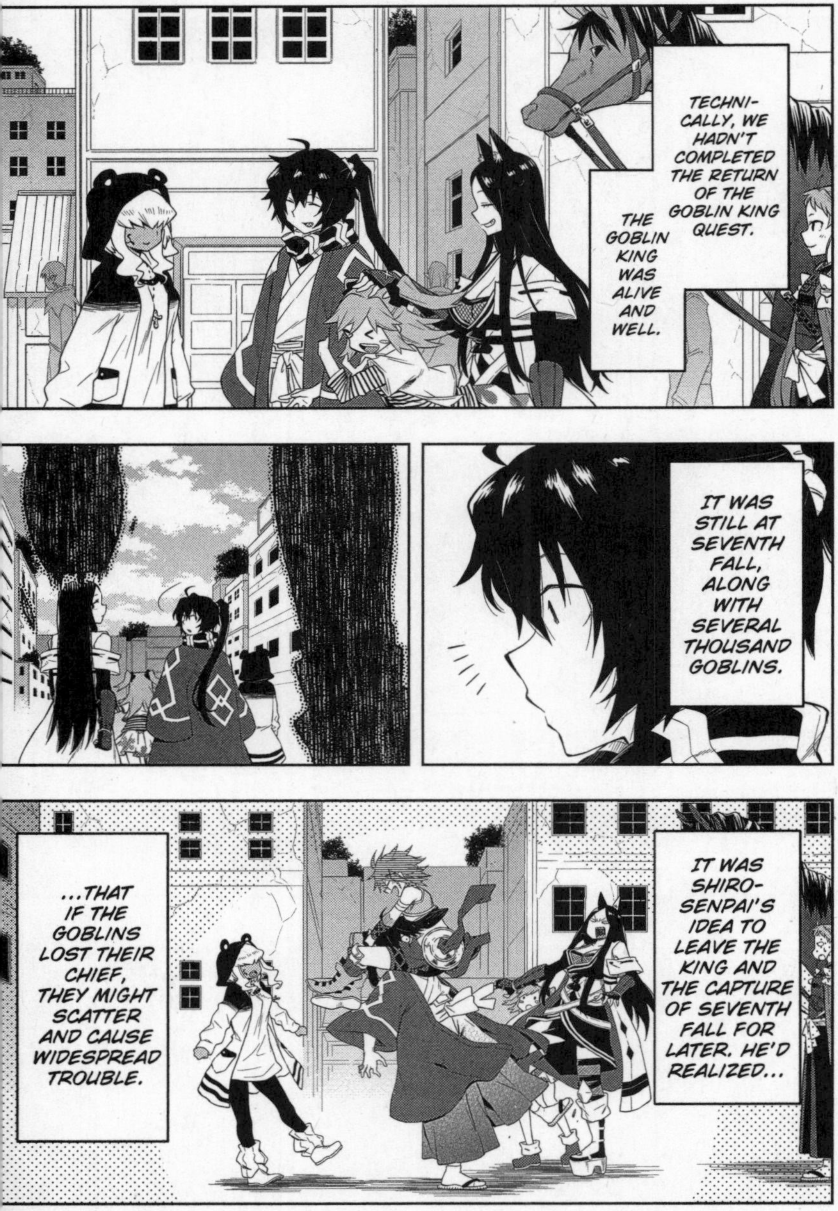
TECHNI-CALLY, WE HADN'T COMPLETED THE RETURN OF THE GOBLIN KING QUEST.
THE GOBLIN KING WAS ALIVE AND WELL.
IT WAS STILL AT SEVENTH FALL, ALONG WITH SEVERAL THOUSAND GOBLINS.
IT WAS SHIRO-SENPAI'S IDEA TO LEAVE THE KING AND THE CAPTURE OF SEVENTH FALL FOR LATER. HE'D REALIZED...
...THAT IF THE GOBLINS LOST THEIR CHIEF, THEY MIGHT SCATTER AND CAUSE WIDESPREAD TROUBLE.

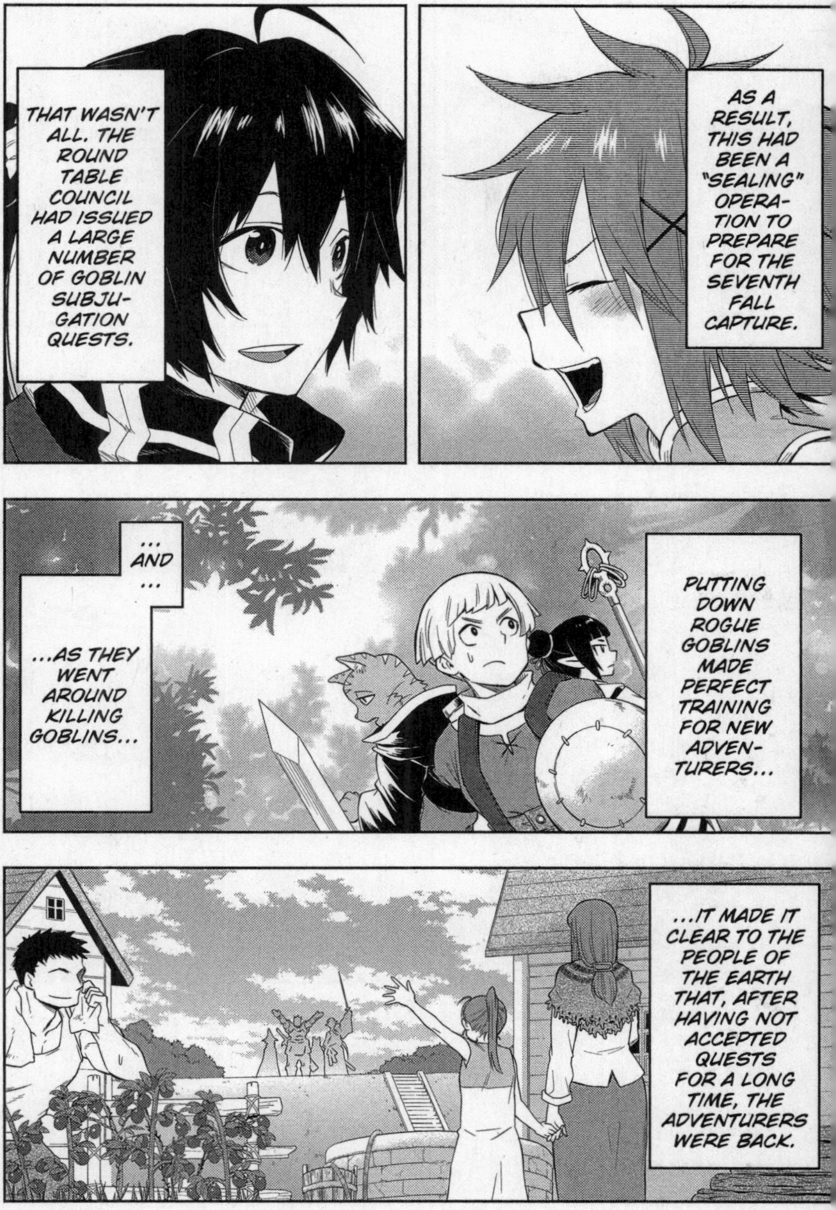
AS A RESULT, THIS HAD BEEN A "SEALING" OPERATION TO PREPARE FOR THE SEVENTH FALL CAPTURE.
THAT WASN'T ALL. THE ROUND TABLE COUNCIL HAD ISSUED A LARGE NUMBER OF GOBLIN SUBJUGATION QUESTS.
PUTTING DOWN ROGUE GOBLINS MADE PERFECT TRAINING FOR NEW ADVENTURERS...
...AND...
...AS THEY WENT AROUND KILLING GOBLINS...
...IT MADE IT CLEAR TO THE PEOPLE OF THE EARTH THAT, AFTER HAVING NOT ACCEPTED QUESTS FOR A LONG TIME, THE ADVENTURERS WERE BACK.

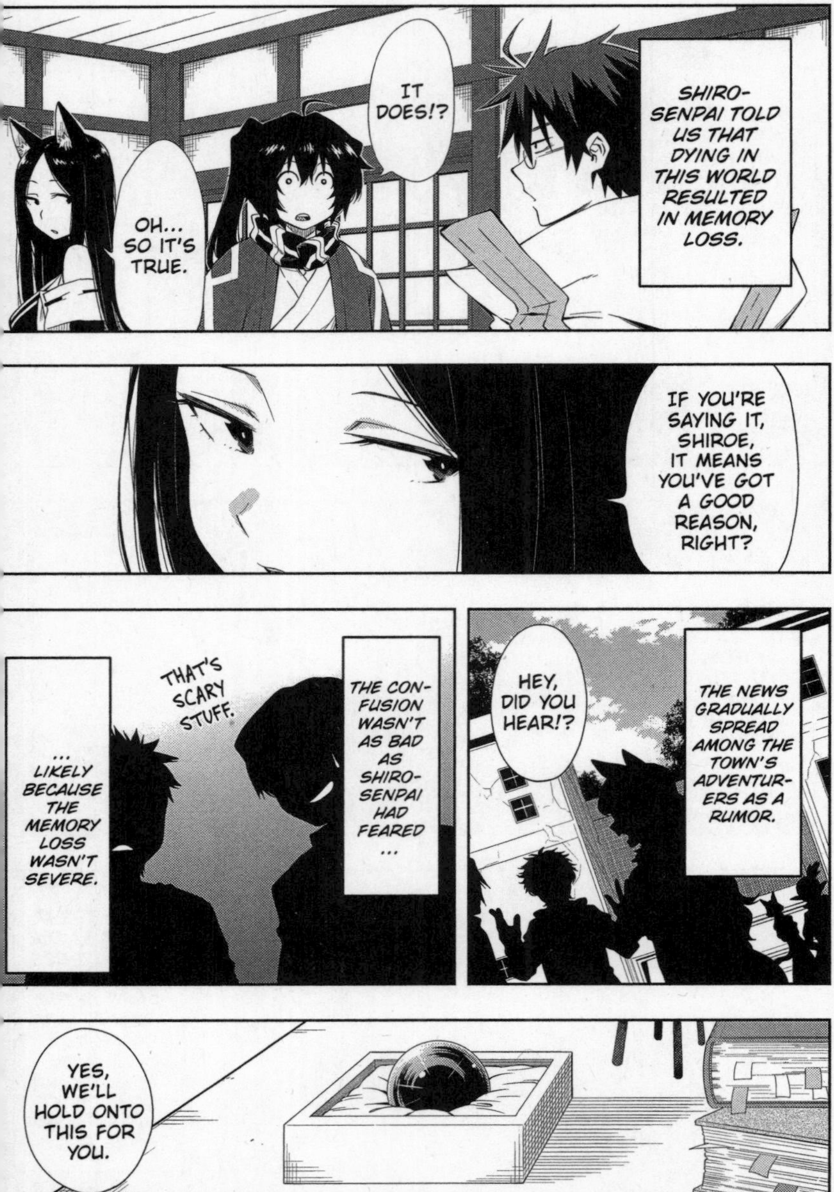
SHIRO-SENPAI TOLD US THAT DYING IN THIS WORLD RESULTED IN MEMORY LOSS.
IT DOES!?
OH... SO IT'S TRUE.
IF YOU'RE SAYING IT, SHIROE, IT MEANS YOU'VE GOT A GOOD REASON, RIGHT?
THE NEWS GRADUALLY SPREAD AMONG THE TOWN'S ADVENTURERS AS A RUMOR.
HEY, DID YOU HEAR!?
THE CONFUSION WASN'T AS BAD AS SHIRO-SENPAI HAD FEARED...
THAT'S SCARY STUFF.
...LIKELY BECAUSE THE MEMORY LOSS WASN'T SEVERE.
YES, WE'LL HOLD ONTO THIS FOR YOU.

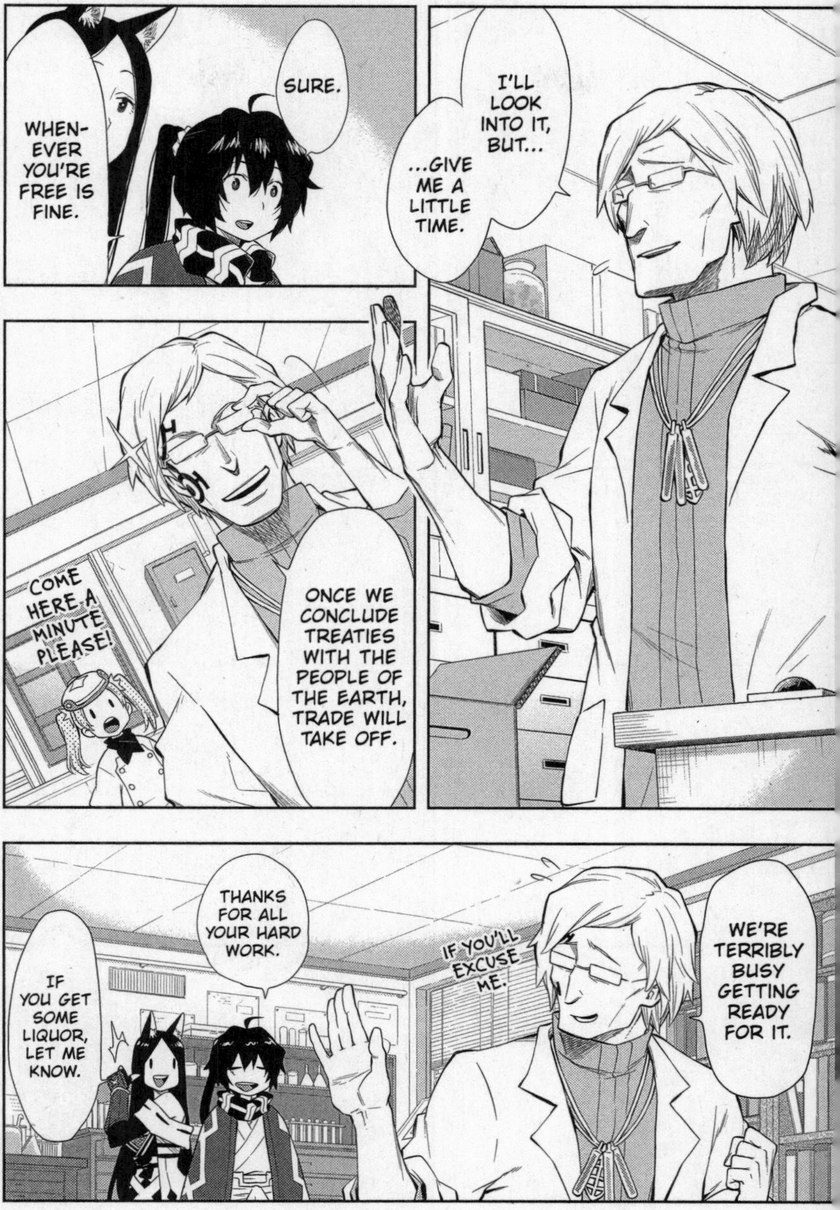
I'LL LOOK INTO IT, BUT...
...GIVE ME A LITTLE TIME.
SURE.
WHEN-EVER YOU'RE FREE IS FINE.
ONCE WE CONCLUDE TREATIES WITH THE PEOPLE OF THE EARTH, TRADE WILL TAKE OFF.
COME HERE A MINUTE PLEASE!
WE'RE TERRIBLY BUSY GETTING READY FOR IT.
IF YOU'LL EXCUSE ME.
THANKS FOR ALL YOUR HARD WORK.
IF YOU GET SOME LIQUOR, LET ME KNOW.

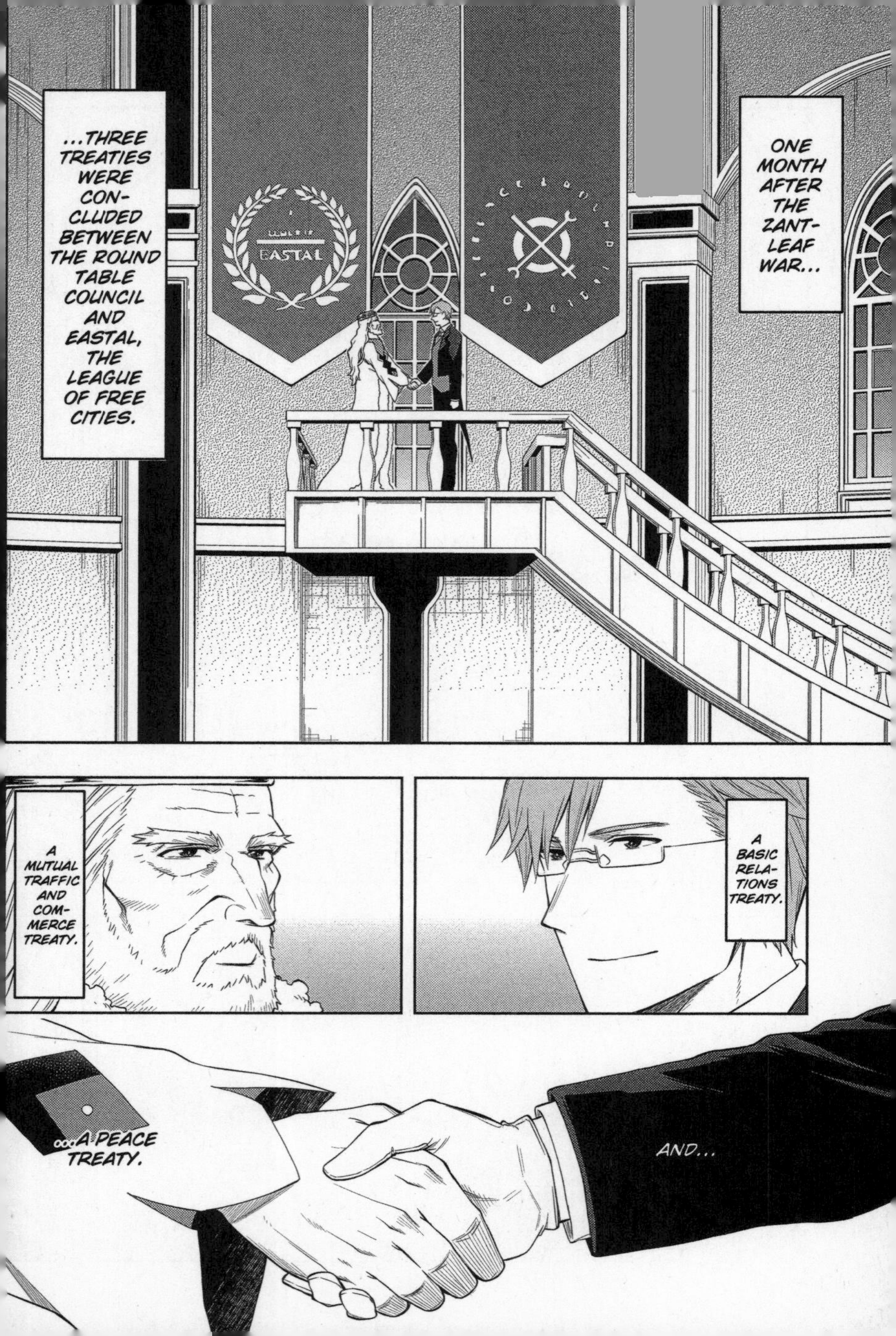
ONE MONTH AFTER THE ZANT-LEAF WAR...
...THREE TREATIES WERE CONCLUDED BETWEEN THE ROUND TABLE COUNCIL AND EASTAL, THE LEAGUE OF FREE CITIES.
EASTAL
A BASIC RELATIONS TREATY.
A MUTUAL TRAFFIC AND COMMERCE TREATY.
AND...
...A PEACE TREATY.

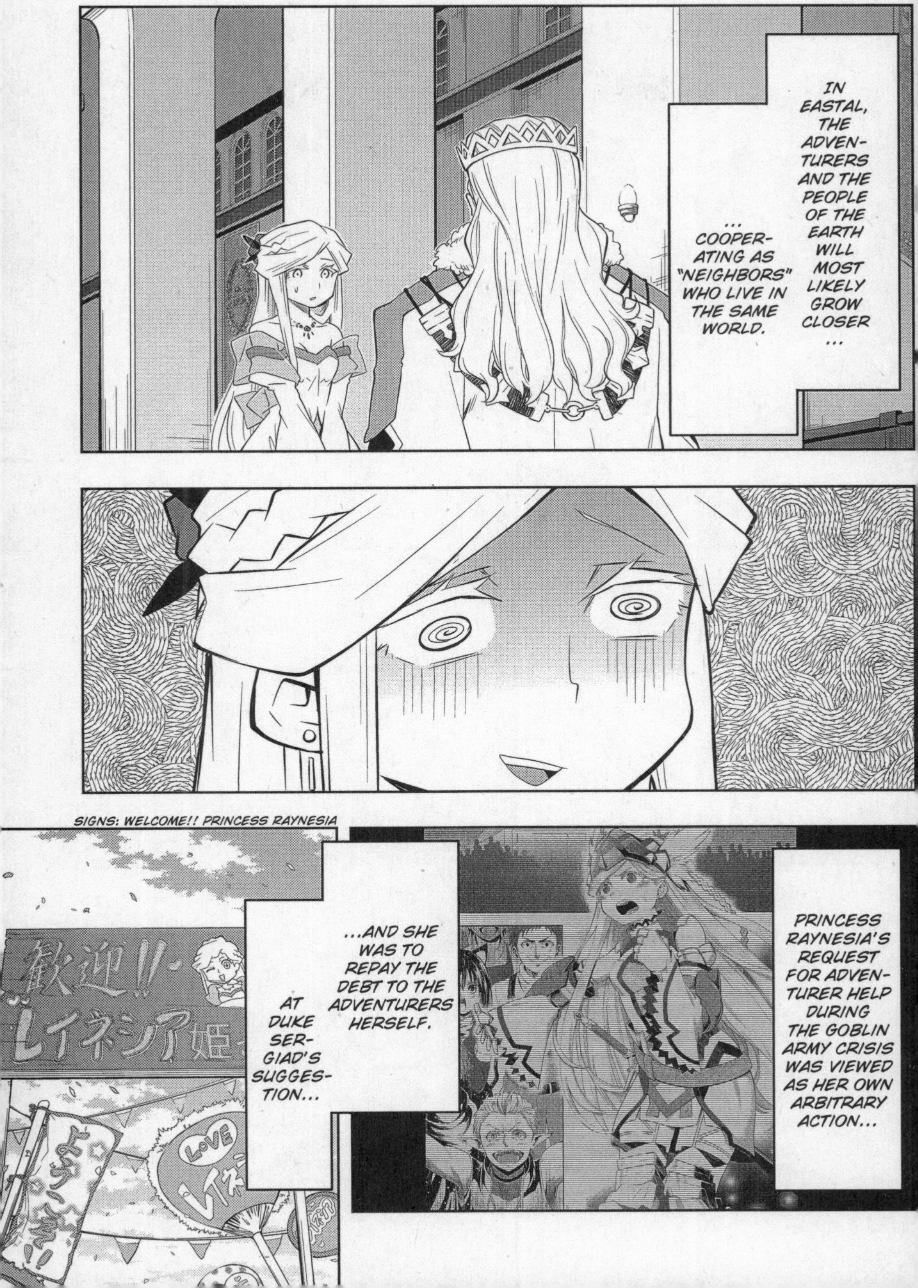
IN EASTAL, THE ADVENTURERS AND THE PEOPLE OF THE EARTH WILL MOST LIKELY GROW CLOSER...
...COOPERATING AS "NEIGHBORS" WHO LIVE IN THE SAME WORLD.
SIGNS: WELCOME!! PRINCESS RAYNESIA
PRINCESS RAYNESIA'S REQUEST FOR ADVENTURER HELP DURING THE GOBLIN ARMY CRISIS WAS VIEWED AS HER OWN ARBITRARY ACTION...
...AND SHE WAS TO REPAY THE DEBT TO THE ADVENTURERS HERSELF.
AT DUKE SERGIAD'S SUGGESTION...

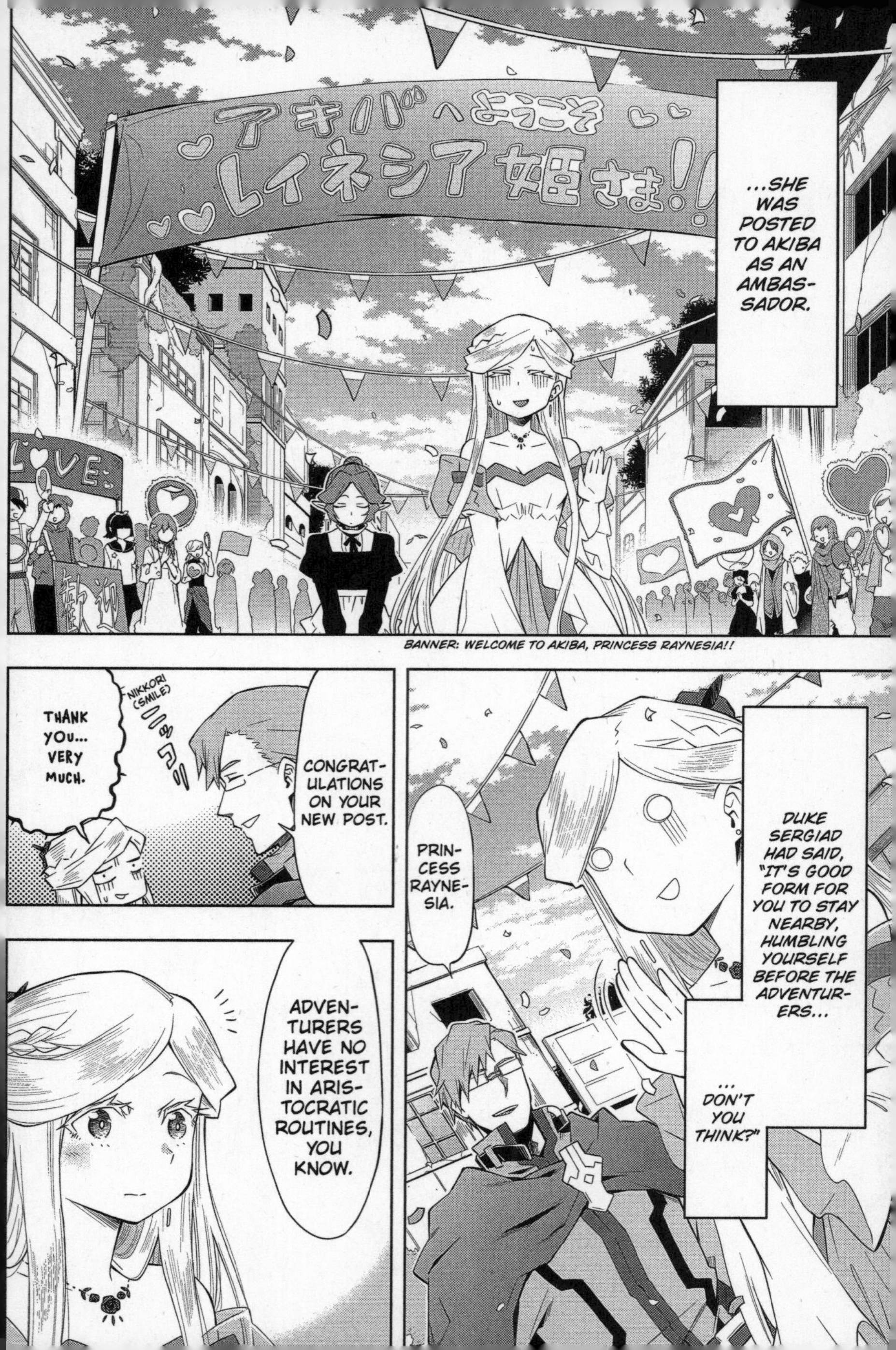
...SHE WAS POSTED TO AKIBA AS AN AMBASSADOR.
アキバへようこそ
レイネシア姫さま!!
LOVE
歓迎
BANNER: WELCOME TO AKIBA, PRINCESS RAYNESIA!!
DUKE SERGIAD HAD SAID, "IT'S GOOD FORM FOR YOU TO STAY NEARBY, HUMBLING YOURSELF BEFORE THE ADVENTURERS...
PRINCESS RAYNESIA.
...DON'T YOU THINK?"
NIKKORI (SMILE)
ニッコリ
CONGRATULATIONS ON YOUR NEW POST.
THANK YOU... VERY MUCH.
ADVENTURERS HAVE NO INTEREST IN ARISTOCRATIC ROUTINES, YOU KNOW.

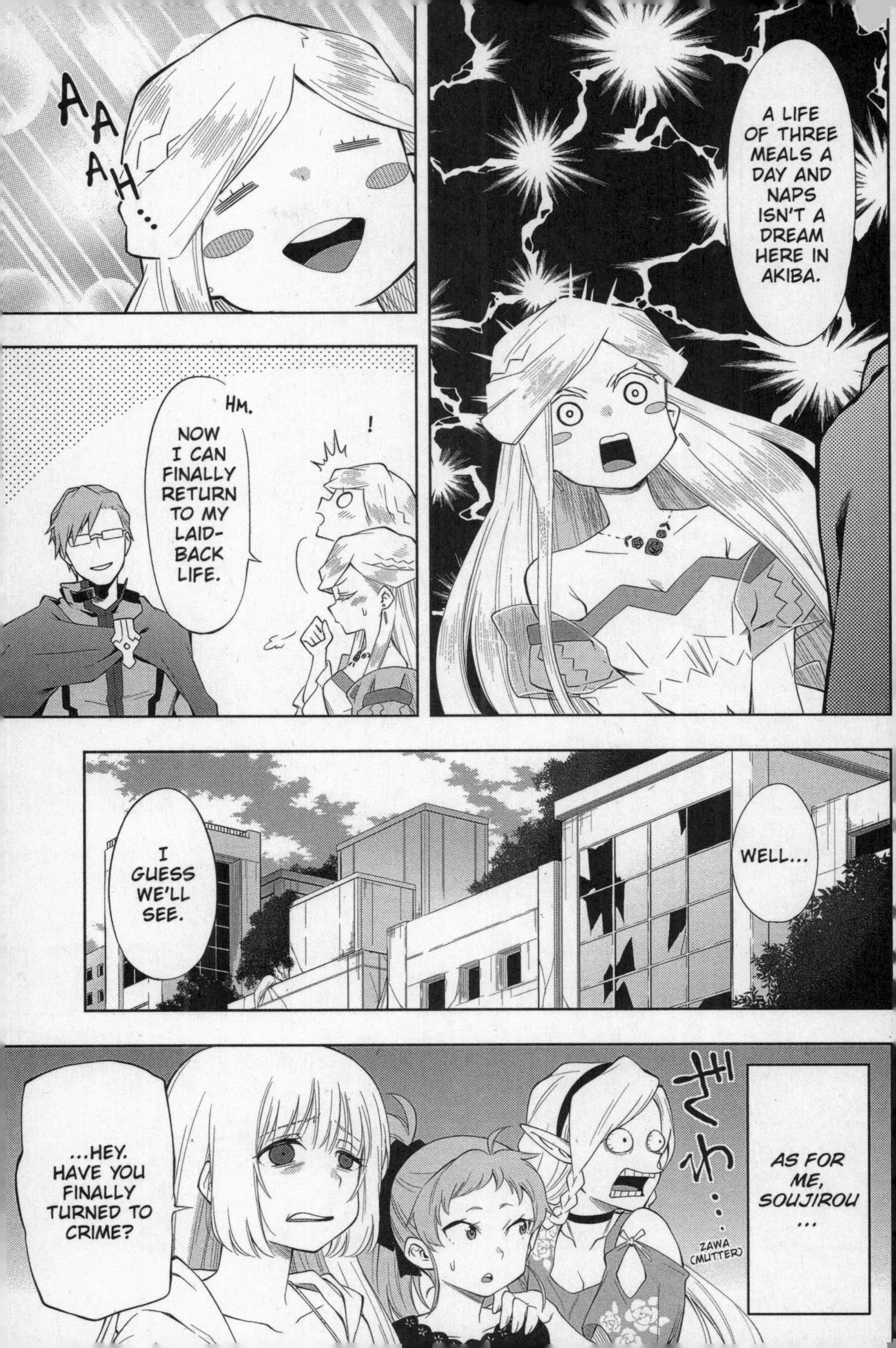
A LIFE OF THREE MEALS A DAY AND NAPS ISN'T A DREAM HERE IN AKIBA.
AAAH...
HM. NOW I CAN FINALLY RETURN TO MY LAID-BACK LIFE.
!
WELL...
I GUESS WE'LL SEE.
AS FOR ME, SOUJIROU...
ざわ…
ZAWA (MUTTER)
...HEY. HAVE YOU FINALLY TURNED TO CRIME?

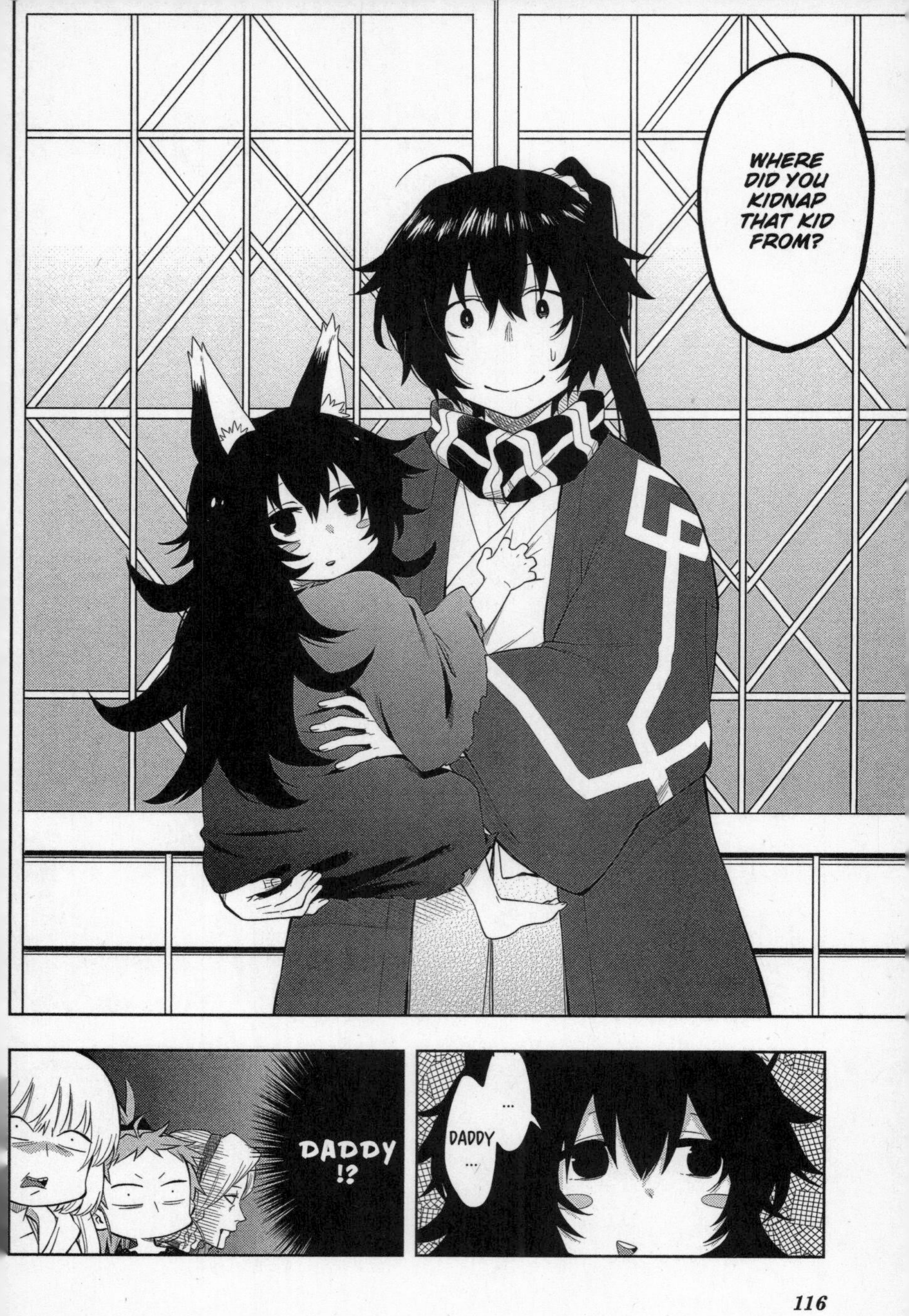
WHERE DID YOU KIDNAP THAT KID FROM?
... DADDY ...
DADDY !?

LOG HORIZON

THE WEST WIND BRIGADE

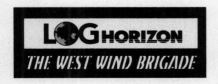

LOG HORIZON
THE WEST WIND BRIGADE

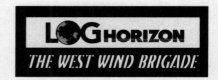

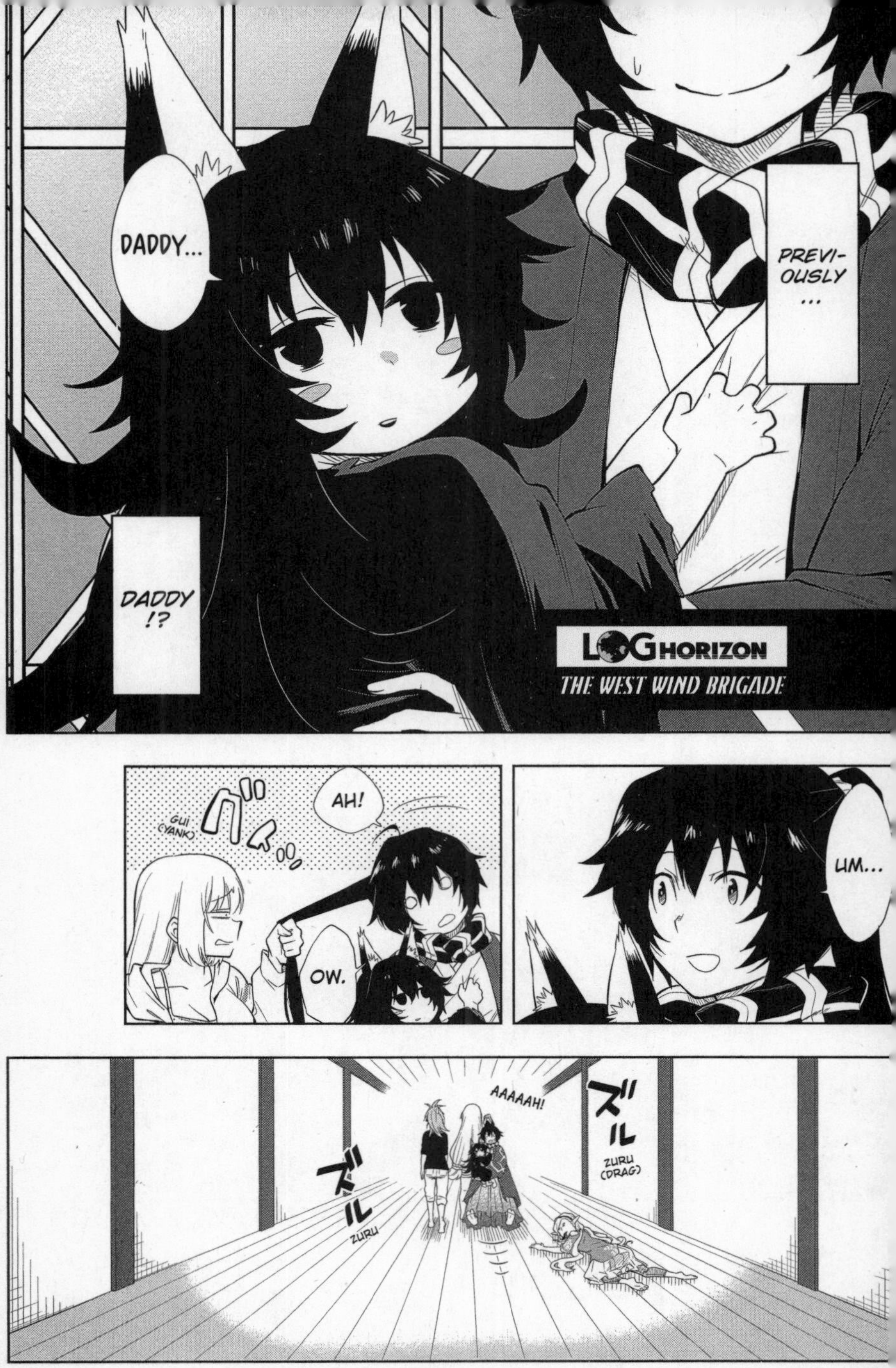
PREVI-
OUSLY
...
DADDY...
DADDY
!?
LOG HORIZON
THE WEST WIND BRIGADE
UM...
AH!
GUI (YANK)
OW.
AAAAAH!
ズル
ZURU (DRAG)
ズル
ZURU

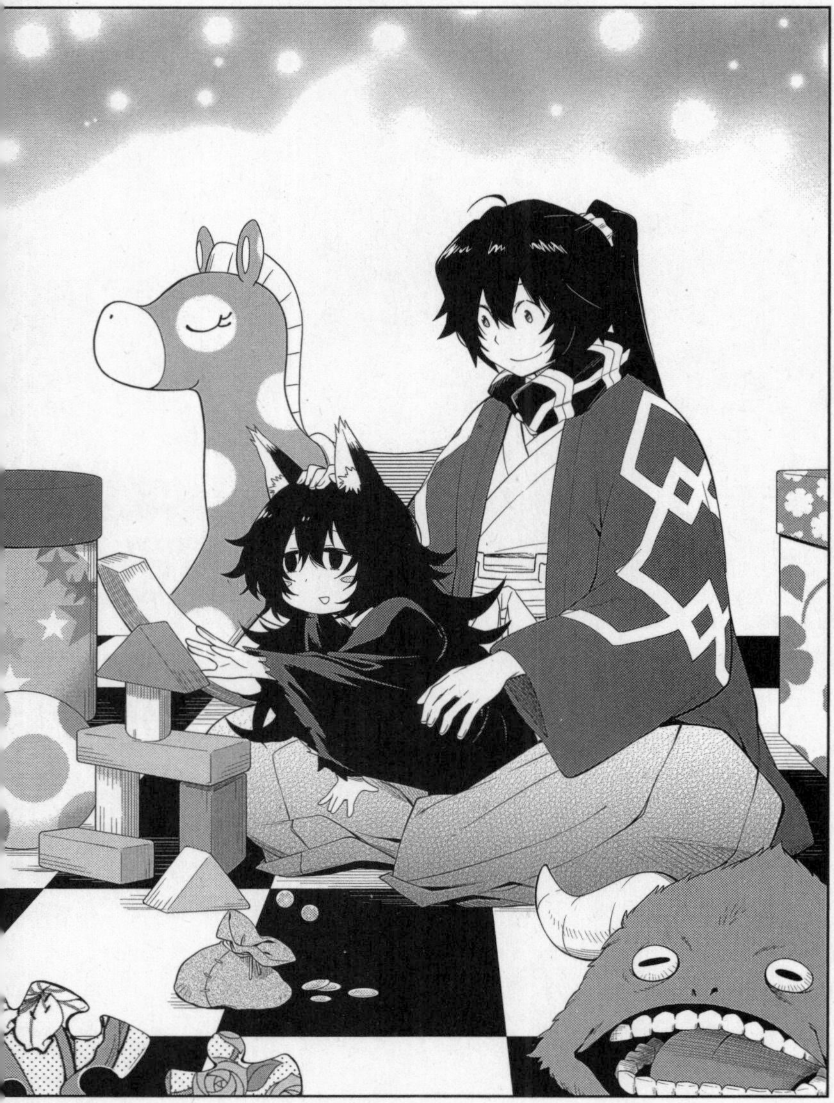

[CHAPTER : 46 **Resurrection**]

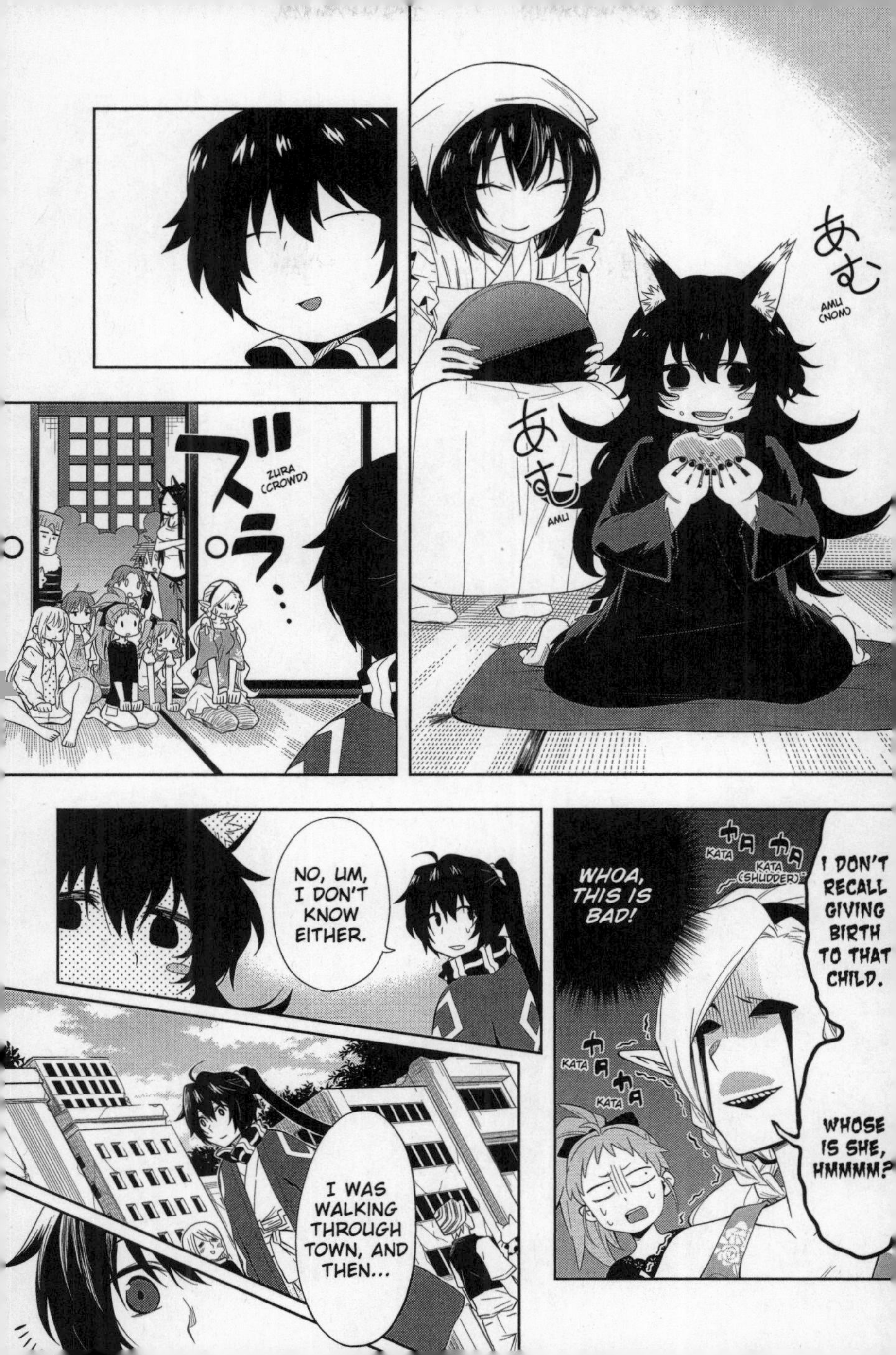
あむ
AMU (NOM)
あむ
AMU
ズラ
ZURA (CROWD)
...
I DON'T RECALL GIVING BIRTH TO THAT CHILD.
カタ カタ
KATA KATA (SHUDDER)
WHOA, THIS IS BAD!
WHOSE IS SHE, HMMMM?
カタ カタ
KATA KATA
NO, UM, I DON'T KNOW EITHER.
I WAS WALKING THROUGH TOWN, AND THEN...

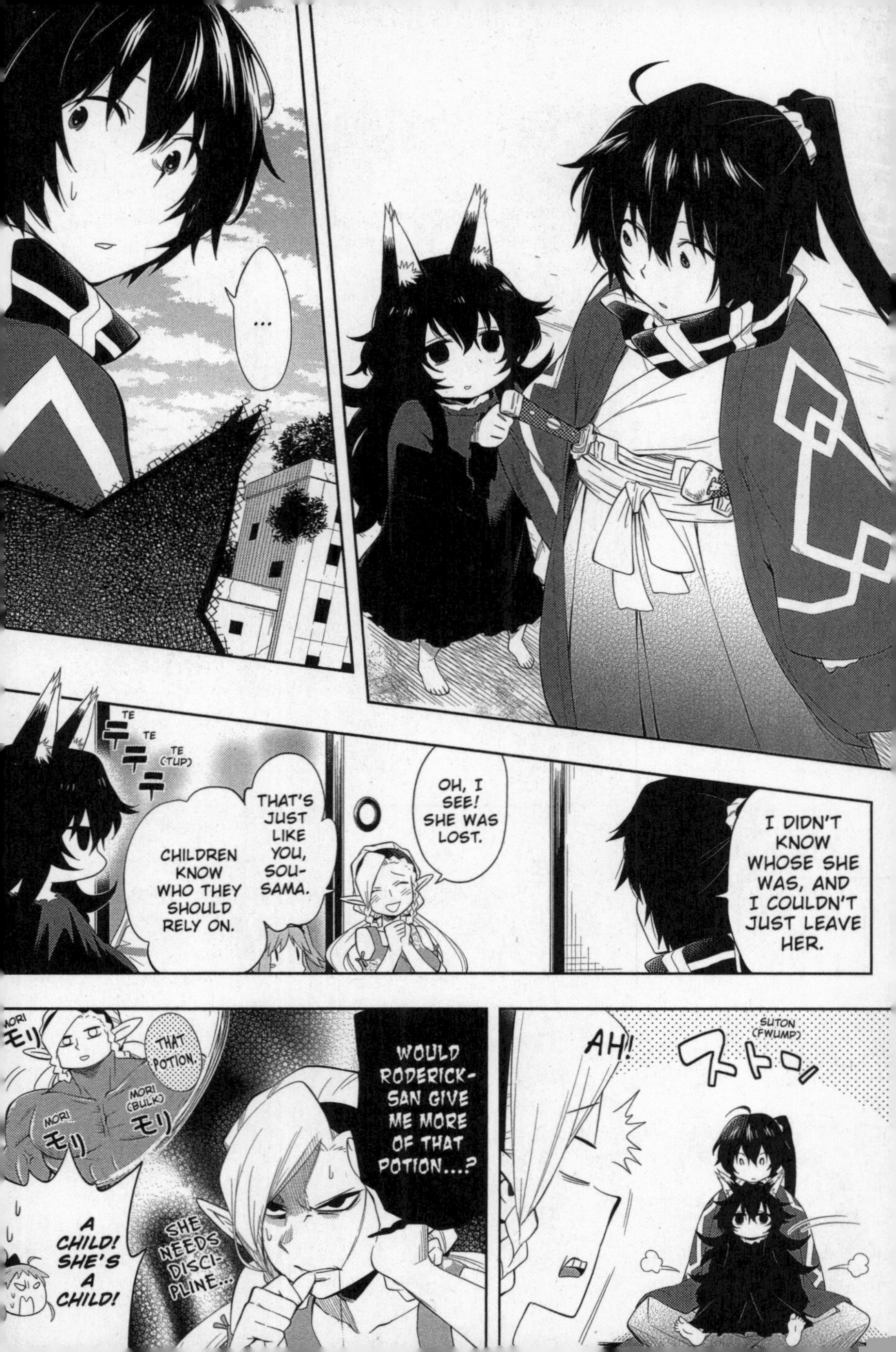
...
I DIDN'T KNOW WHOSE SHE WAS, AND I COULDN'T JUST LEAVE HER.
OH, I SEE! SHE WAS LOST.
THAT'S JUST LIKE YOU, SOU-SAMA.
CHILDREN KNOW WHO THEY SHOULD RELY ON.
TE テ TE テ TE テ (TUP)
SUTON (FWUMP) ストン
AH!
WOULD RODERICK-SAN GIVE ME MORE OF THAT POTION...?
SHE NEEDS DISCI-PLINE...
THAT POTION.
MORI モリ MORI モリ MORI (BULK) モリ
A CHILD! SHE'S A CHILD!

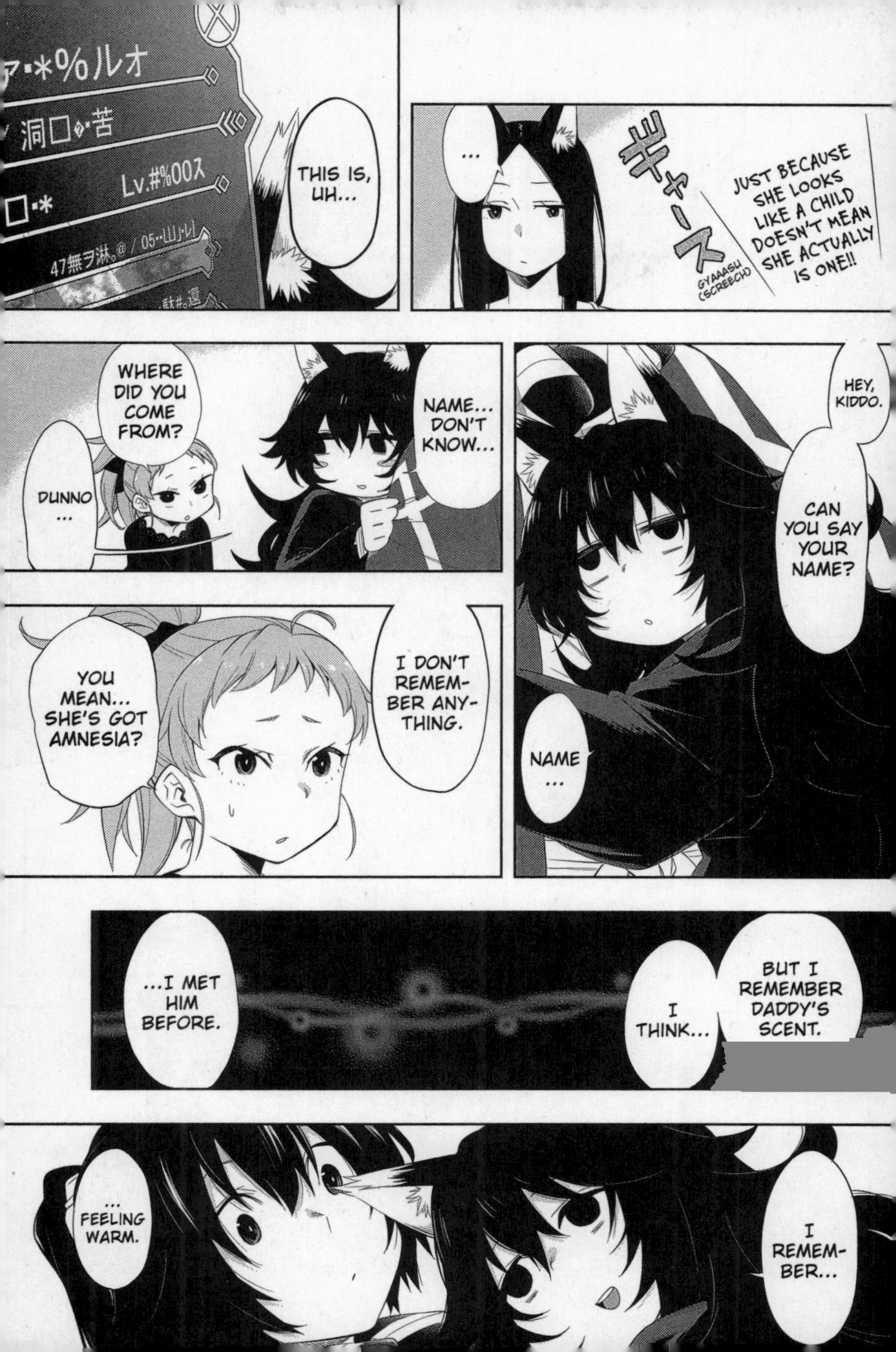
...
ギャース
GYAAASU (SCREECH)
JUST BECAUSE SHE LOOKS LIKE A CHILD DOESN'T MEAN SHE ACTUALLY IS ONE!!
THIS IS, UH...
HEY, KIDDO.
CAN YOU SAY YOUR NAME?
NAME ...
NAME... DON'T KNOW...
WHERE DID YOU COME FROM?
DUNNO ...
I DON'T REMEMBER ANYTHING.
YOU MEAN... SHE'S GOT AMNESIA?
BUT I REMEMBER DADDY'S SCENT.
I THINK...
...I MET HIM BEFORE.
I REMEMBER...
... FEELING WARM.

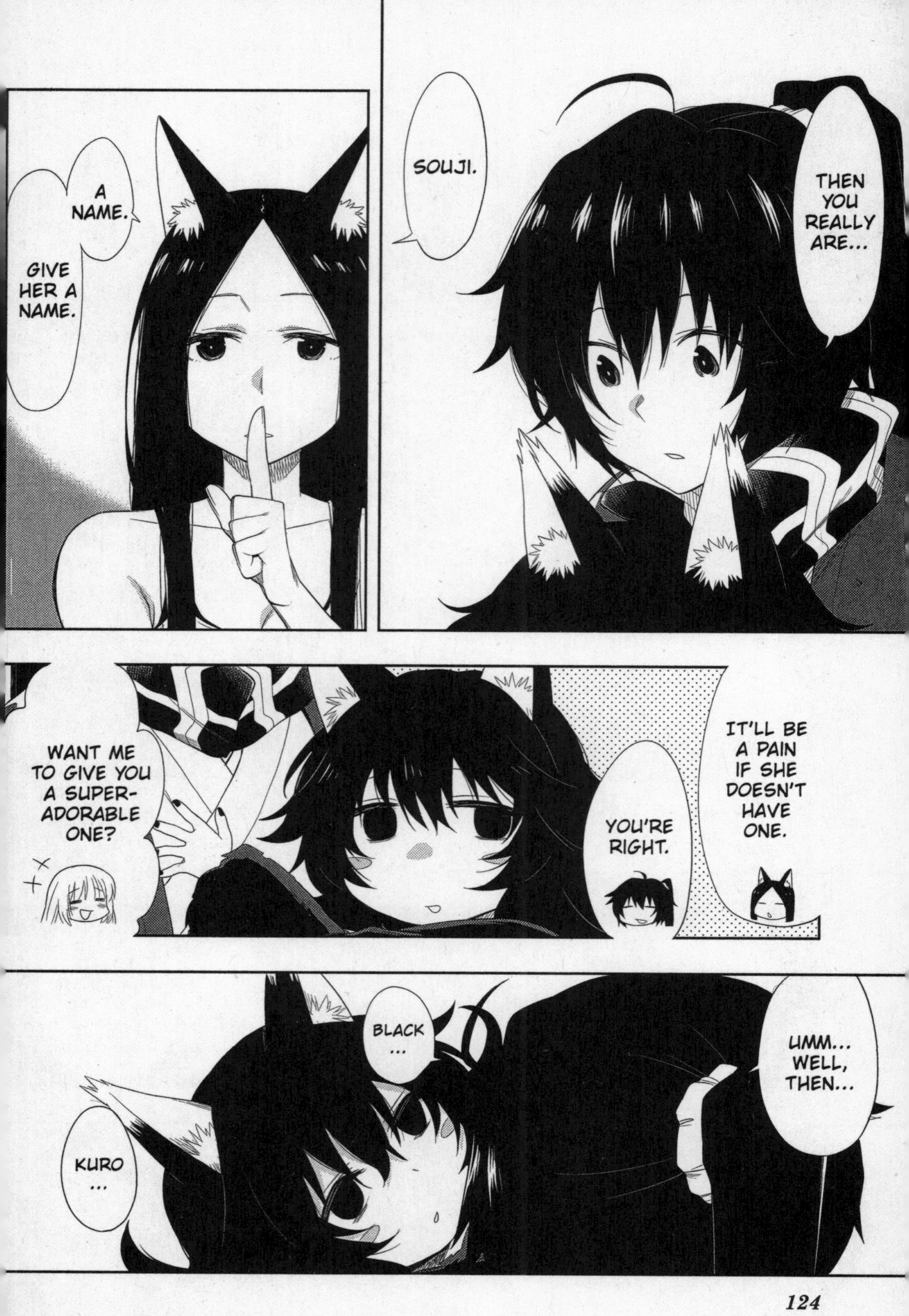
THEN YOU REALLY ARE...
SOUJI.
A NAME.
GIVE HER A NAME.
IT'LL BE A PAIN IF SHE DOESN'T HAVE ONE.
YOU'RE RIGHT.
WANT ME TO GIVE YOU A SUPER-ADORABLE ONE?
UMM... WELL, THEN...
BLACK...
KURO...

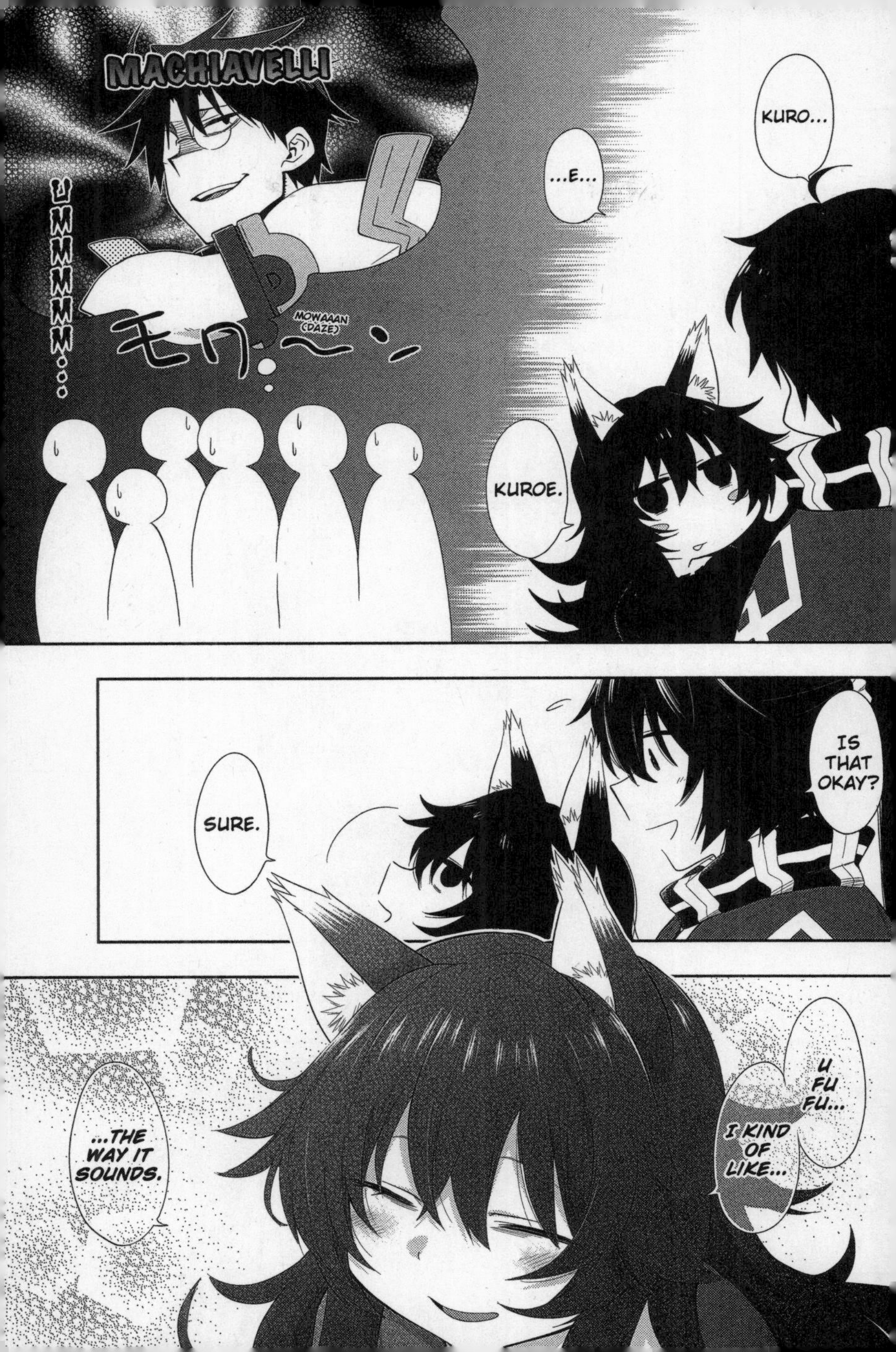
KURO...
...E...
KUROE.
MACHIAVELLI
UMMMMMM...
モワ～
MOWAAAN (DAZE)
IS THAT OKAY?
SURE.
UFUFU...
I KIND OF LIKE...
...THE WAY IT SOUNDS.

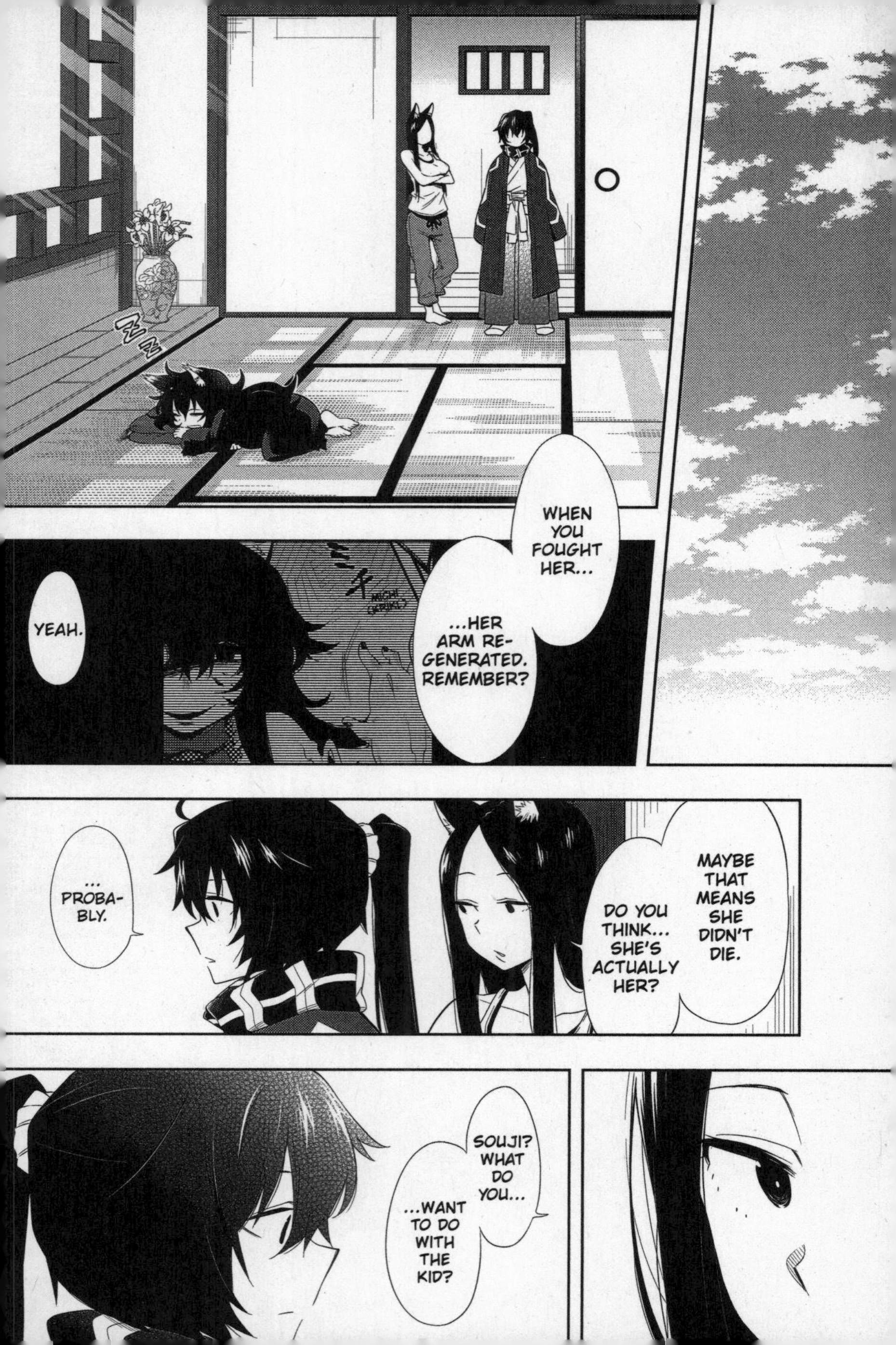
WHEN YOU FOUGHT HER...
...HER ARM RE-GENERATED. REMEMBER?
MICHI (GRIP)
YEAH.
MAYBE THAT MEANS SHE DIDN'T DIE.
DO YOU THINK... SHE'S ACTUALLY HER?
...PROBA-BLY.
SOUJI? WHAT DO YOU...
...WANT TO DO WITH THE KID?

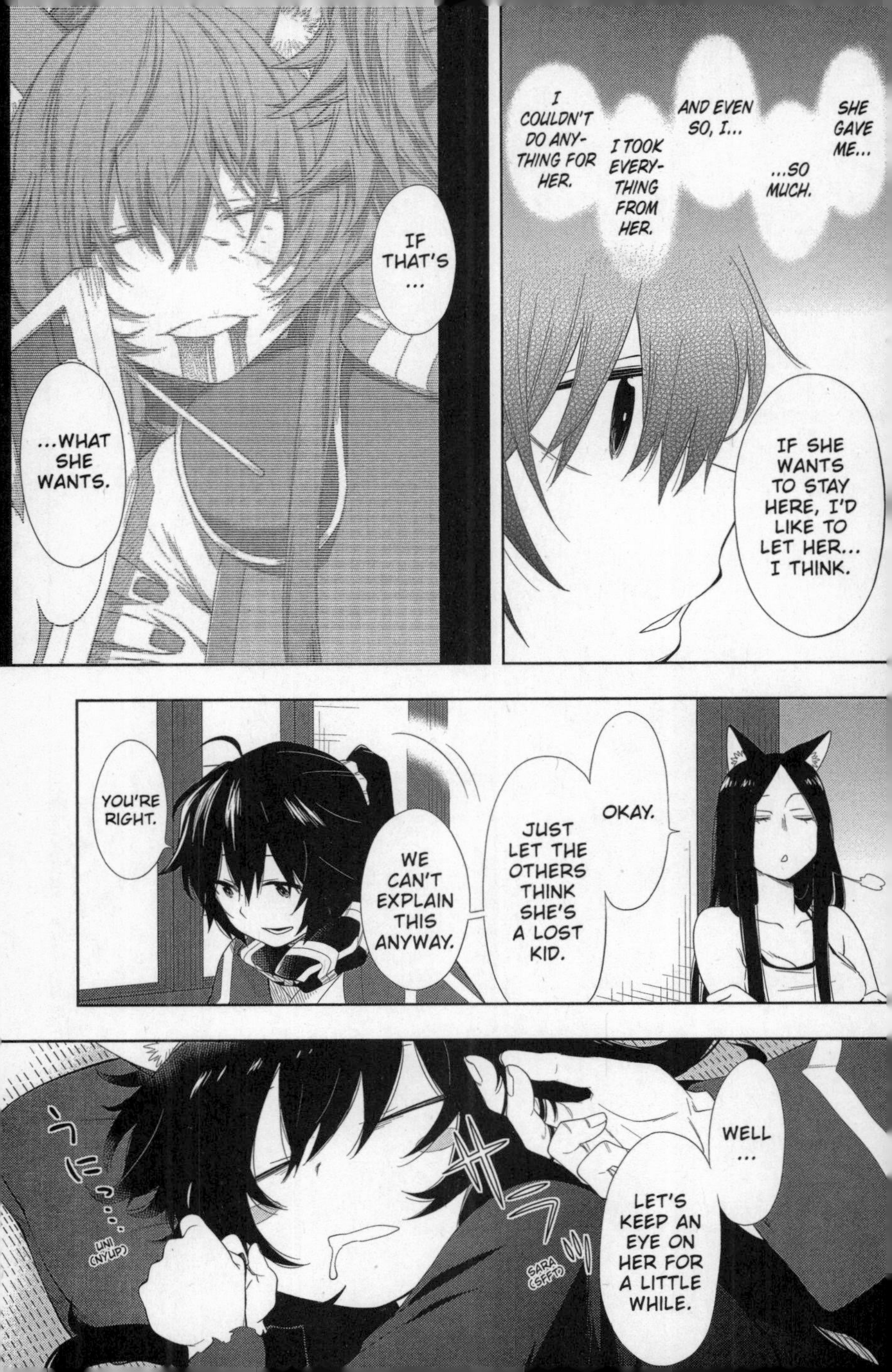
SHE GAVE ME...
...SO MUCH.
AND EVEN SO, I...
I TOOK EVERYTHING FROM HER.
I COULDN'T DO ANYTHING FOR HER.
IF SHE WANTS TO STAY HERE, I'D LIKE TO LET HER... I THINK.
IF THAT'S...
...WHAT SHE WANTS.
OKAY.
JUST LET THE OTHERS THINK SHE'S A LOST KID.
WE CAN'T EXPLAIN THIS ANYWAY.
YOU'RE RIGHT.
WELL...
LET'S KEEP AN EYE ON HER FOR A LITTLE WHILE.
SARA (SFFT)
UNI (NYUP)

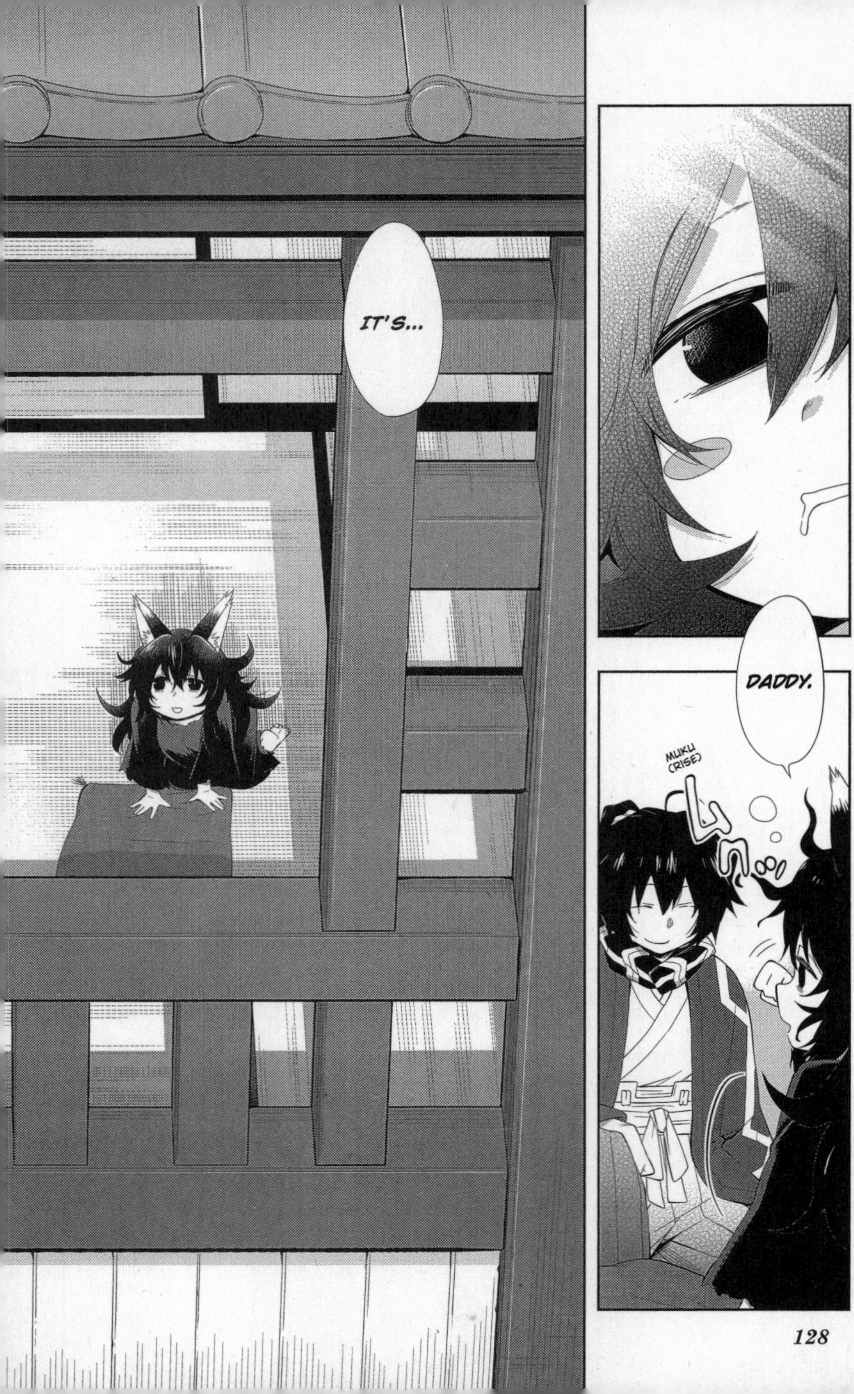
IT'S...
DADDY.
MUKU (RISE)

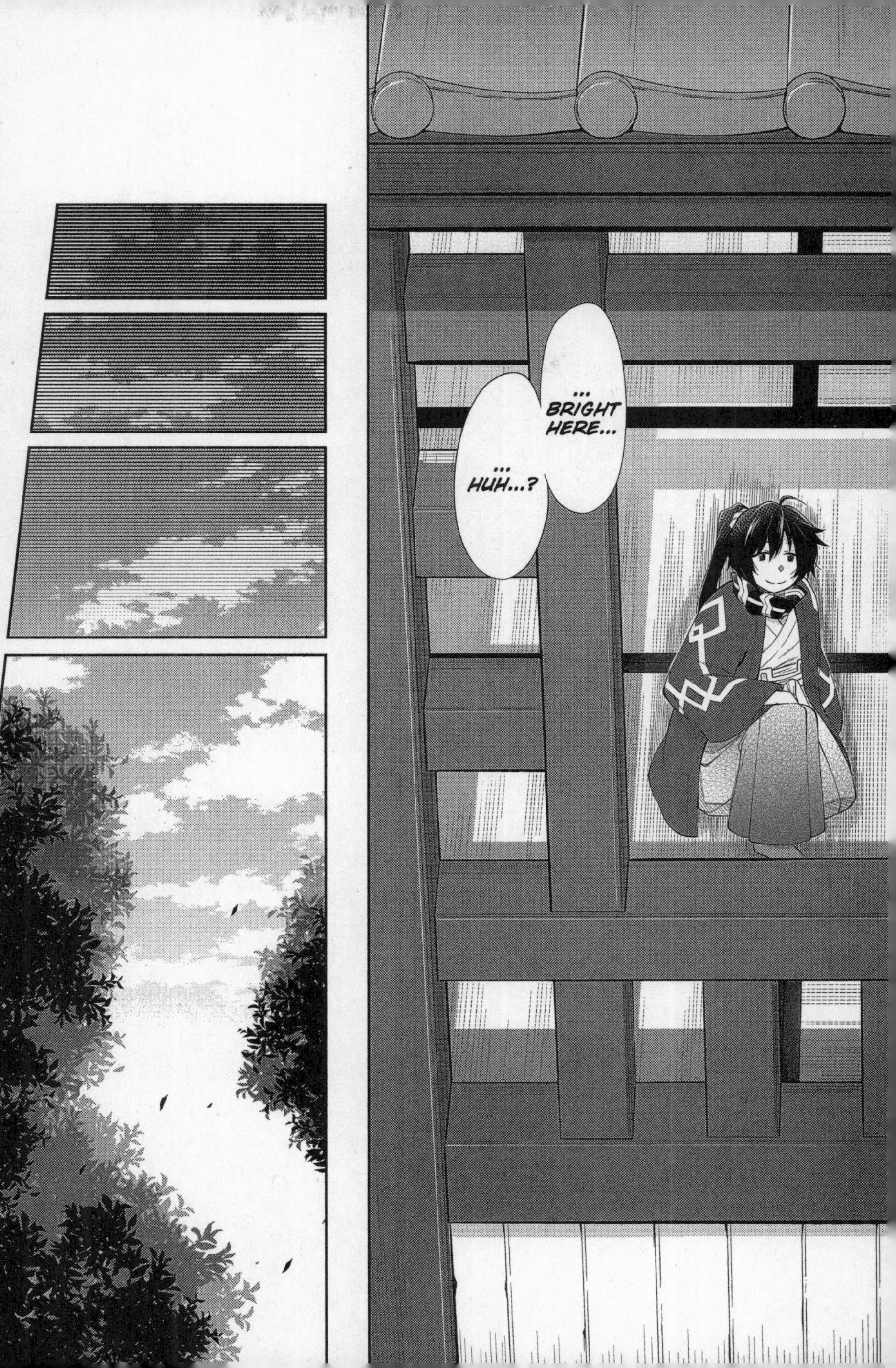
... BRIGHT HERE...
... HUH...?

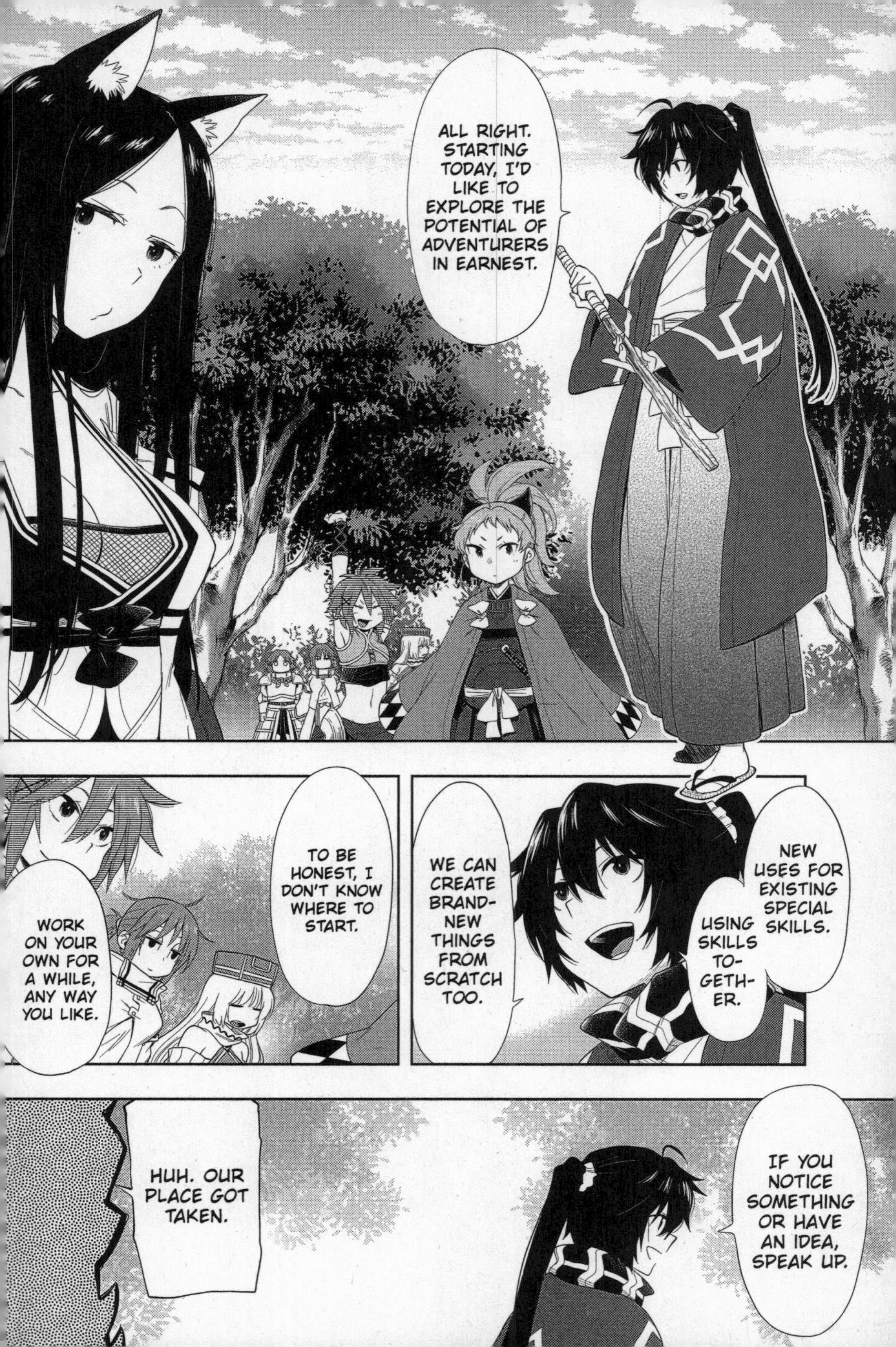
ALL RIGHT. STARTING TODAY, I'D LIKE TO EXPLORE THE POTENTIAL OF ADVENTURERS IN EARNEST.
NEW USES FOR EXISTING SPECIAL SKILLS.
USING SKILLS TOGETHER.
WE CAN CREATE BRAND-NEW THINGS FROM SCRATCH TOO.
TO BE HONEST, I DON'T KNOW WHERE TO START.
WORK ON YOUR OWN FOR A WHILE, ANY WAY YOU LIKE.
IF YOU NOTICE SOMETHING OR HAVE AN IDEA, SPEAK UP.
HUH. OUR PLACE GOT TAKEN.

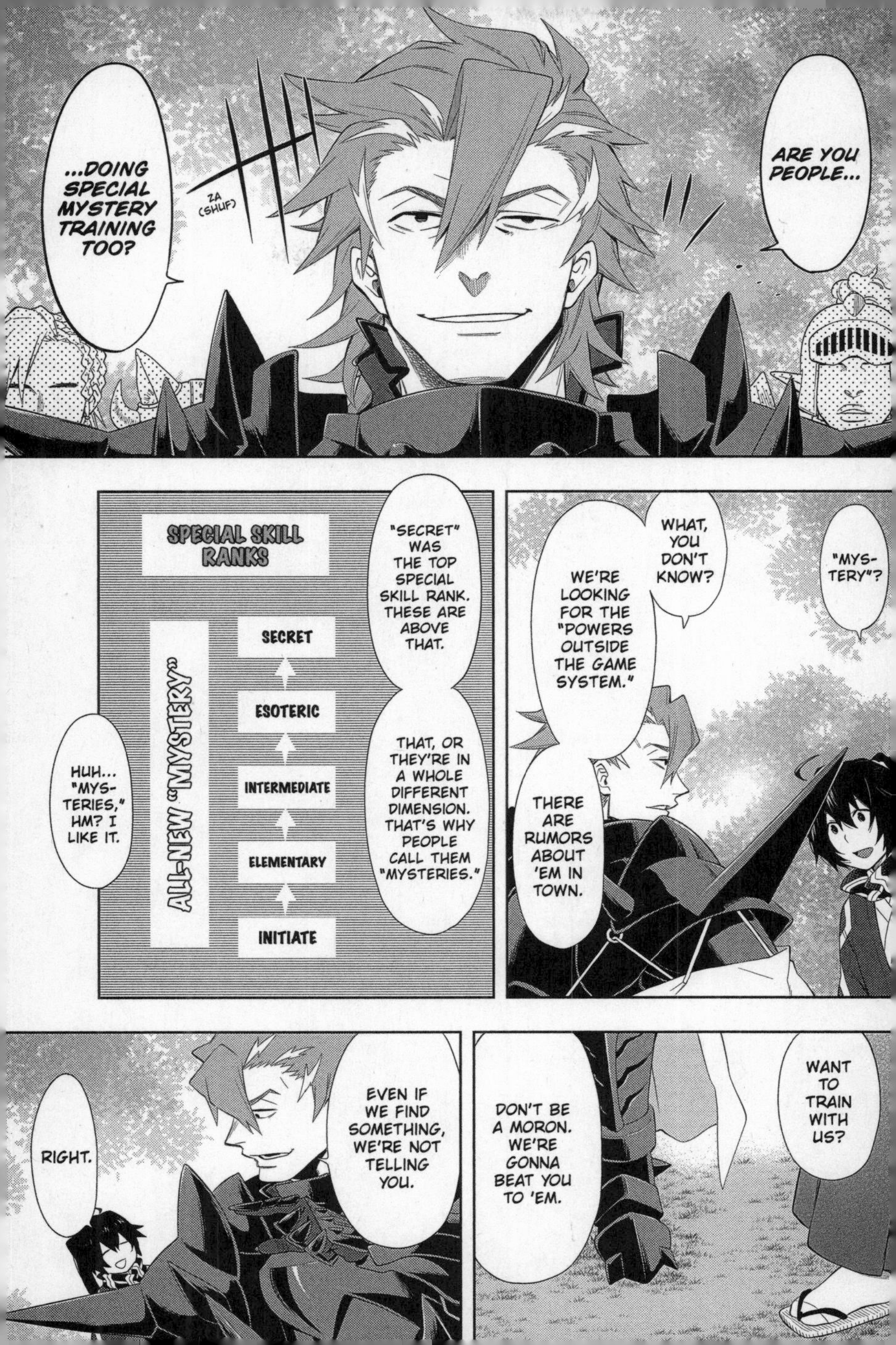
ARE YOU PEOPLE...
ZA (SHUF)
...DOING SPECIAL MYSTERY TRAINING TOO?
"MYS-TERY"?
WHAT, YOU DON'T KNOW?
WE'RE LOOKING FOR THE "POWERS OUTSIDE THE GAME SYSTEM."
THERE ARE RUMORS ABOUT 'EM IN TOWN.
"SECRET" WAS THE TOP SPECIAL SKILL RANK. THESE ARE ABOVE THAT.
THAT, OR THEY'RE IN A WHOLE DIFFERENT DIMENSION. THAT'S WHY PEOPLE CALL THEM "MYSTERIES."
SPECIAL SKILL RANKS
ALL-NEW "MYSTERY"
SECRET
ESOTERIC
INTERMEDIATE
ELEMENTARY
INITIATE
HUH... "MYS-TERIES," HM? I LIKE IT.
WANT TO TRAIN WITH US?
DON'T BE A MORON. WE'RE GONNA BEAT YOU TO 'EM.
EVEN IF WE FIND SOMETHING, WE'RE NOT TELLING YOU.
RIGHT.

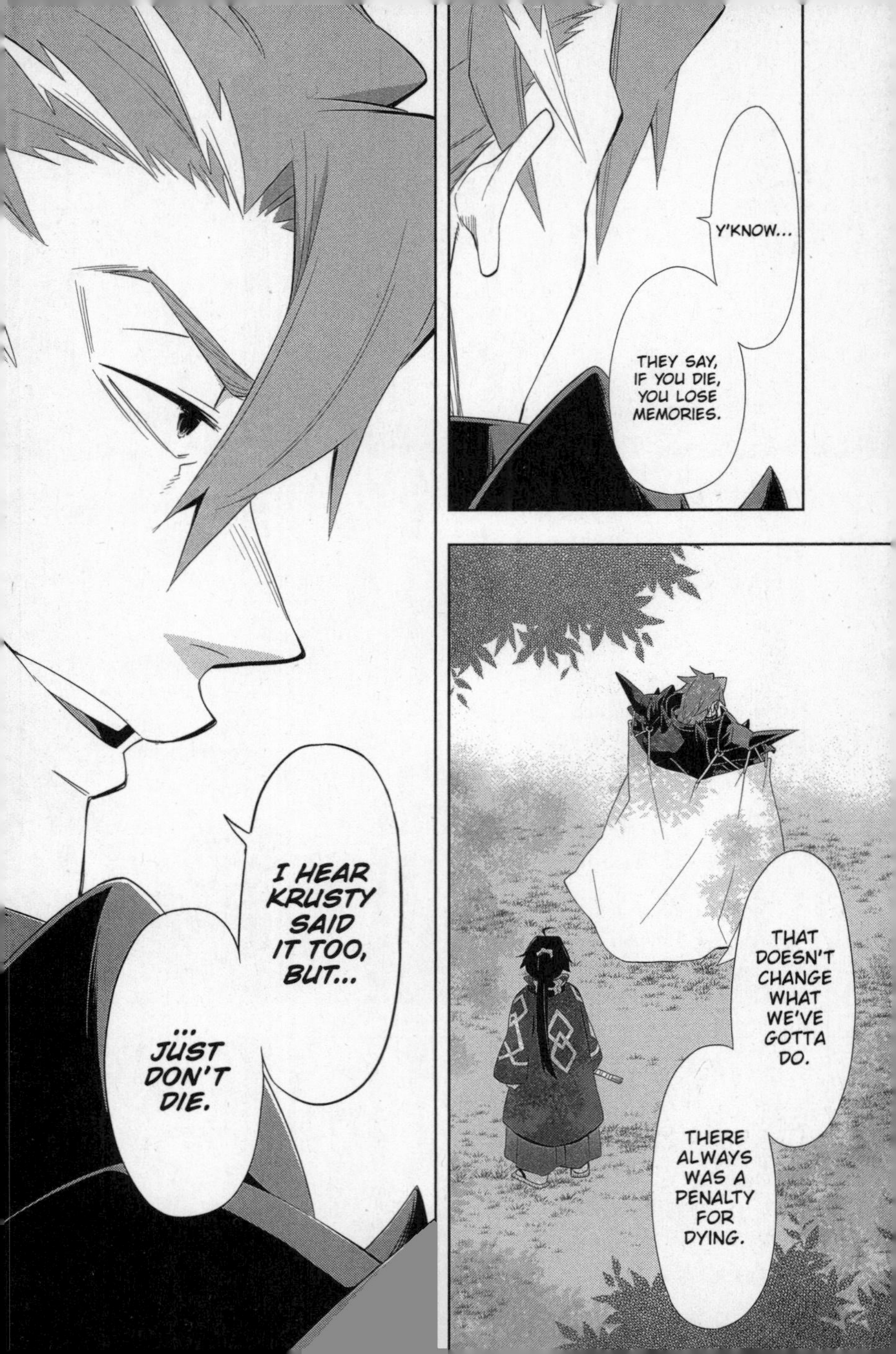
Y'KNOW...
THEY SAY, IF YOU DIE, YOU LOSE MEMORIES.
THAT DOESN'T CHANGE WHAT WE'VE GOTTA DO.
THERE ALWAYS WAS A PENALTY FOR DYING.
I HEAR KRUSTY SAID IT TOO, BUT...
... JUST DON'T DIE.

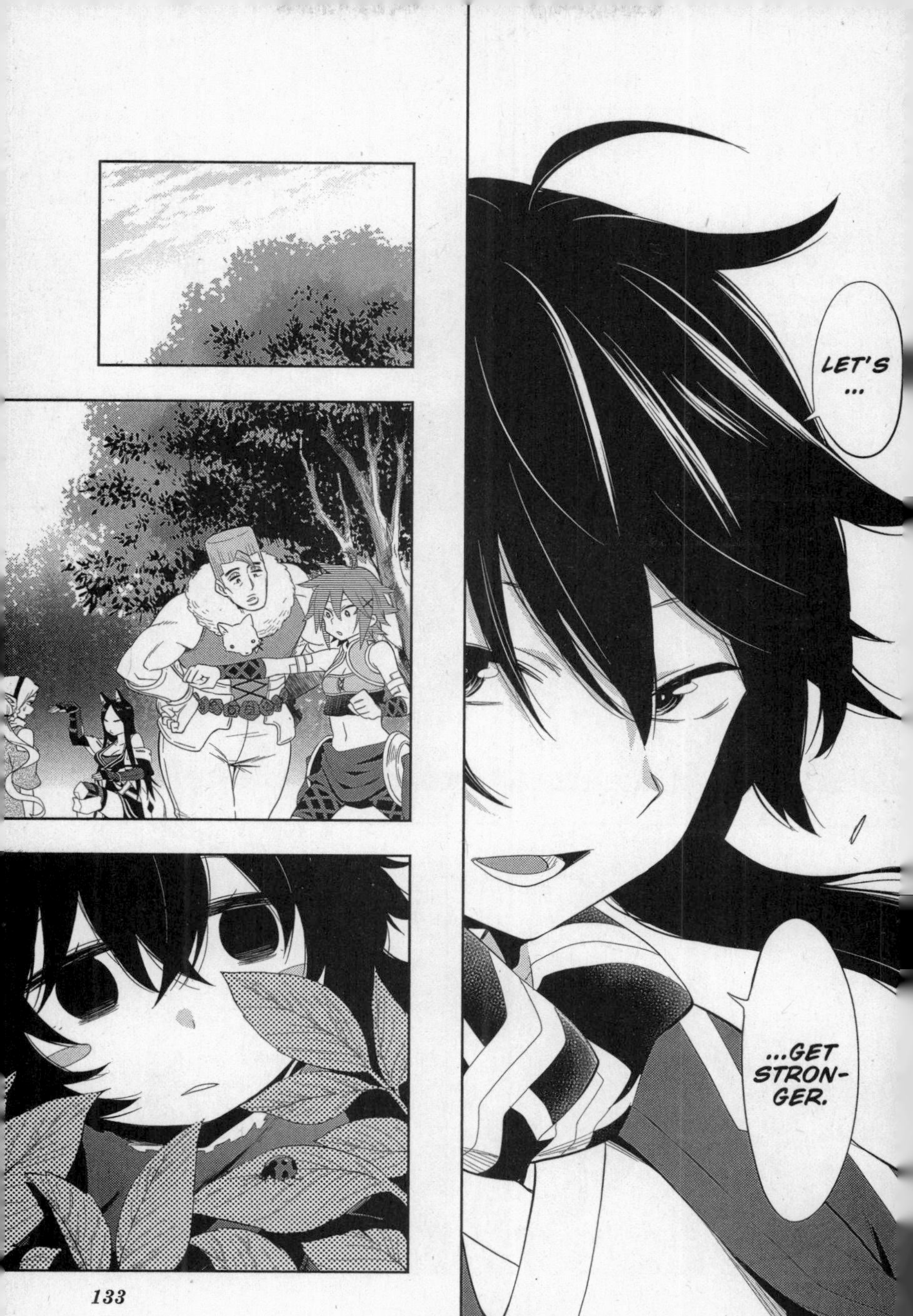
LET'S ...
...GET STRONGER.

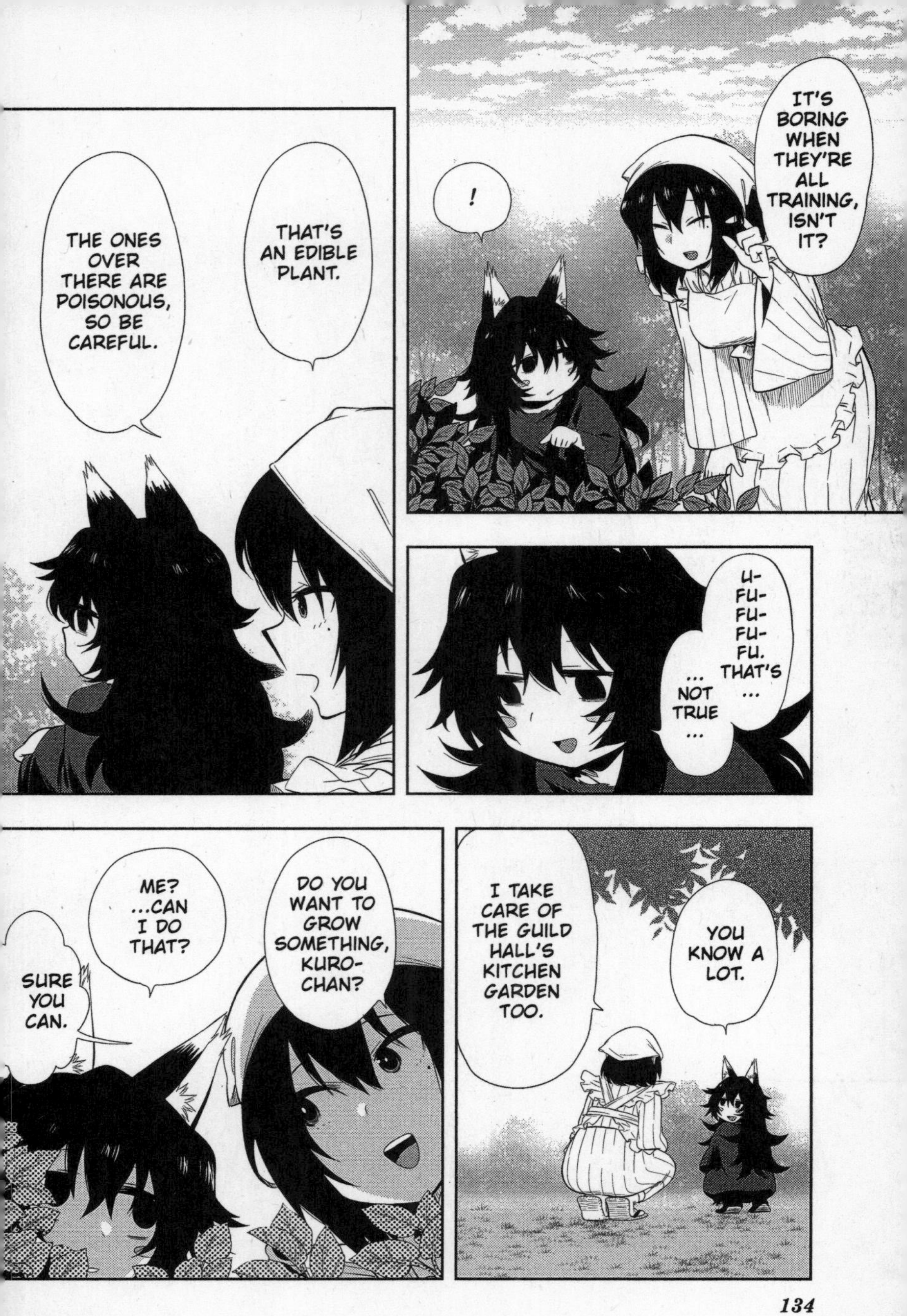
IT'S BORING WHEN THEY'RE ALL TRAINING, ISN'T IT?
!
U-FU-FU-FU-FU. THAT'S ...
... NOT TRUE ...
THAT'S AN EDIBLE PLANT.
THE ONES OVER THERE ARE POISONOUS, SO BE CAREFUL.
YOU KNOW A LOT.
I TAKE CARE OF THE GUILD HALL'S KITCHEN GARDEN TOO.
DO YOU WANT TO GROW SOMETHING, KURO-CHAN?
ME? ...CAN I DO THAT?
SURE YOU CAN.

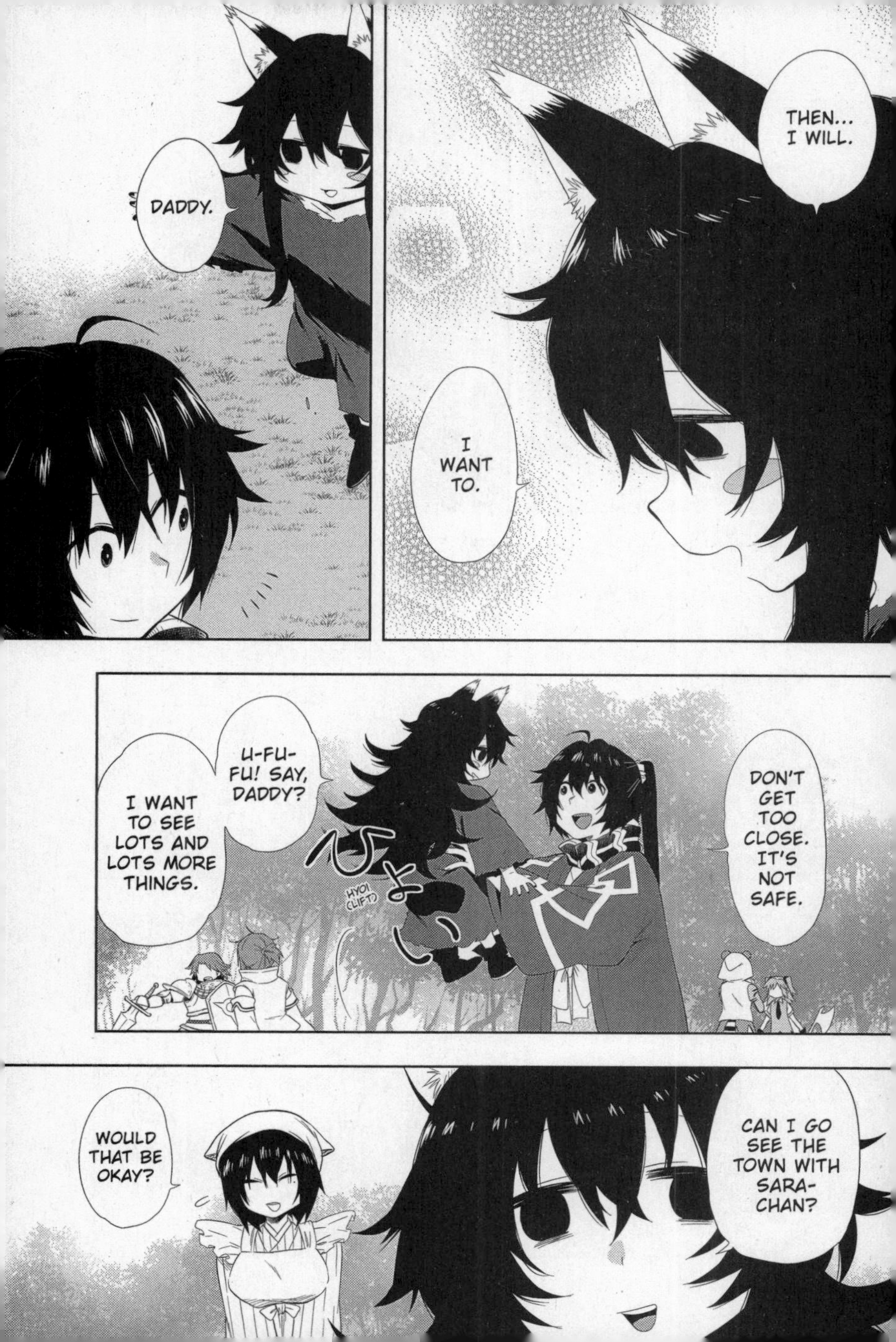
THEN... I WILL.
I WANT TO.
DADDY.
DON'T GET TOO CLOSE. IT'S NOT SAFE.
U-FU-FU! SAY, DADDY?
I WANT TO SEE LOTS AND LOTS MORE THINGS.
HYOI (LIFT?)
CAN I GO SEE THE TOWN WITH SARA-CHAN?
WOULD THAT BE OKAY?

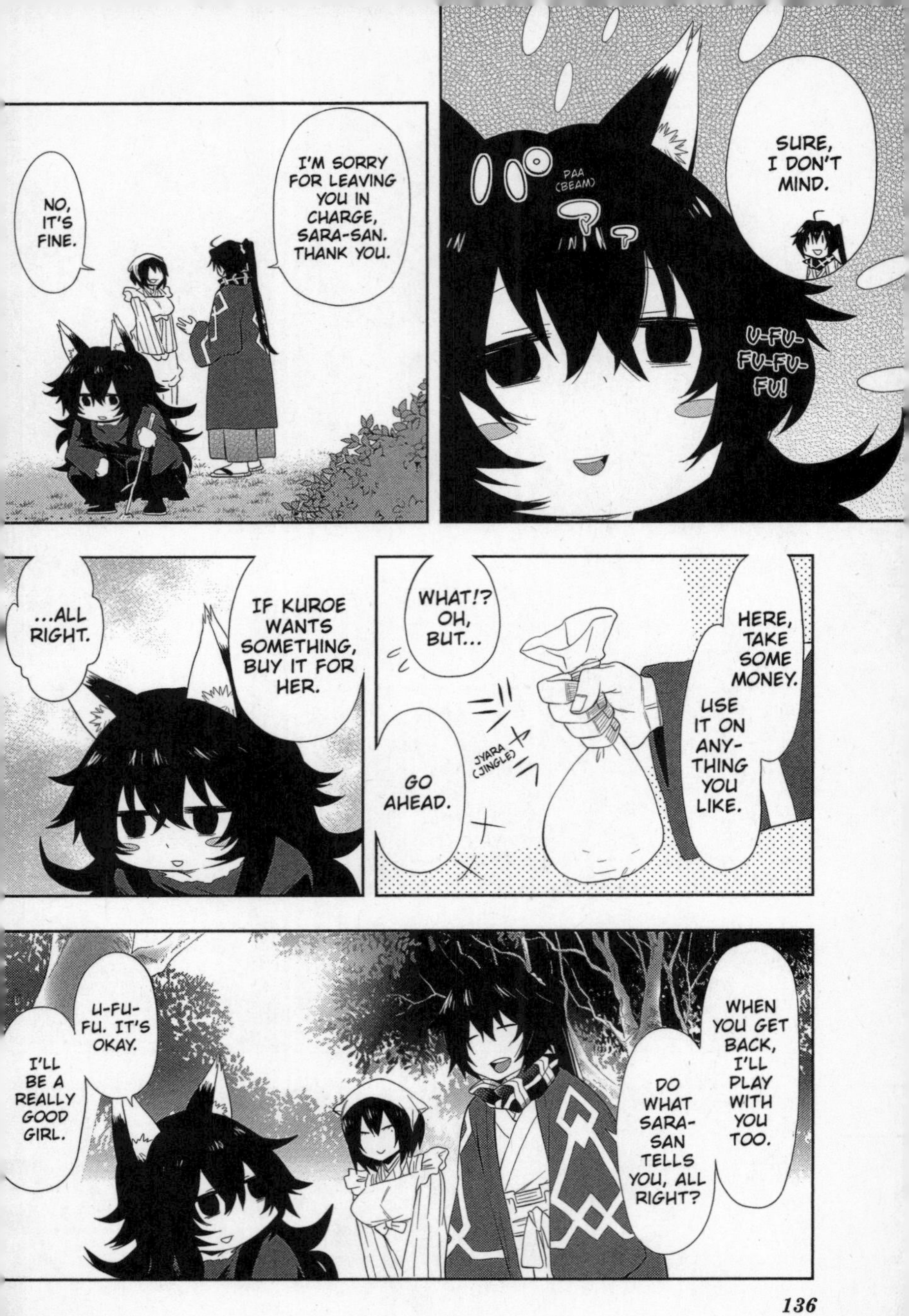
SURE, I DON'T MIND.
PAA (BEAM)
U-FU-FU-FU-FU!
I'M SORRY FOR LEAVING YOU IN CHARGE, SARA-SAN. THANK YOU.
NO, IT'S FINE.
HERE, TAKE SOME MONEY.
USE IT ON ANY-THING YOU LIKE.
JYARA (JINGLE)
WHAT!? OH, BUT...
GO AHEAD.
IF KUROE WANTS SOMETHING, BUY IT FOR HER.
...ALL RIGHT.
WHEN YOU GET BACK, I'LL PLAY WITH YOU TOO.
DO WHAT SARA-SAN TELLS YOU, ALL RIGHT?
U-FU-FU. IT'S OKAY.
I'LL BE A REALLY GOOD GIRL.

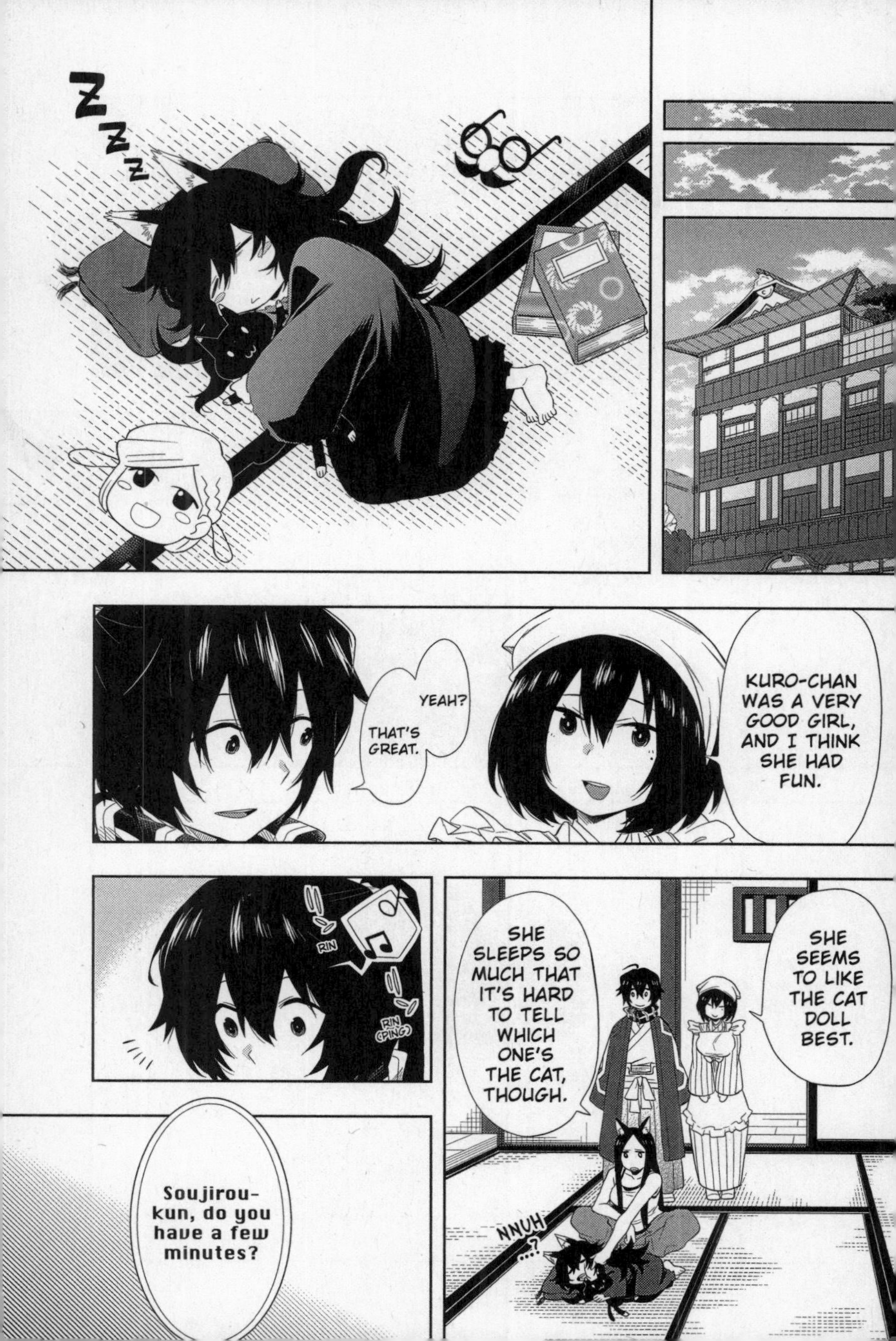
ZZZ
KURO-CHAN WAS A VERY GOOD GIRL, AND I THINK SHE HAD FUN.
YEAH? THAT'S GREAT.
SHE SEEMS TO LIKE THE CAT DOLL BEST.
SHE SLEEPS SO MUCH THAT IT'S HARD TO TELL WHICH ONE'S THE CAT, THOUGH.
NNUH...?
RIN
RIN (PING)
Soujirou-kun, do you have a few minutes?

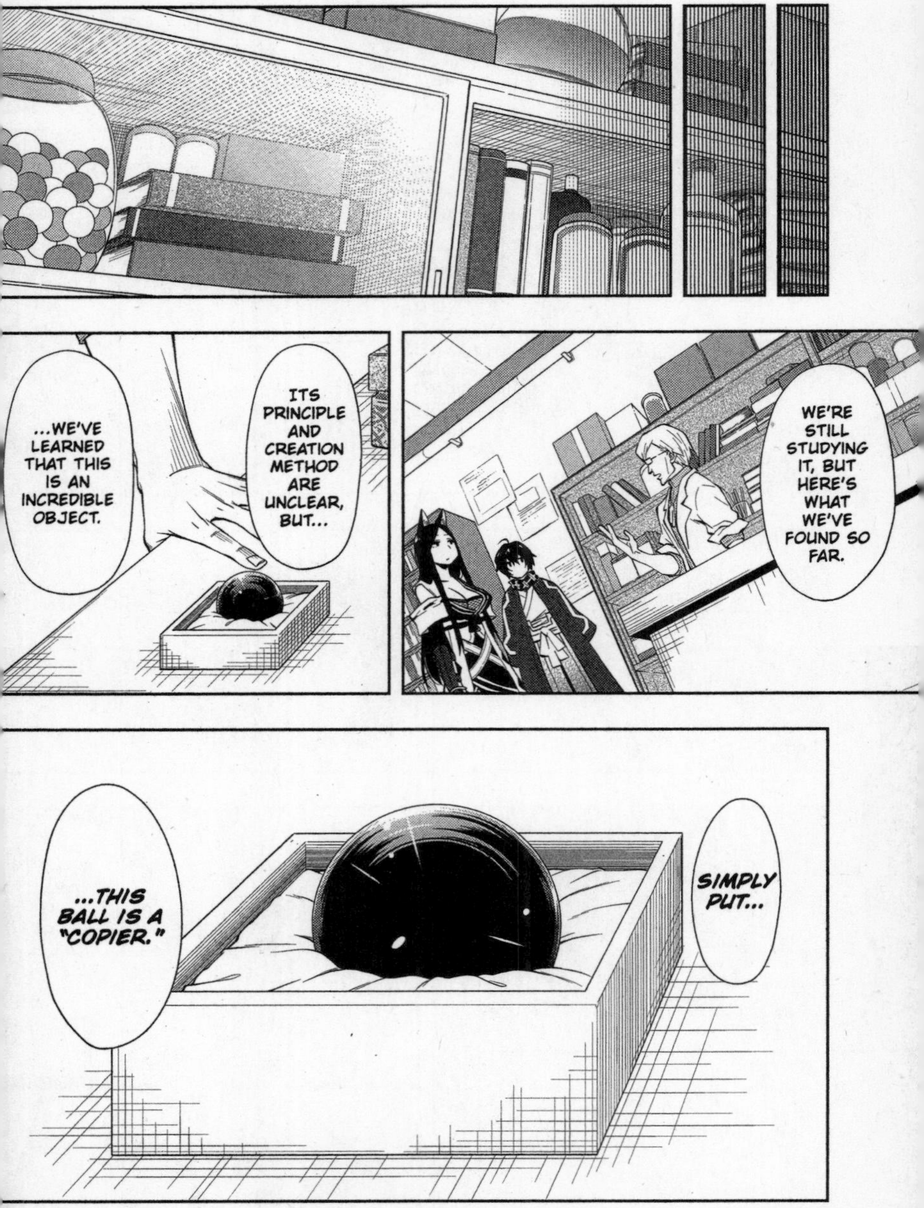
WE'RE STILL STUDYING IT, BUT HERE'S WHAT WE'VE FOUND SO FAR.
ITS PRINCIPLE AND CREATION METHOD ARE UNCLEAR, BUT...
...WE'VE LEARNED THAT THIS IS AN INCREDIBLE OBJECT.
SIMPLY PUT...
...THIS BALL IS A "COPIER."

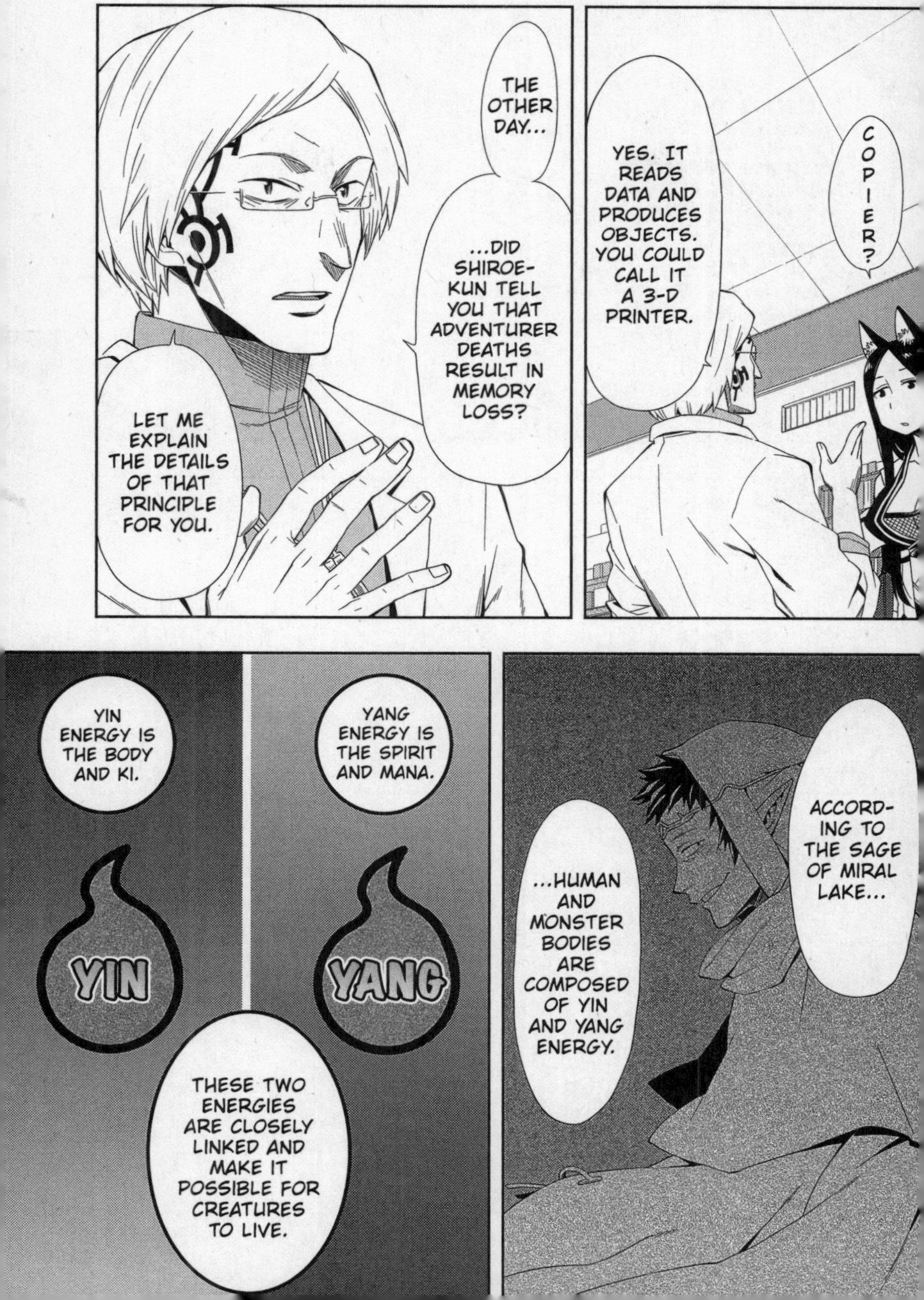
COPIER?
YES. IT READS DATA AND PRODUCES OBJECTS. YOU COULD CALL IT A 3-D PRINTER.
THE OTHER DAY...
...DID SHIROE-KUN TELL YOU THAT ADVENTURER DEATHS RESULT IN MEMORY LOSS?
LET ME EXPLAIN THE DETAILS OF THAT PRINCIPLE FOR YOU.
ACCORDING TO THE SAGE OF MIRAL LAKE...
...HUMAN AND MONSTER BODIES ARE COMPOSED OF YIN AND YANG ENERGY.
YANG ENERGY IS THE SPIRIT AND MANA.
YANG
YIN ENERGY IS THE BODY AND KI.
YIN
THESE TWO ENERGIES ARE CLOSELY LINKED AND MAKE IT POSSIBLE FOR CREATURES TO LIVE.

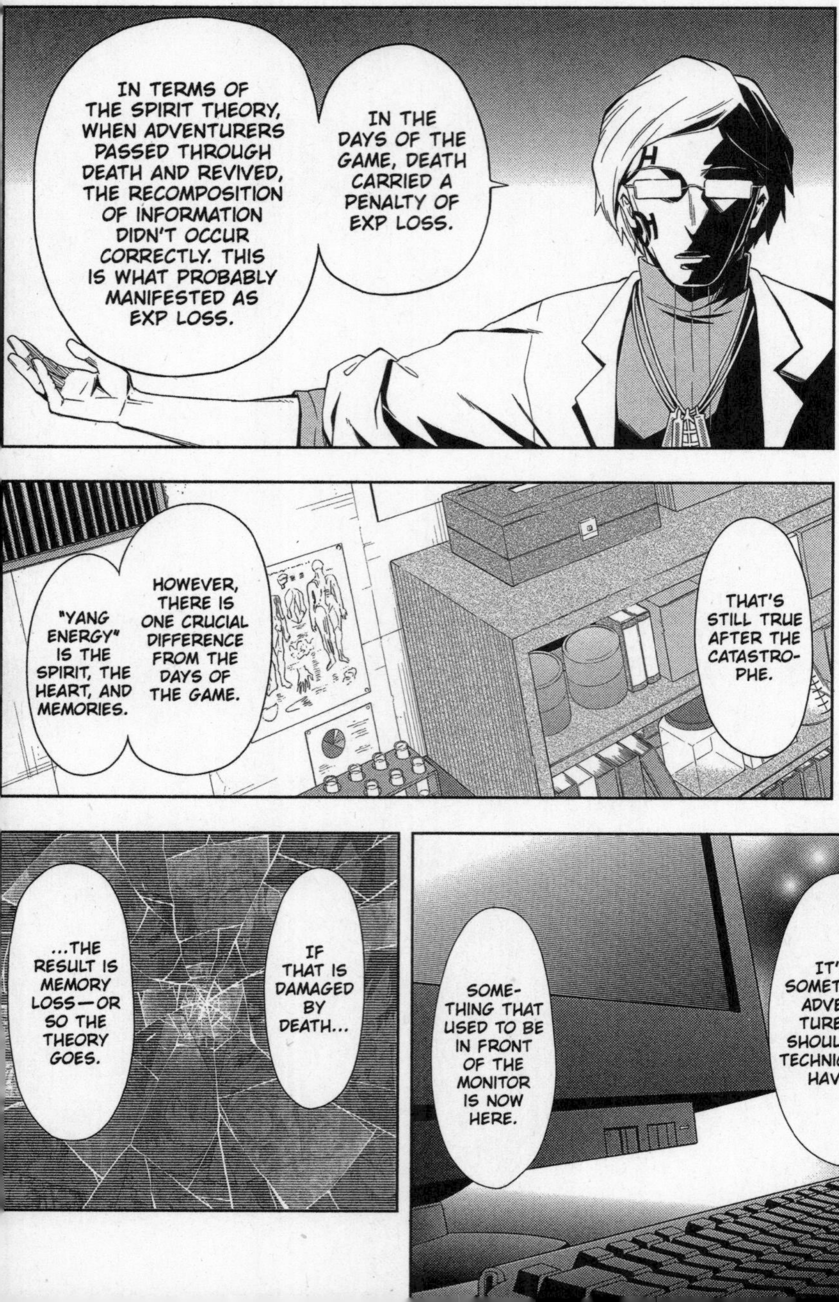
IN THE DAYS OF THE GAME, DEATH CARRIED A PENALTY OF EXP LOSS.
IN TERMS OF THE SPIRIT THEORY, WHEN ADVENTURERS PASSED THROUGH DEATH AND REVIVED, THE RECOMPOSITION OF INFORMATION DIDN'T OCCUR CORRECTLY. THIS IS WHAT PROBABLY MANIFESTED AS EXP LOSS.
THAT'S STILL TRUE AFTER THE CATASTRO-PHE.
HOWEVER, THERE IS ONE CRUCIAL DIFFERENCE FROM THE DAYS OF THE GAME.
"YANG ENERGY" IS THE SPIRIT, THE HEART, AND MEMORIES.
IT'S SOMETHING ADVEN-TURERS SHOULDN'T TECHNICALLY HAVE.
SOME-THING THAT USED TO BE IN FRONT OF THE MONITOR IS NOW HERE.
IF THAT IS DAMAGED BY DEATH...
...THE RESULT IS MEMORY LOSS—OR SO THE THEORY GOES.

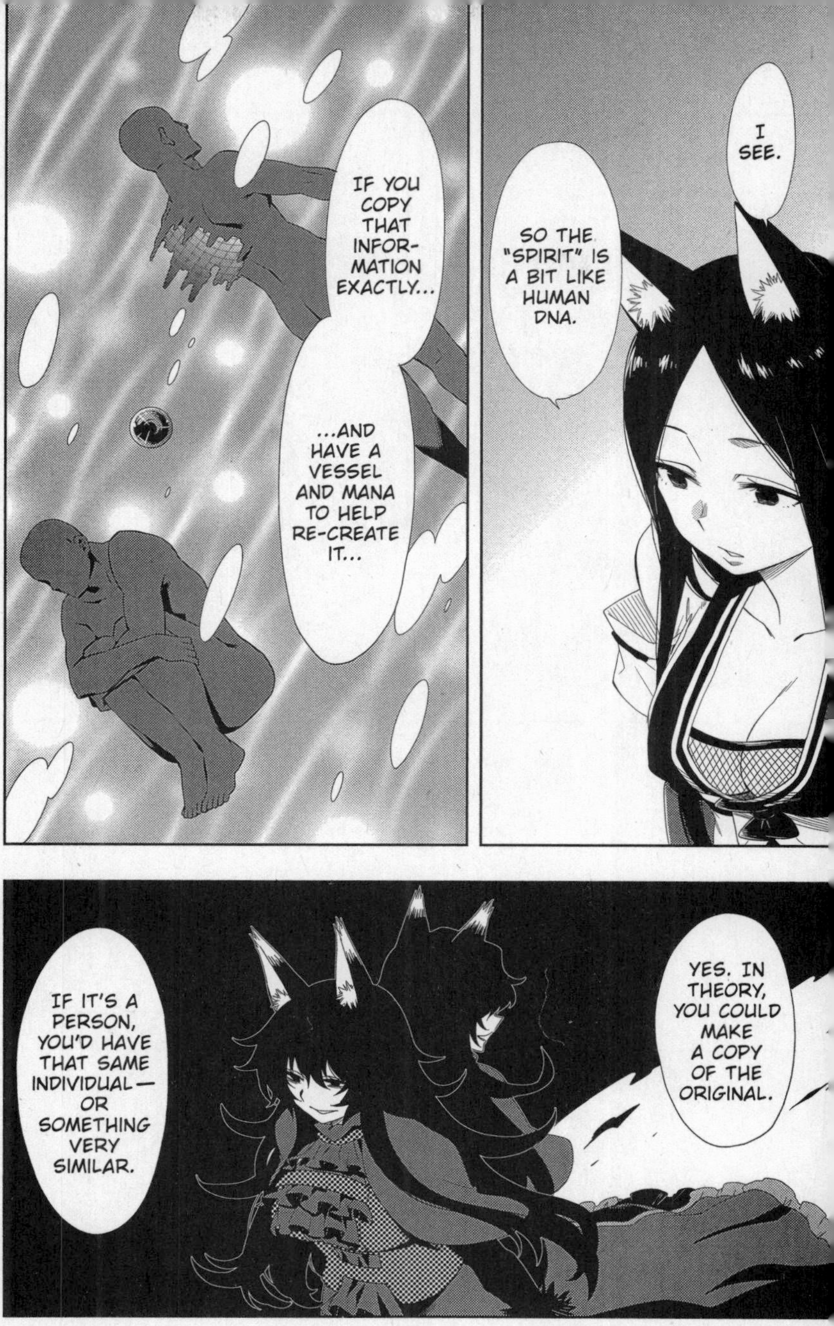
I SEE.
SO THE "SPIRIT" IS A BIT LIKE HUMAN DNA.
IF YOU COPY THAT INFOR-MATION EXACTLY...
...AND HAVE A VESSEL AND MANA TO HELP RE-CREATE IT...
YES. IN THEORY, YOU COULD MAKE A COPY OF THE ORIGINAL.
IF IT'S A PERSON, YOU'D HAVE THAT SAME INDIVIDUAL—OR SOMETHING VERY SIMILAR.

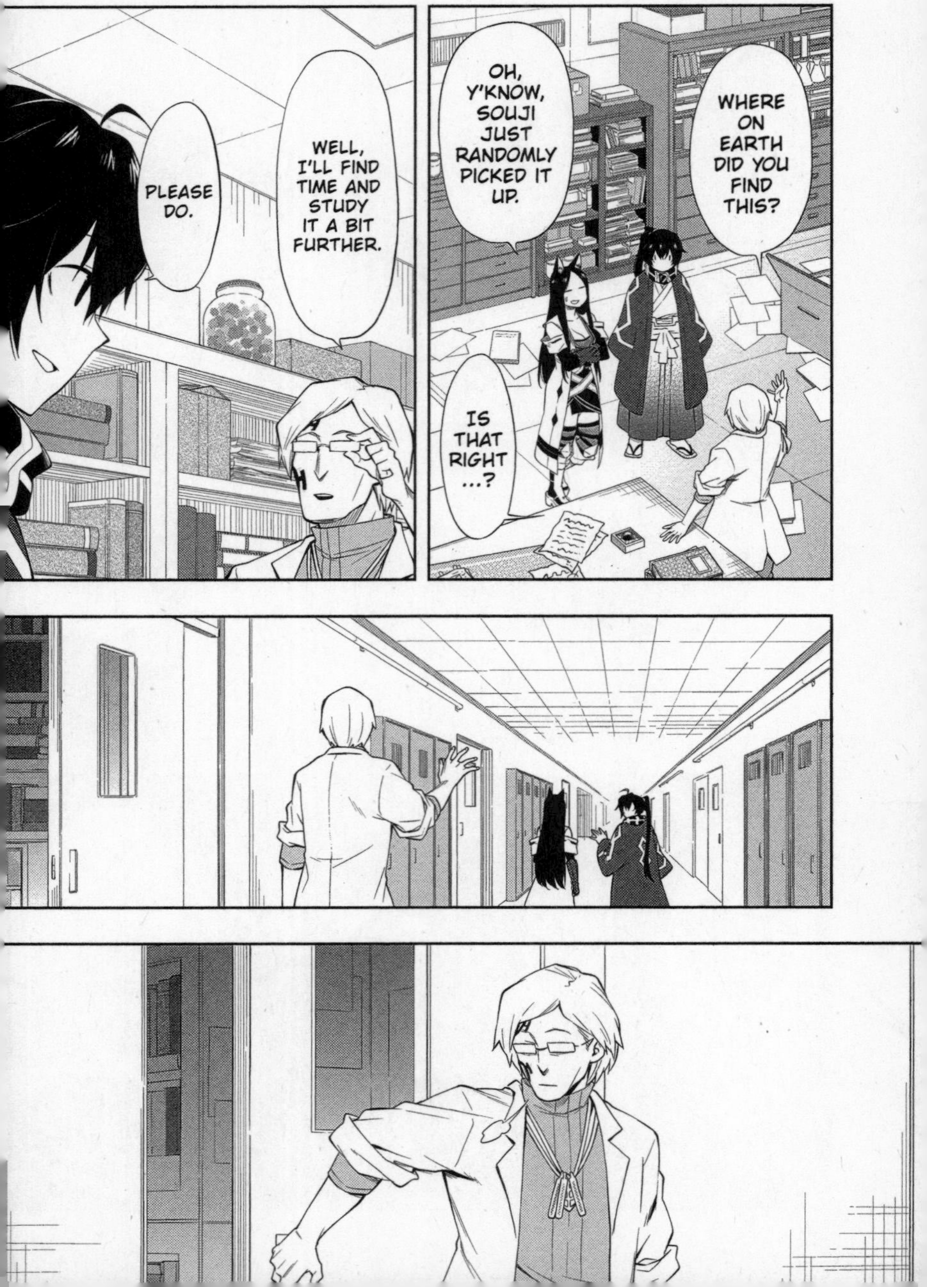
WHERE ON EARTH DID YOU FIND THIS?
OH, Y'KNOW, SOUJI JUST RANDOMLY PICKED IT UP.
IS THAT RIGHT ...?
WELL, I'LL FIND TIME AND STUDY IT A BIT FURTHER.
PLEASE DO.

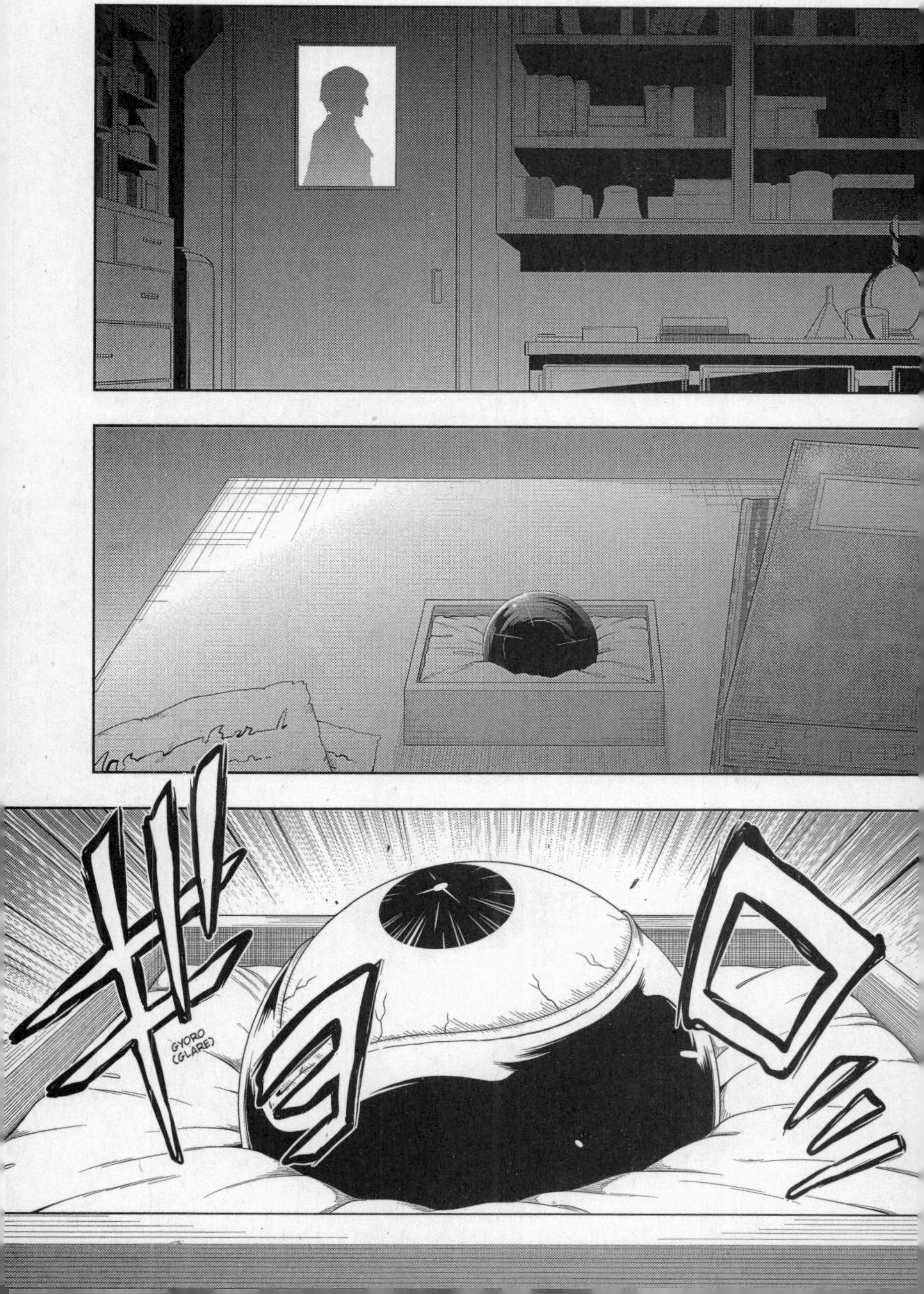
GYORO
(GLARE)

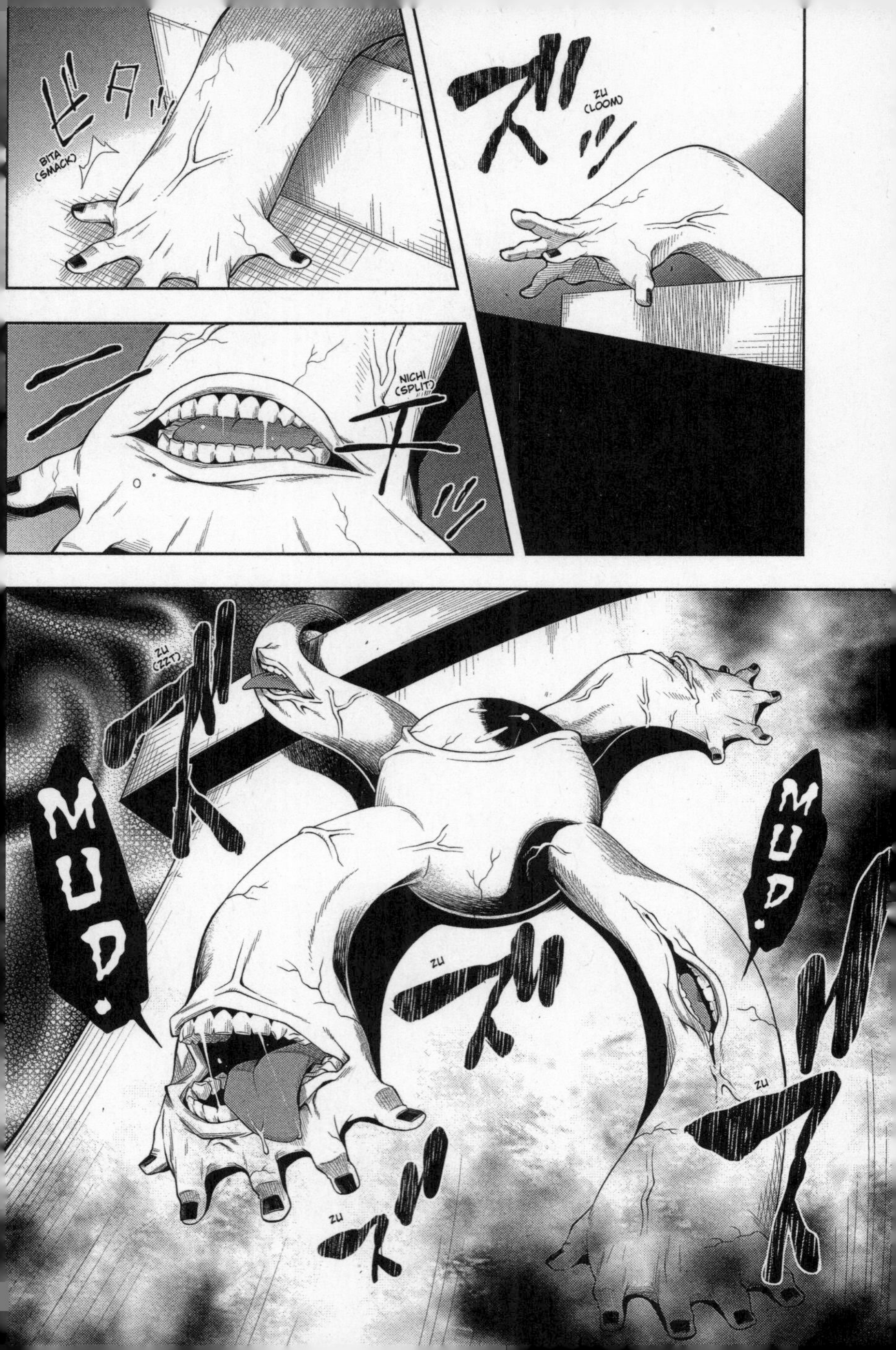
ZU (LOOM)
BITA (SMACK)
NICHI (SPLIT)
MUD.
ZU (ZZT)
MUD.
ZU
ZU
ZU

LOG HORIZON

THE WEST WIND BRIGADE

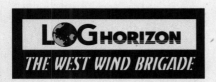

LOG HORIZON

THE WEST WIND BRIGADE

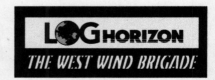

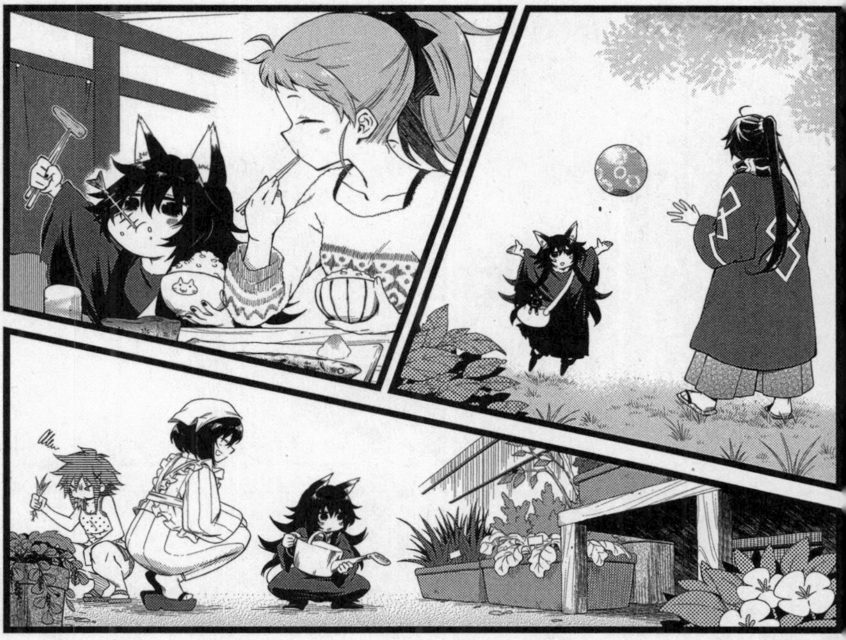

CHAPTER : 47 Searching For...

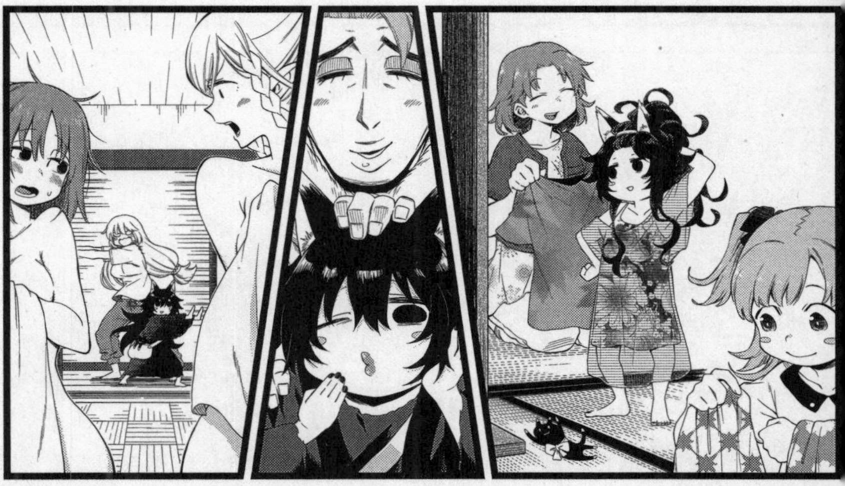

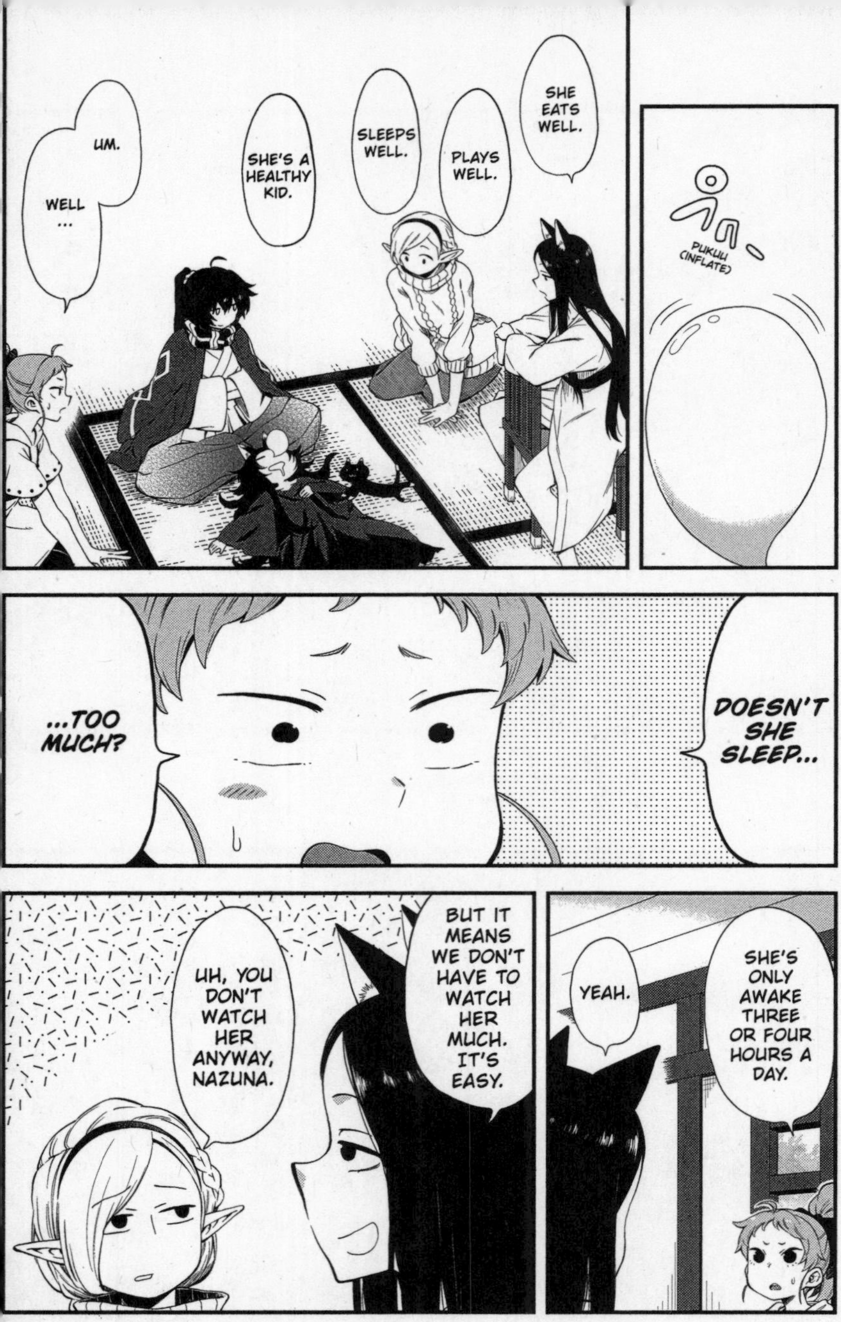
PUKUU (INFLATE)
SHE EATS WELL.
PLAYS WELL.
SLEEPS WELL.
SHE'S A HEALTHY KID.
UM. WELL ...
DOESN'T SHE SLEEP...
...TOO MUCH?
SHE'S ONLY AWAKE THREE OR FOUR HOURS A DAY.
YEAH.
BUT IT MEANS WE DON'T HAVE TO WATCH HER MUCH. IT'S EASY.
UH, YOU DON'T WATCH HER ANYWAY, NAZUNA.

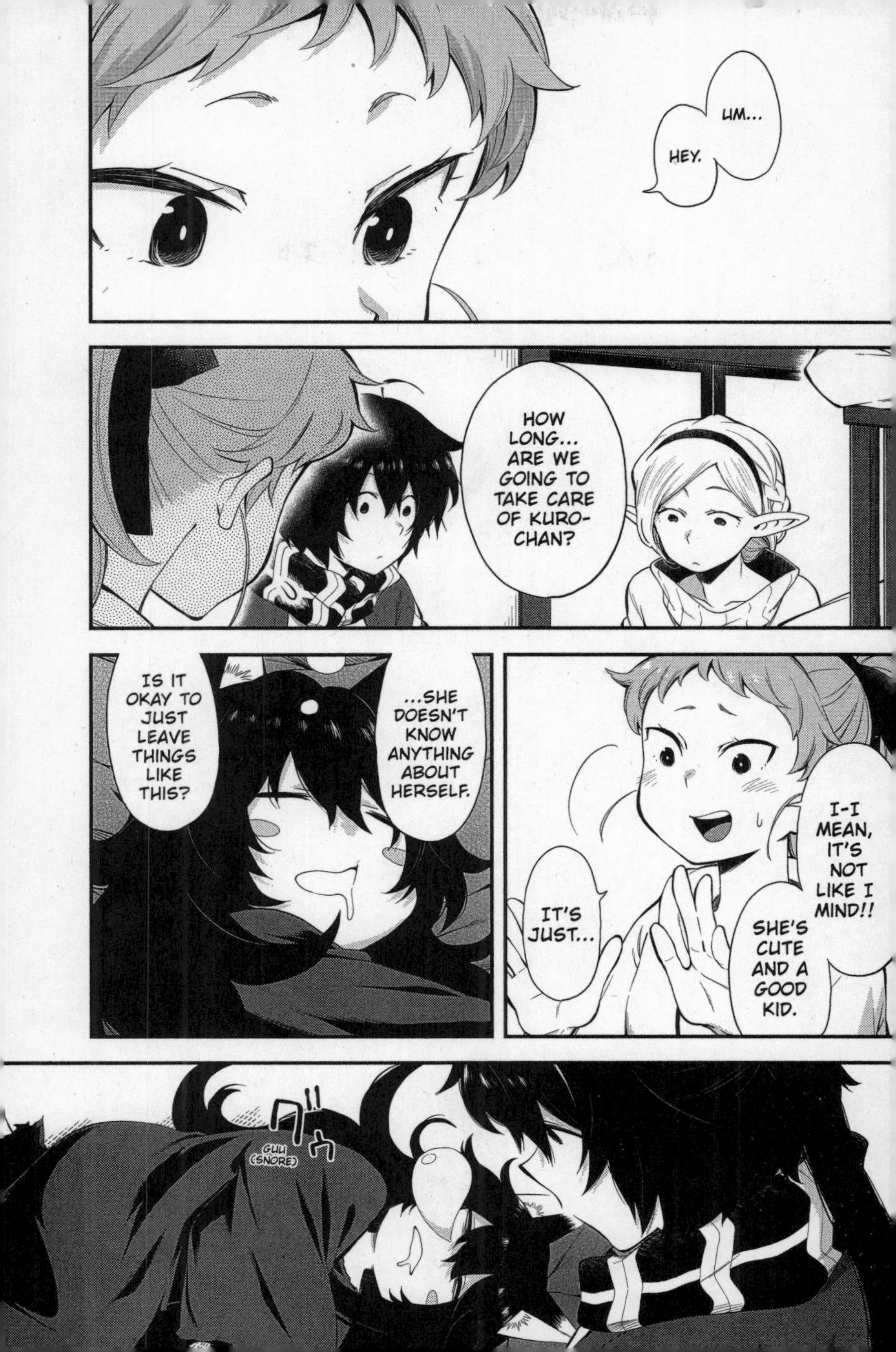
UM...
HEY.
HOW LONG... ARE WE GOING TO TAKE CARE OF KURO-CHAN?
I-I MEAN, IT'S NOT LIKE I MIND!!
SHE'S CUTE AND A GOOD KID.
IT'S JUST...
...SHE DOESN'T KNOW ANYTHING ABOUT HERSELF.
IS IT OKAY TO JUST LEAVE THINGS LIKE THIS?
GUU (SNORE)

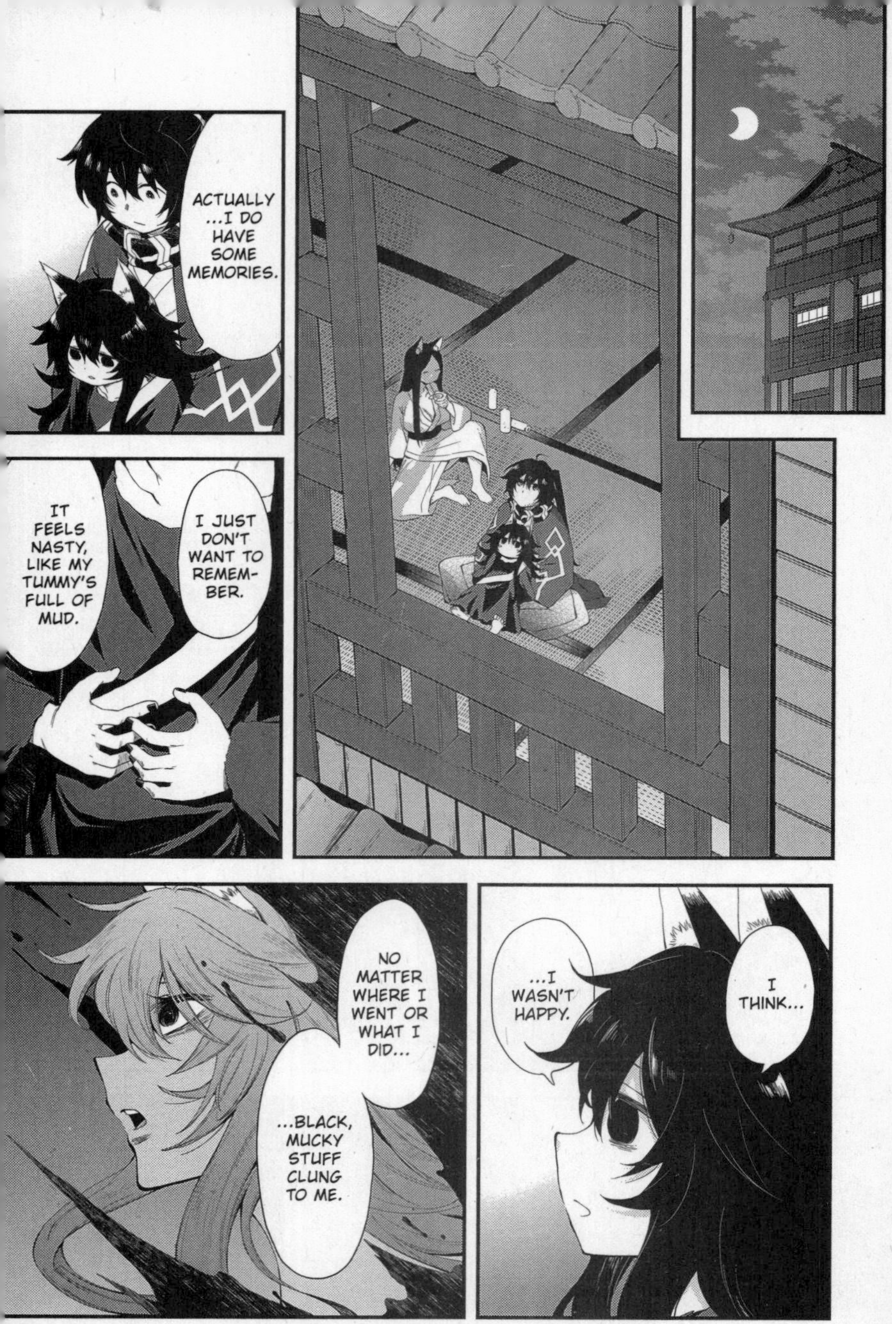
ACTUALLY ...I DO HAVE SOME MEMORIES.
I JUST DON'T WANT TO REMEMBER.
IT FEELS NASTY, LIKE MY TUMMY'S FULL OF MUD.
I THINK...
...I WASN'T HAPPY.
NO MATTER WHERE I WENT OR WHAT I DID...
...BLACK, MUCKY STUFF CLUNG TO ME.

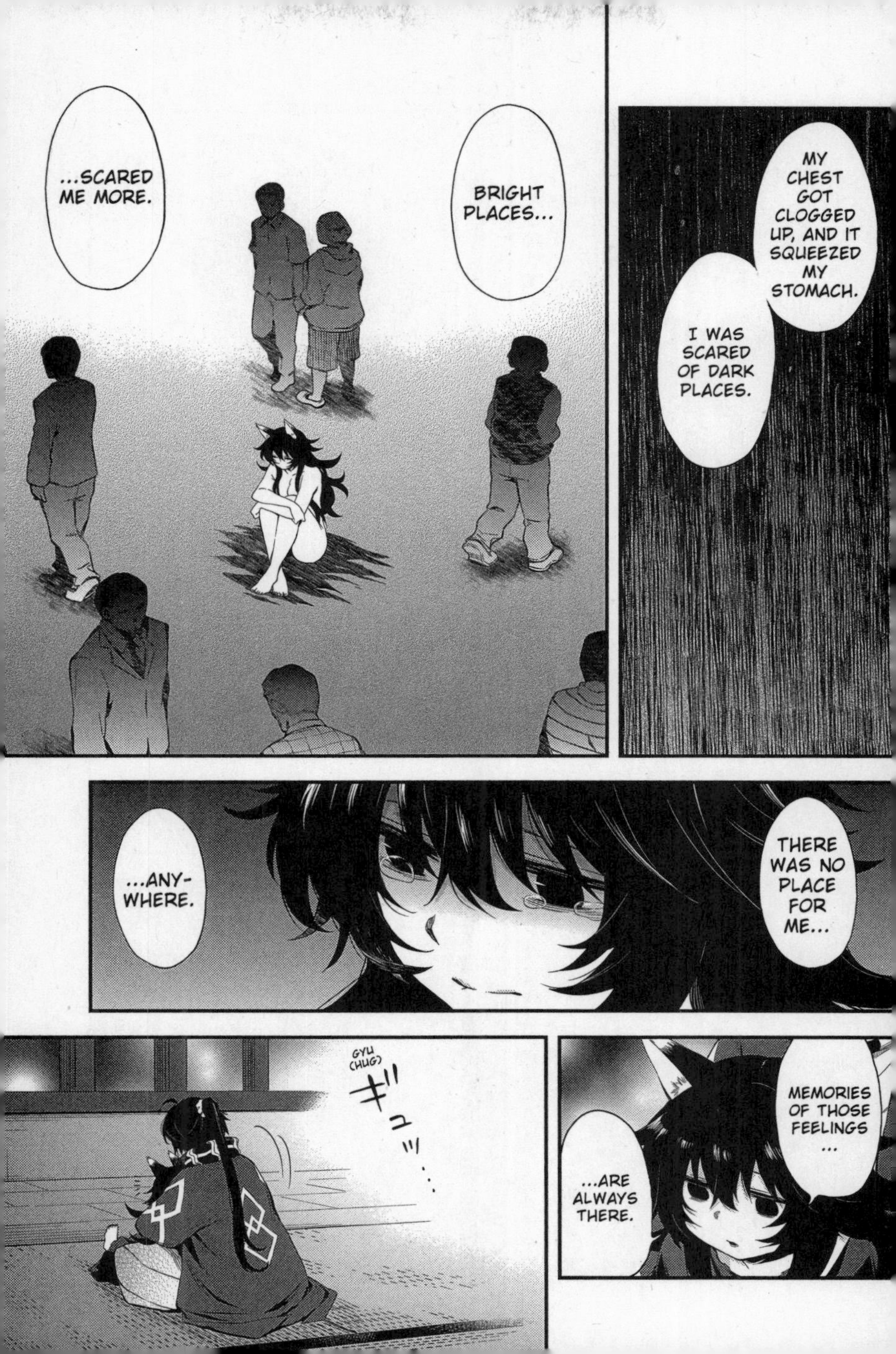
MY CHEST GOT CLOGGED UP, AND IT SQUEEZED MY STOMACH.
I WAS SCARED OF DARK PLACES.
BRIGHT PLACES...
...SCARED ME MORE.
THERE WAS NO PLACE FOR ME...
...ANYWHERE.
MEMORIES OF THOSE FEELINGS ...
...ARE ALWAYS THERE.
GYU (HUG)
ギュッ…

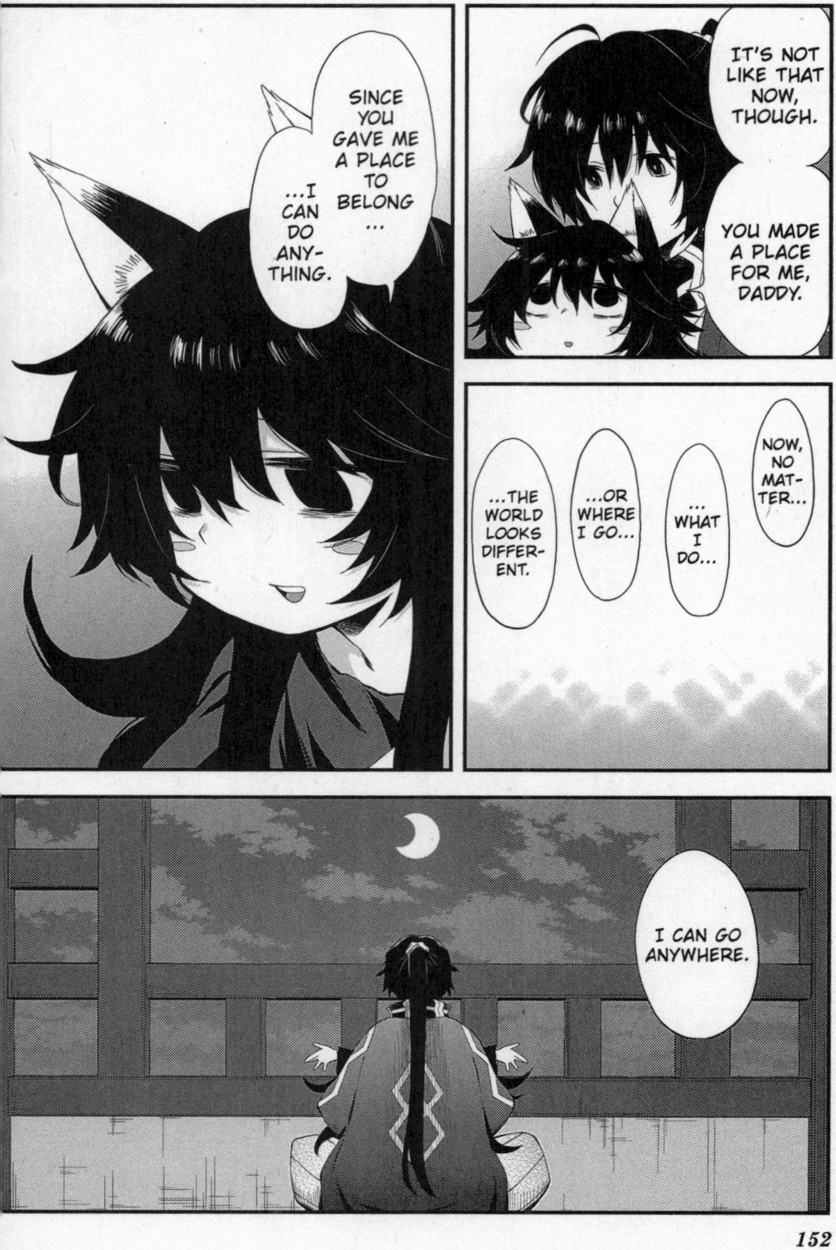
IT'S NOT LIKE THAT NOW, THOUGH.
YOU MADE A PLACE FOR ME, DADDY.
NOW, NO MATTER...
...WHAT I DO...
...OR WHERE I GO...
...THE WORLD LOOKS DIFFER-ENT.
SINCE YOU GAVE ME A PLACE TO BELONG...
...I CAN DO ANY-THING.
I CAN GO ANYWHERE.

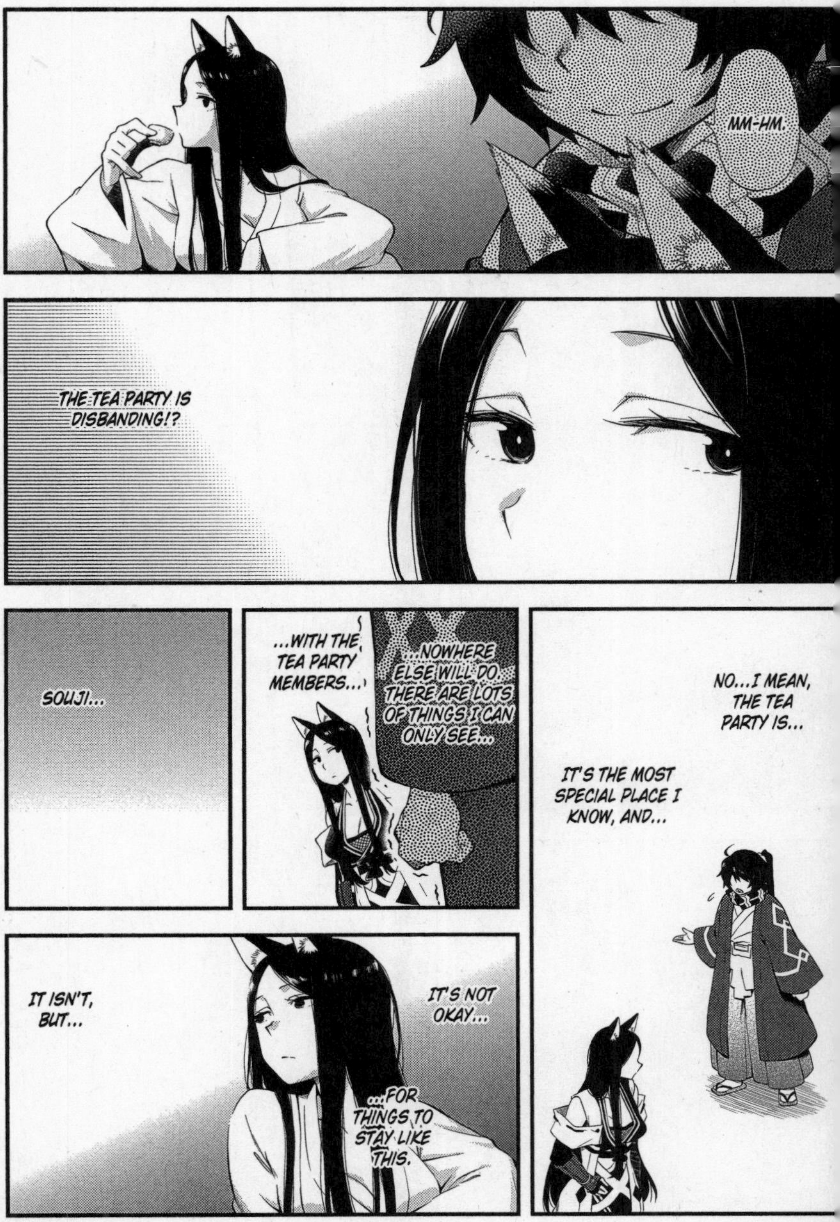
MM-HM.
THE TEA PARTY IS DISBANDING!?
NO...I MEAN, THE TEA PARTY IS...
IT'S THE MOST SPECIAL PLACE I KNOW, AND...
...NOWHERE ELSE WILL DO. THERE ARE LOTS OF THINGS I CAN ONLY SEE...
...WITH THE TEA PARTY MEMBERS...
SOUJI...
IT'S NOT OKAY...
...FOR THINGS TO STAY LIKE THIS.
IT ISN'T, BUT...

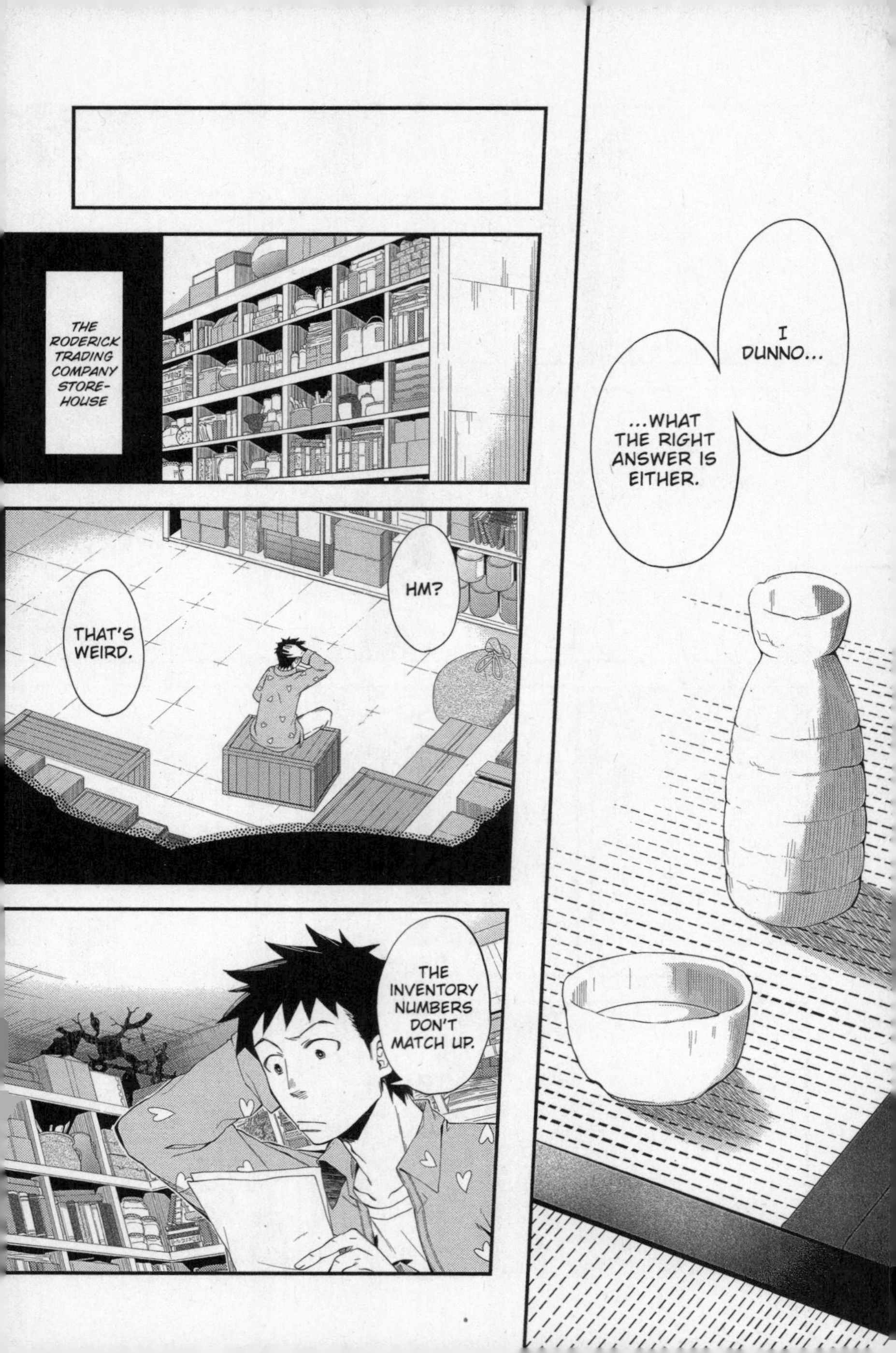
I DUNNO...
...WHAT THE RIGHT ANSWER IS EITHER.
THE RODERICK TRADING COMPANY STORE-HOUSE
HM?
THAT'S WEIRD.
THE INVENTORY NUMBERS DON'T MATCH UP.

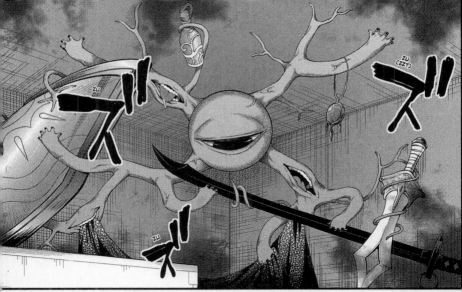

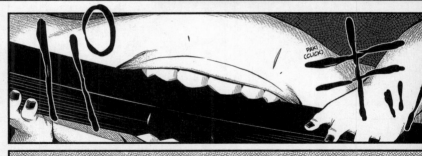

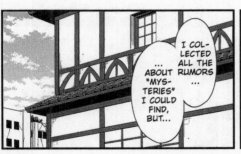

ZU (ZZT)
ZU
ZU
PAKI (CLICK)
PASA (RUSTLE)
I COLLECTED ALL THE RUMORS...
... ABOUT "MYSTERIES" I COULD FIND, BUT...

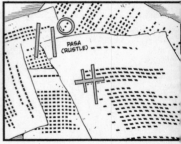

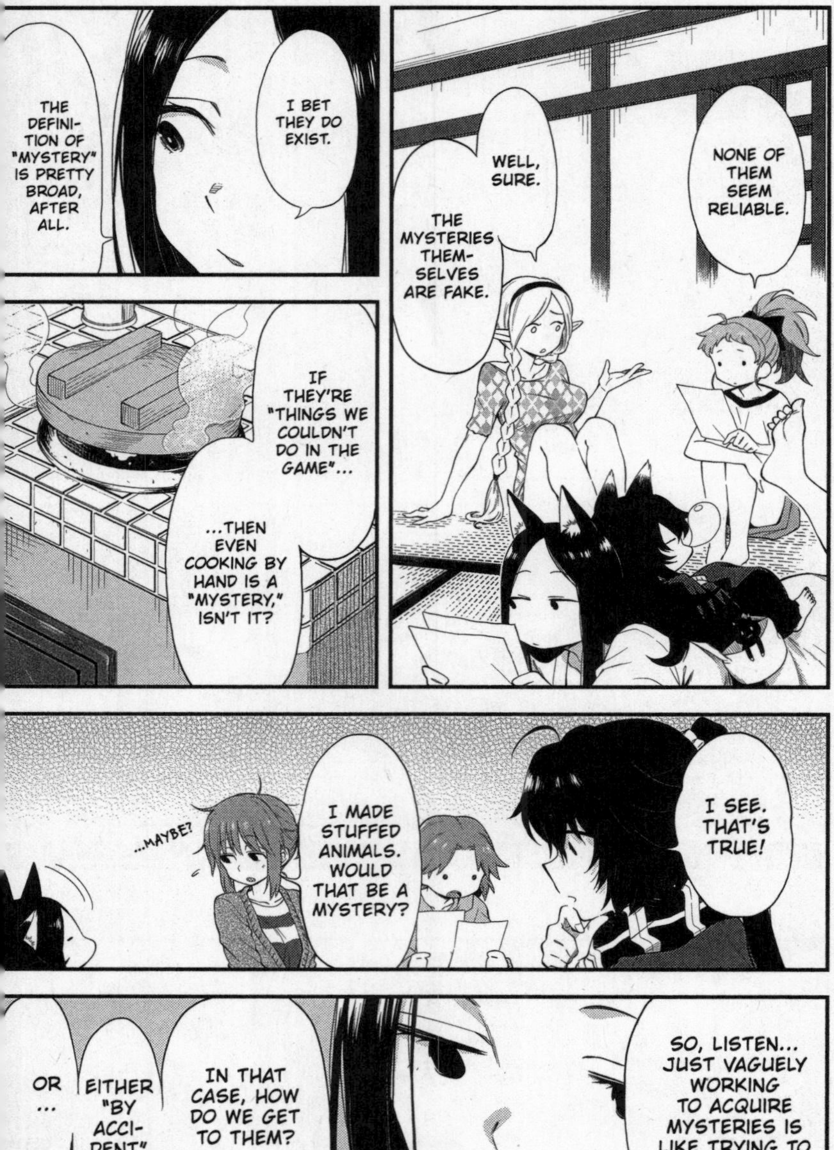
NONE OF THEM SEEM RELIABLE.
WELL, SURE.
THE MYSTERIES THEMSELVES ARE FAKE.
I BET THEY DO EXIST.
THE DEFINITION OF "MYSTERY" IS PRETTY BROAD, AFTER ALL.
IF THEY'RE "THINGS WE COULDN'T DO IN THE GAME"...
...THEN EVEN COOKING BY HAND IS A "MYSTERY," ISN'T IT?
I SEE. THAT'S TRUE!
I MADE STUFFED ANIMALS. WOULD THAT BE A MYSTERY?
...MAYBE?
SO, LISTEN... JUST VAGUELY WORKING TO ACQUIRE MYSTERIES IS LIKE TRYING TO GRAB CLOUDS.
IN THAT CASE, HOW DO WE GET TO THEM?
EITHER "BY ACCIDENT"...
OR...

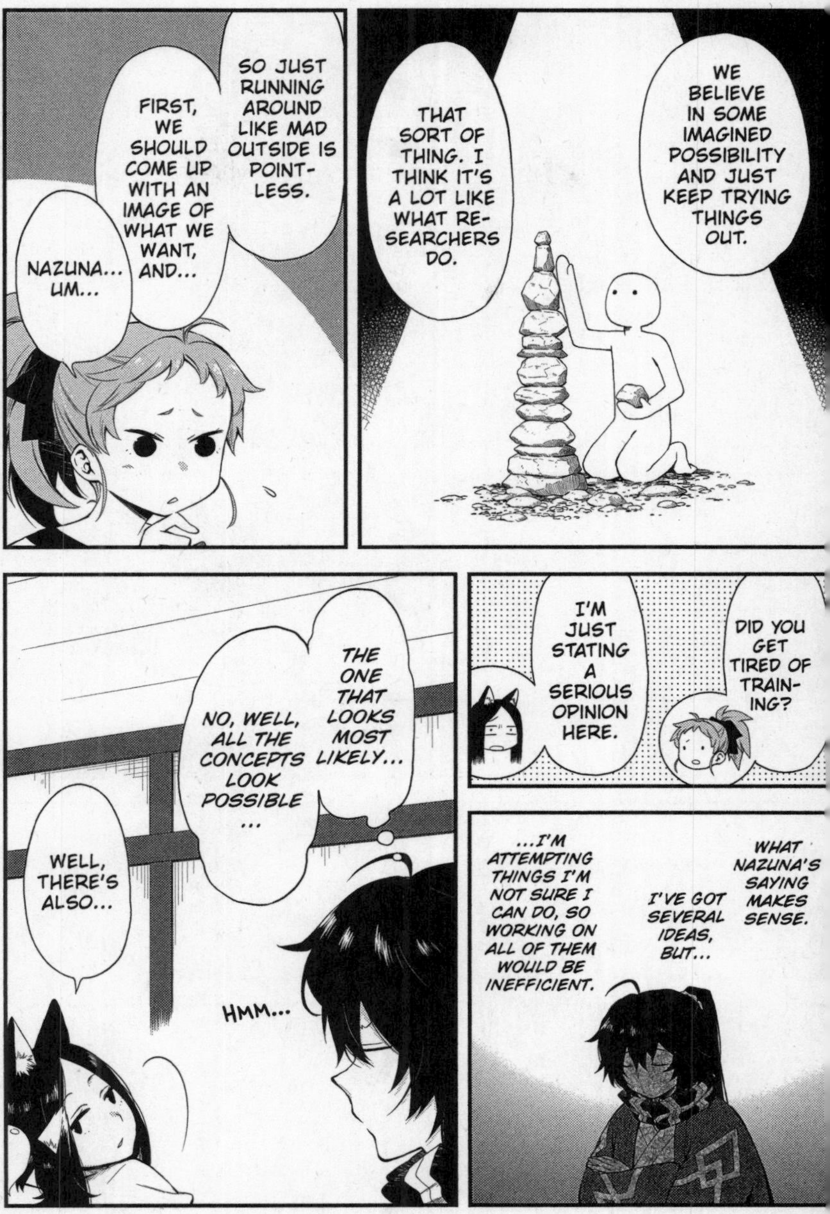
WE BELIEVE IN SOME IMAGINED POSSIBILITY AND JUST KEEP TRYING THINGS OUT.
THAT SORT OF THING. I THINK IT'S A LOT LIKE WHAT RE-SEARCHERS DO.
SO JUST RUNNING AROUND LIKE MAD OUTSIDE IS POINT-LESS.
FIRST, WE SHOULD COME UP WITH AN IMAGE OF WHAT WE WANT, AND...
NAZUNA... UM...
DID YOU GET TIRED OF TRAIN-ING?
I'M JUST STATING A SERIOUS OPINION HERE.
WHAT NAZUNA'S SAYING MAKES SENSE.
I'VE GOT SEVERAL IDEAS, BUT...
...I'M ATTEMPTING THINGS I'M NOT SURE I CAN DO, SO WORKING ON ALL OF THEM WOULD BE INEFFICIENT.
THE ONE THAT LOOKS MOST LIKELY...
NO, WELL, ALL THE CONCEPTS LOOK POSSIBLE ...
WELL, THERE'S ALSO...
HMM...

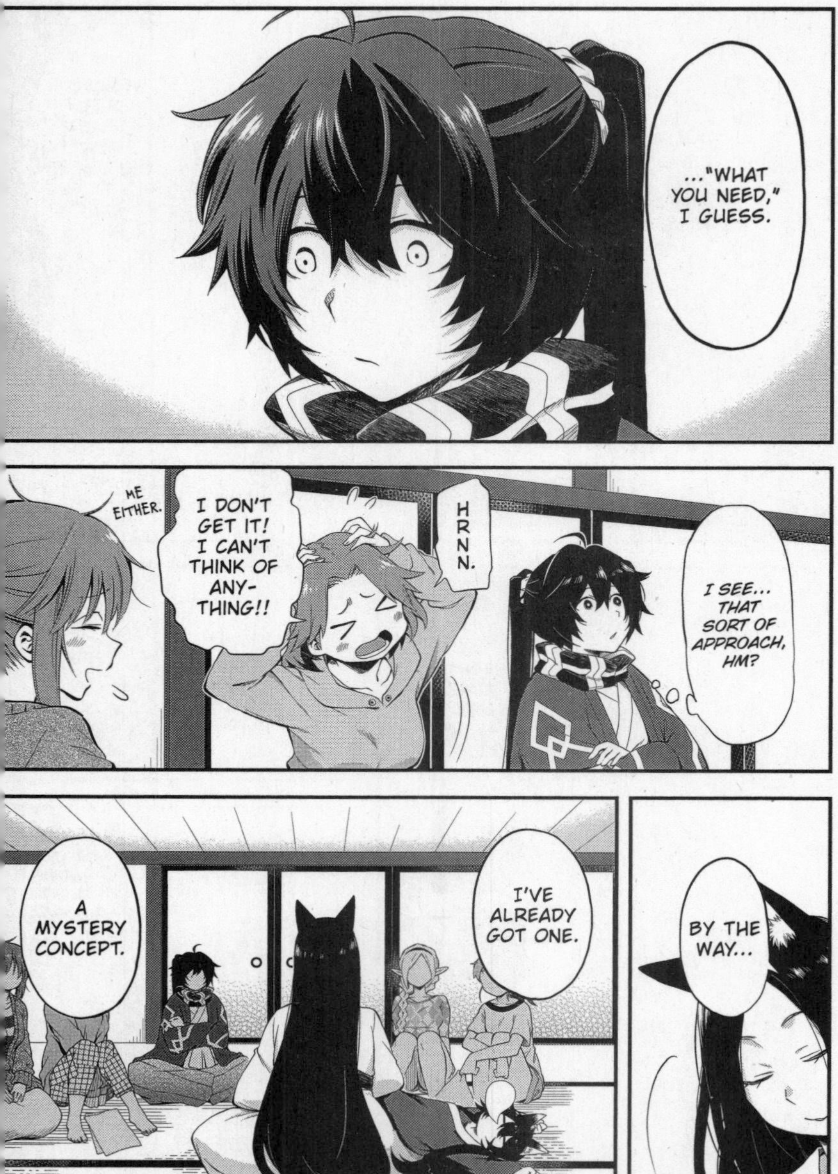
..."WHAT YOU NEED," I GUESS.
I SEE... THAT SORT OF APPROACH, HM?
HRNN.
I DON'T GET IT! I CAN'T THINK OF ANY-THING!!
ME EITHER.
BY THE WAY...
I'VE ALREADY GOT ONE.
A MYSTERY CONCEPT.

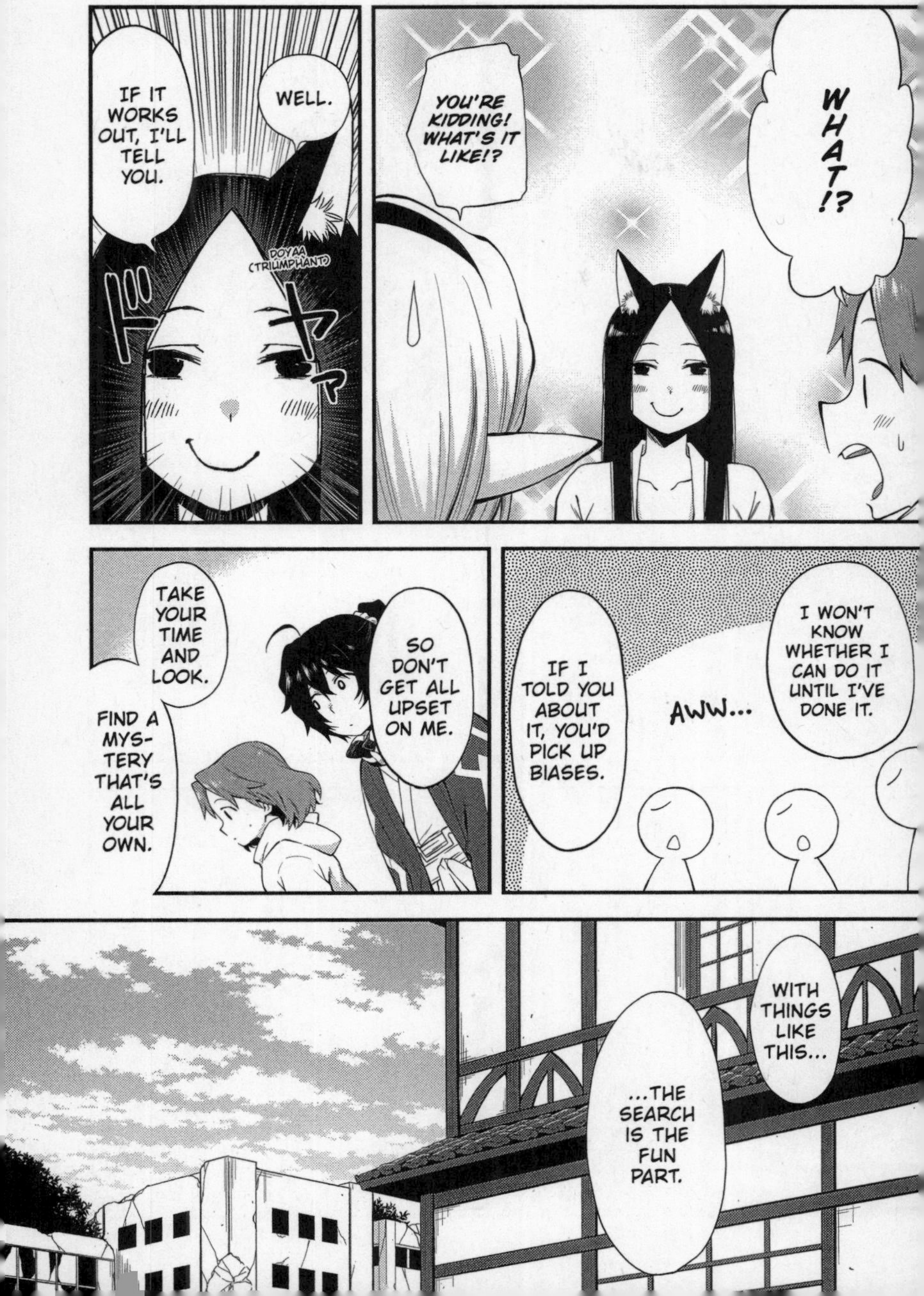
WHAT!?
YOU'RE KIDDING! WHAT'S IT LIKE!?
WELL.
IF IT WORKS OUT, I'LL TELL YOU.
ドヤァ
DOYAA (TRIUMPHANT)
I WON'T KNOW WHETHER I CAN DO IT UNTIL I'VE DONE IT.
AWW...
IF I TOLD YOU ABOUT IT, YOU'D PICK UP BIASES.
SO DON'T GET ALL UPSET ON ME.
TAKE YOUR TIME AND LOOK.
FIND A MYSTERY THAT'S ALL YOUR OWN.
WITH THINGS LIKE THIS...
...THE SEARCH IS THE FUN PART.

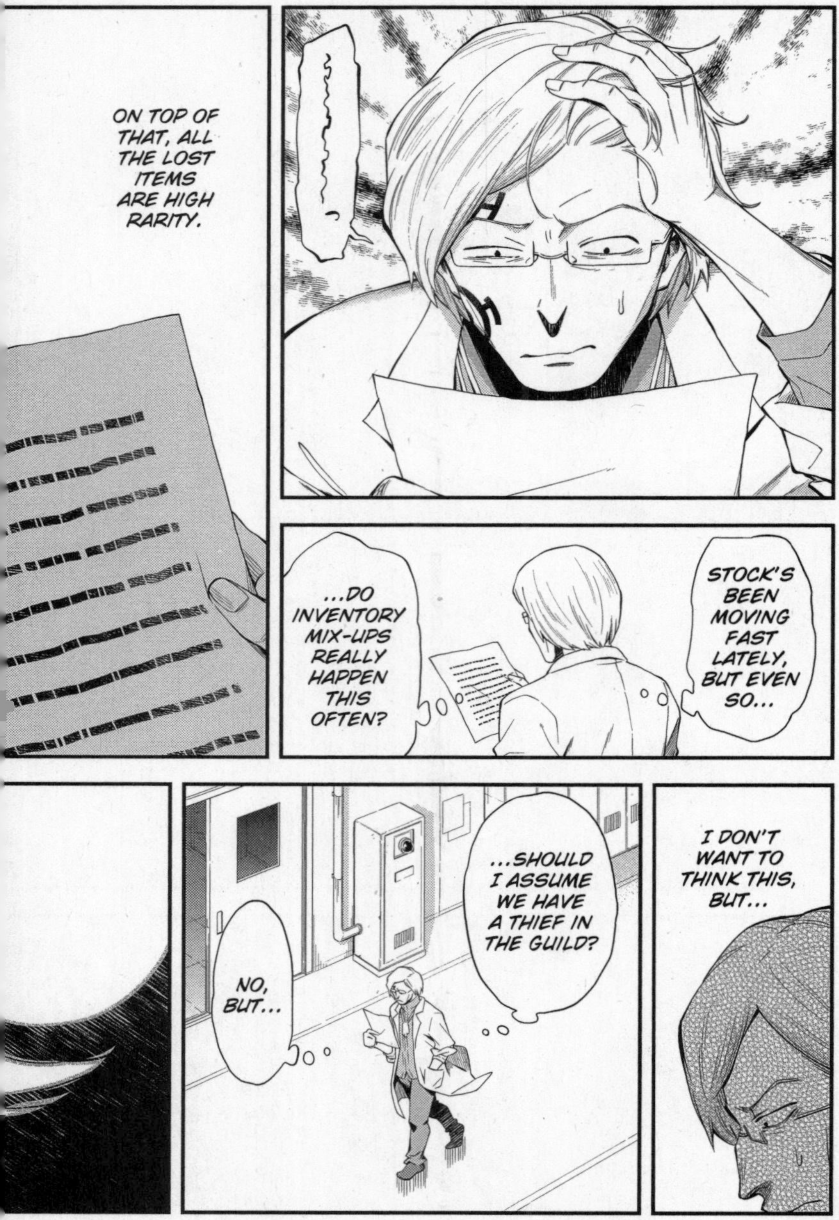
STOCK'S BEEN MOVING FAST LATELY, BUT EVEN SO...
...DO INVENTORY MIX-UPS REALLY HAPPEN THIS OFTEN?
ON TOP OF THAT, ALL THE LOST ITEMS ARE HIGH RARITY.
I DON'T WANT TO THINK THIS, BUT...
...SHOULD I ASSUME WE HAVE A THIEF IN THE GUILD?
NO, BUT...

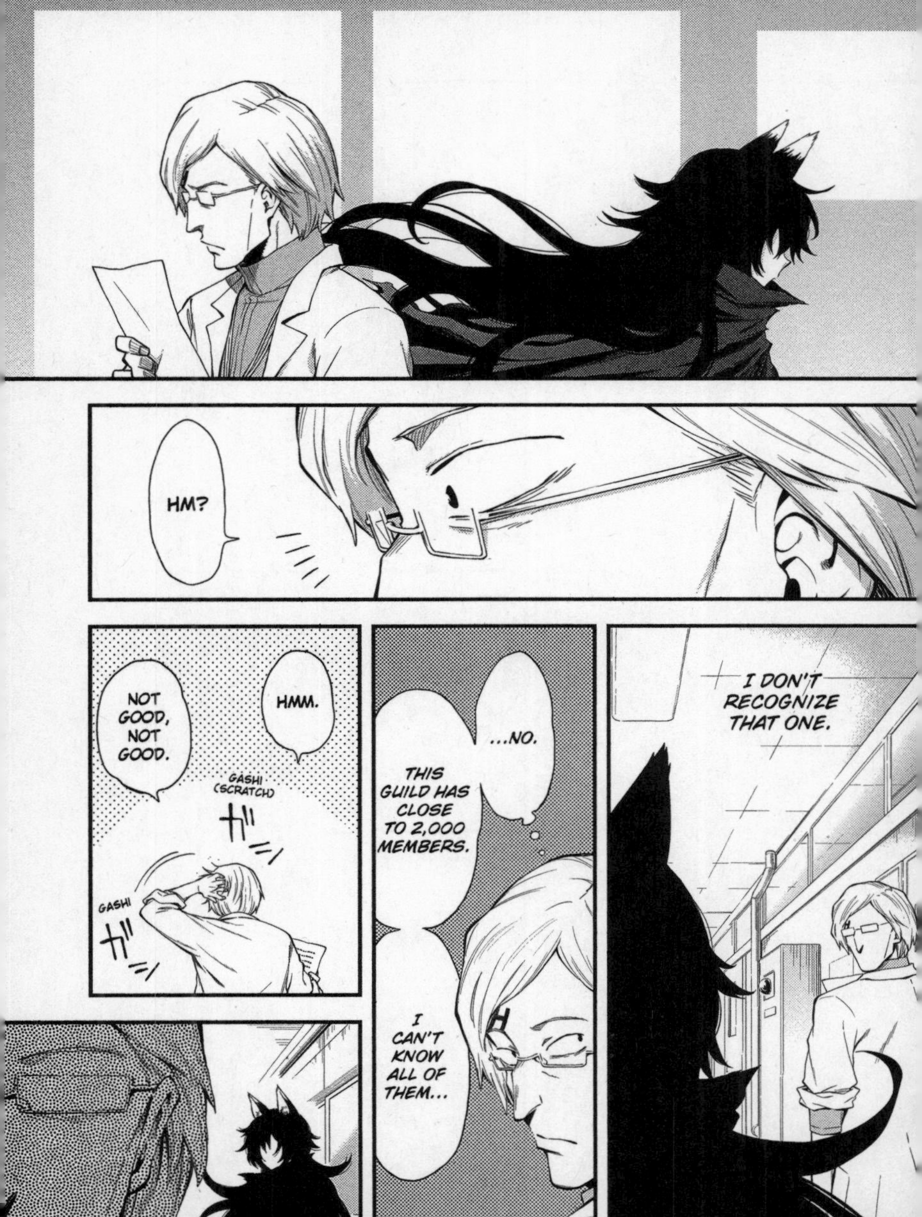
HM?
I DON'T RECOGNIZE THAT ONE.
...NO.
THIS GUILD HAS CLOSE TO 2,000 MEMBERS.
I CAN'T KNOW ALL OF THEM...
HMM.
NOT GOOD, NOT GOOD.
GASHI (SCRATCH)
GASHI

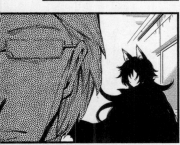

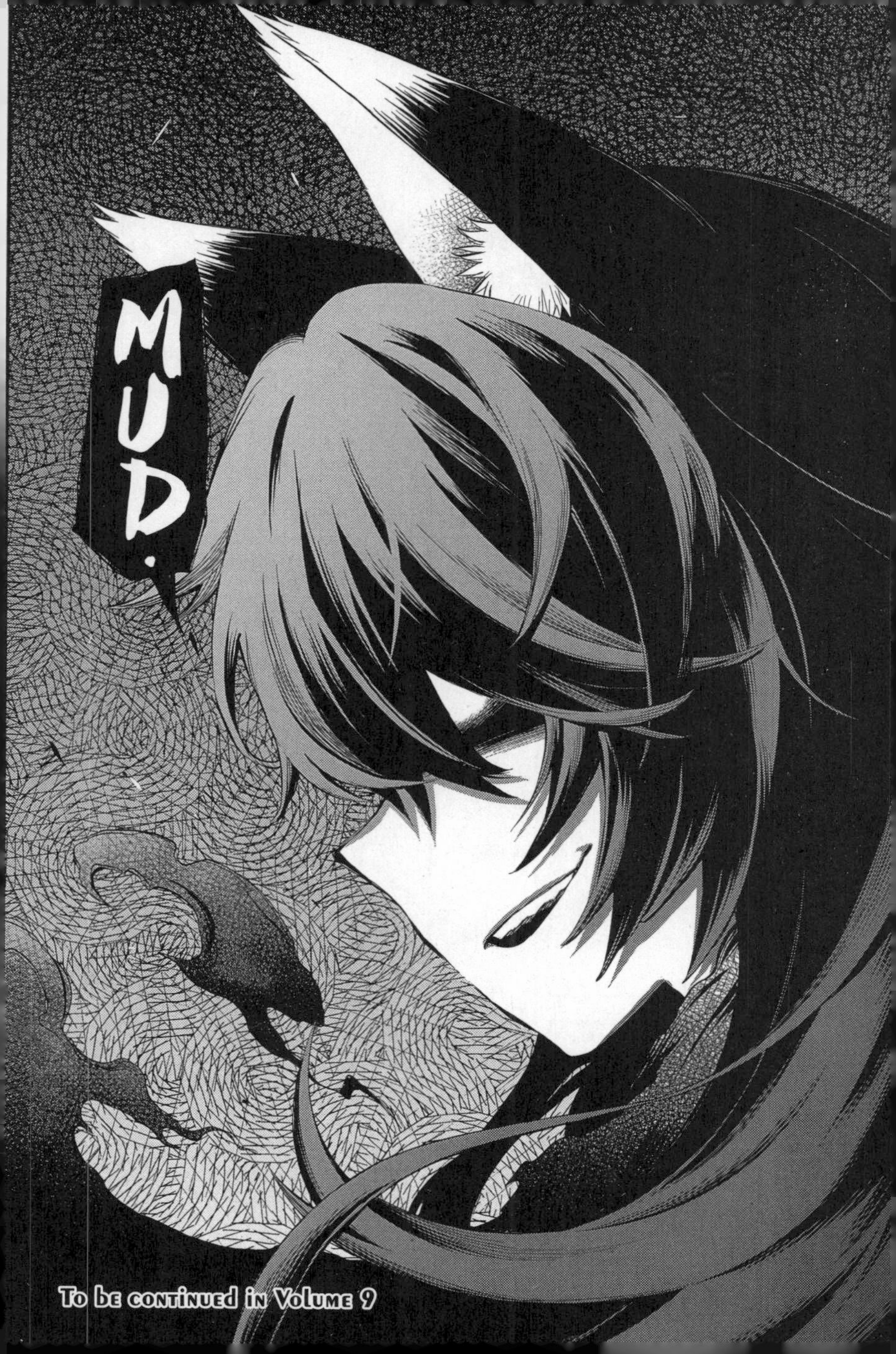
MUD.

To be continued in Volume 9